Jordan Boldt

THE PRINCETON REVIEW

WORD SMART

BUILDING AN EDUCATED VOCABULARY

By Adam Robinson
and the Staff of The Princeton Review

Random House, Inc.
New York 1997
http://www.randomhouse.com

Princeton Review Publishing, L.L.C.
2315 Broadway, 3rd Floor
New York, NY 10024
E-mail: info@review.com

Library of Congress Cataloging-in-Publication Data

Robinson, Adam.
        Word smart.
        At head of title: The Princeton Review.
        1. Vocabulary. 2. Scholastic aptitude test
Study guides. I. Princeton Review (Firm)
II. Title.   III. Title: Princeton Review:
word smart.
PE1449.R63   1988 428.1   87-40580

ISBN 0-679-74589-0

Manufactured in the United States of America

    12 14 16 18 20 B 19 17 15 13 11

ACKNOWLEDGMENTS

A very special thanks to Lee Harper Marshall and Erica Judge. We couldn't have finished on time without you.

Thanks also to our editor, Diane Reverand, for her continued support and guidance, and to her able assistant, Emily Bestler, for her patient prodding.

Finally, thanks to those meticulous readers who have written in with suggestions, politely reminding us of our human fallibility.

CONTENTS

INTRODUCTION

YOUR VOCABULARY HAS BEEN TALKING ABOUT YOU BEHIND YOUR BACK

The words you use say a lot about you. Some words say that you are smart, persuasive, and informed. Others say that you don't know what you are talking about. Knowing which words to use and understanding how to use them are keys to getting the most out of your mind.

People often say, in frustration, "I know what I mean but I don't know how to say it." They are almost always incorrect. If they don't know how to say it, they usually don't know what they mean. We use words not just to speak but also to think. If the right words aren't there, the right ideas can't get through.

Your vocabulary is the foundation of your ability to think and your ability to share your thoughts with other people. When you improve your vocabulary, you improve your ability to bring your intelligence to bear on the world around you.

BIGGER ISN'T NECESSARILY BETTER

When people say that someone has a "good vocabulary," they usually mean that he or she uses a lot of big, important-sounding words—words like *jactitation, demulcent,* and *saxicolous.* But a vocabulary consisting of words like this isn't necessarily a "good" vocabulary at all.

Why?

Because almost no one knows what *jactitation, demulcent,* and *saxicolous* mean. If you used these words in conversation, the chances are that no one listening to you would know what you were talking about. Big, difficult words have very important uses, but improving a vocabulary involves much more than merely decorating your speech or your writing with a few polysyllabic zingers.

The goal of communication is clarity. We write and speak in order to make ourselves understood. A good vocabulary is one that makes communication easy and efficient. One mark of an effective speaker or writer is an ability to express complex ideas with relatively simple words.

Most discourse among educated people is built on words that are fairly ordinary—words you've heard before, even if you aren't exactly certain what they mean. The best way to improve your vocabulary isn't to comb the dictionary for a handful of tongue-twisters to throw at unsuspecting strangers. Instead, you need to hone your understanding of words that turn up again and again in intelligent communication. A person who had a clear understanding of every word in an issue of The New York *Times, The Wall Street Journal,* or *The Atlantic* would have a very powerful vocabulary—vocabulary sophisticated enough to impress almost any teacher, admissions officer, colleague, or employer.

An Educated Vocabulary

An educated vocabulary is one that enables you to convey ideas easily. Do you know what *inveterate* means? Do you know the difference between *flaunt* and *flout*? Do you know why an artist might be insulted if you called his or her work *artful*?

None of these words is particularly difficult. But each has its own meaning or meanings. If you misuse these words, you tell an educated person that you are in over your head. Using them correctly can identify you as a member of that most elite of elites: people who know what they're talking about.

What's the Problem?

When people get into trouble with words, it usually isn't because they don't know the meaning of a seldom-used word like *termagant* but because they are confused about the meaning of a much more common word—a word they hear, read, and even use with regularity.

Peruse, for example. Many people think that it means "skim" or "glance over." But it doesn't. In fact, it means very nearly the opposite. To peruse a document is to read it carefully.

Confusion about the meaning of this useful word is one of the most common vocabulary errors we encounter in our SAT-preparation students. A great many high school students could probably improve their SAT scores simply by learning the meaning of this word.

The number of words you know is less important than the care you have taken in learning the ones you really use. Speaking or writing well doesn't require an enormous vocabulary—but it does require a confident one. And the way to gain confidence in your vocabulary is to buckle down and learn the words you need to make yourself clearly understood.

Why You Need This Book

There are a lot of vocabulary books out there. Most of them, we believe, aren't very useful. Some contain too many words. Others contain too many absurdly difficult words. Some claim to be based on surefire tricks or "painless" learning methods. Most aren't very good at helping people learn new words of any kind.

This book is different.

THE PRINCETON REVIEW APPROACH

The Princeton Review is the largest SAT-preparation course in the country. We've been in the business for just seven years, but we already have branches in more than thirty cities. We've grown as rapidly as we have because we are good at what we do. At the end of our six-week course, our students improve their SAT scores an average of 150 points. Many of our students raise their scores more than 200 points. We're proud to compare our results with those of any preparation course in the nation.

In preparing students for the SAT and other standardized tests, we spend much of our time working on vocabulary. Despite what many people think, most "intelligence" or "aptitude" tests are largely tests of vocabulary. In fact, most of the questions on such tests are vocabulary questions, such as the analogy and sentence-completion items that make up the bulk of the verbal SAT.

The students who earn high scores on such tests are the students who know the right words. The success of our school is in part a result of our success in teaching vocabulary.

NEW WORDS IN A HURRY

Because our course lasts only a few weeks, we don't have much time to teach our students the words they need to know in order to do well on the SAT. As a result, we've put a lot of thought into how people learn—and retain—new words.

The methods we have developed are easy to use and, we believe, extremely effective. There's nothing particularly startling about them. They rely mostly on common sense. But they do work. And although they were developed primarily for high school students, they can be used profitably by anyone who wants to build a stronger, smarter vocabulary.

HOW THIS BOOK IS ORGANIZED

In the next section, we'll describe our basic principles of vocabulary building. We'll also explain our general techniques for learning new words. You should apply these techniques as you work through the rest of the book. The more carefully you work, the more rapidly you'll enhance your ability to use words effectively.

The heart of *Word Smart* is the large central section containing the thousand or so words we think an intelligent person ought to know. Each word is accompanied by a definition, and one or more examples intended to help you understand how to use the word properly.

Many entries also include discussions of related words or certain shades of meaning. Scattered throughout the book are drills that should help you strengthen your new vocabulary and make it possible for you to assess your progress as you work along.

At the end of the book are several specialized lists of words, including our famous Hit Parade. This is the vocabulary list we use to help our students boost their verbal scores on the SAT. It contains the words most frequently tested on the SAT, in the order of their importance on the test.

Our SAT-preparation students use the Hit Parade to boost their scores on the verbal SAT. Sometimes simply knowing that a particular word is included on the Hit Parade is enough to lead our students to a correct answer on the SAT, since it emphasizes words appearing in correct answer choices.

Other specialized lists include frequently misused words, useful foreign words and phrases, common abbreviations, and words associated with computers, finance, the arts, and science. If you learn the words on these lists, you'll be able to follow important articles in the nation's best-written newspapers and magazines and to keep up your end of conversations with your (undoubtedly) well-educated friends.

Toward the end of this book is a Final Exam covering all the words in the main section. You can use this test to help you firm up your new vocabulary knowledge and to help ensure that you'll retain all the new words you've learned.

You can also use the test as a diagnostic tool. By trying your hand at the questions *before* working your way through the book, you'll give yourself a good idea of which words are causing you the most trouble. And if you're preparing for a major standardized test, such as the SAT, you and one or more friends can use the Final Exam as a handy review device.

How We Chose These Words

We assemble our Hit Parade by entering into a computer all the words from released editions of the SAT, sorting them by frequency, weighting them, as mentioned earlier, to give more emphasis to words appearing in correct answer choices, and eliminating words that are too simple to cause problems for most students. The result is a list of the most important words tested on the SAT, in order of their importance.

We have assembled our other *Word Smart* lists in much the same way. We have monitored a broad sampling of literate publications, looking for challenging words that appear regularly. For the primary *Word Smart* list, we selected the 823 difficult words that appeared most frequently.

We have also sought the advice of teachers, writers, and others. In brief, we have assessed all available sources in an effort to compile a powerful working vocabulary that will help you communicate.

How to Use This Book

Don't try to read this book in a single sitting. You'll learn much more if you tackle it a little at a time. You may feel comfortable with a number of the words already. You don't need to spend much time on these, but be certain you really *do* know a word as well as you think you do before you skip ahead. Some of the most embarrassing vocabulary blunders occur when we boldly misuse words we felt certain we understood.

The words in *Word Smart* are arranged alphabetically. You'll find a Quick Quiz every ten words or so. You may find it convenient to tackle words in the main list in ten-word chunks, pausing at each Quick Quiz to make certain you have retained what you just learned. Don't forget to check your answers.

If you're trying to build your vocabulary in preparation for a test, you should set a schedule for yourself and work methodically from beginning to end. If you're simply trying to improve your vocabulary, you may find it more interesting to dip into the text at random. You can also use the book as a companion to your dictionary, to help you zero in on the meanings of new words you've encountered in your reading or in conversation.

About *Word Smart II*

If you're like most people, you'll want to learn words as efficiently and as rapidly as possible. The list of words that forms the main portion of this book will provide a foundation on which you can build your own educated vocabulary.

Word Smart II picks up where this book leaves off. So many of you finished this book and looked up from your plate demanding "More words!" that we compiled a second list.

In *Word Smart II* we place more emphasis on pronunciation, and we also extend our SAT and GRE Hit Parades. The words in *Word Smart II* are somewhat more difficult, and don't appear quite so frequently, but otherwise they are just as important for you to know.

When you finish this book, and certainly when you finish *Word Smart II,* you will have a working vocabulary better than that of most college graduates. But don't stop there. Continue to expand your vocabulary by mastering the new words you encounter.

Start reading!

THE PRINCETON REVIEW

WORD
SMART

BUILDING AN
EDUCATED VOCABULARY

CHAPTER 1

LEARNING
NEW
WORDS

BUILDING A VOCABULARY IS CHILD'S PLAY

Young children learn new words by imitating the speakers around them. When a three-year-old hears a new word that catches her interest, she may use it repeatedly for a day or two until she feels comfortable with it. She establishes its meaning from context, often by trial and error. She adds new words to her vocabulary because she needs them to make herself understood.

Children have an easier time learning new words than most adults do. As we grow beyond childhood, our brains seem to lose their magical ability to soak up language from the environment. But adults can still learn a great deal from the way children learn new words.

HOW CHILDREN DO IT

Young children don't learn the meanings of new words by looking them up. Sometimes they ask grown-ups directly, but more often they simply infer meanings from context. They figure out what a new word means by paying attention to how it is used.

You need to do the same. You need to make your mind receptive to new words by actively seeking to understand them. When you encounter an unfamiliar word in the newspaper, don't skim over it. Stop and try to figure out what it means. The words that surround it should provide a few clues. Put your mind to work on it.

A WORD IS USEFUL ONLY IF YOU USE IT

Children learn words by using them. Adults who want to build their vocabularies must do the same. You can't incorporate a new word into your vocabulary unless you give it a thorough workout, and then keep it in shape through regular exercise.

We tell our students to use new words over and over—at the dinner table, at school, among their friends—even at the risk of making themselves annoying. Even at the risk of making mistakes and appearing foolish.

If a word isn't useful to you, you'll never remember it. Our students have a powerful incentive for learning the words we teach them: if they learn them carefully, they'll do better on the SAT or GRE and improve their chances of being admitted to the schools they want to attend. An added bonus is that their writing and speaking skills improve along with their vocabulary, often leading to better grades. Adults and other nonstudents may have other vocabulary needs, but the same general rule applies. With vocabulary, as with many other things in life, you have to use it if you don't want to lose it. Remember that the size and quality of a person's vocabulary correlate powerfully with his or her success in school, at work, and beyond.

LEARNING NEW WORDS CAN BE FUN

We also try to make learning fun. We give our students decks of playing cards with Hit Parade words and definitions printed on them, so that they can learn even while they're playing. (We call these decks of cards Hit Packs.)

We think this book makes learning new words fun, too. You'll have to work, but if you approach the task in the proper frame of mind, you'll find that learning new words can be a pleasure. For one thing, you'll get to read a lot of good books.

READ, READ, READ!

The best way to build a solid, sophisticated vocabulary is to read voraciously.

Careful reading not only brings you into contact with new words, it also forces you to use your head to figure out what those new words mean. If you read widely enough, you will find that your vocabulary will build itself. New words are contagious if you give yourself enough exposure to them. Reading any good book is better for your vocabulary than is watching television. Reading well-written magazines and newspapers can help, too. *The New York Times, The New Yorker, The Wall Street Journal, The Atlantic, Time, Newsweek, The New Republic,* and any number of other intelligent publications can help boost your vocabulary.

READING ISN'T ENOUGH, THOUGH

We aren't the only people who think that avid reading is the key to building an educated vocabulary. You've probably heard the same thing from your parents and teachers, and with good reason. But reading isn't enough.

Reading the writing of respected authors will expose you to a large stock of words and a variety of writing styles.

But honestly now, when you encounter a word you don't know, what do you do?

You probably don't labor over the word, trying to determine its meaning from context. You skip over the words you don't know, and somehow you muddle through with more or less vague comprehension. If you're serious about understanding what you read, as well as improving your vocabulary, you'll have to use the dictionary.

THE DANGERS OF RELYING ON CONTEXT ALONE

The natural way to learn words, as we observed earlier, is to see how other people use them—that is, to see or hear the word in context. While context may tell you how to use the word, relying on context is not without pitfalls.

First, when you encounter a new word, you can't be certain how to pronounce it unless you hear it spoken by someone whose pronunciation is authoritative. You also can't be certain the word is being used correctly. Even skillful writers and speakers occasionally misuse language. A writer or speaker may even misuse a word intentionally, perhaps for dramatic or comic effect.

Even more important, most words have many different meanings or shades of meanings. Sometimes the difference between one meaning and another can be tiny; sometimes it can be enormous. Even if you deduce the meaning from the context, you have no way of knowing whether the meaning you've deduced will apply in other cases.

Finally, context can be misleading. Here is an example of what we mean. It's a dialogue we find ourselves having over and over again with our students. The dialogue concerns the meaning of the word *formidable,* although you can substitute just about any medium-difficult word:

Us:	Do you know what *formidable* means?
STUDENT:	Sure, of course.
Us:	Good. Define it.
STUDENT:	Okay. A *formidable* opponent is someone...
Us:	Sorry to cut you off. We want the definition of *formidable,* not an example of how to use it in a sentence. Can you please define the word *formidable* for us?
STUDENT:	Sure. Ummm, let's see... (The student is still thinking of the phrase *formidable opponent.*) *Formidable* means *good* or *skillful.* Maybe *big, aggressive.* What about *tremendous*?
Us:	Nice try, but it means *frightening.*
STUDENT:	Really? I didn't know that. I thought it meant something else.
Us:	Well, it also means *awe-inspiring.*

WHAT'S THE POINT?

The point is that context can be misleading. Have you ever played the game Mad Libs? In it, one player is given a text from which a number of words are missing, and the other player is asked to supply those missing words without looking at the text. The result is often very funny.

But something similar—and much less funny—can happen when you rely exclusively on context to supply you with the meanings of new words. You may hit upon a meaning that seems to fit the context, only to discover later that your guess was far wide of the mark.

To keep this from happening, you need to use a dictionary.

THE BIG BOOK

Some ambitious students try to build their vocabularies by sitting down with the dictionary, opening to the first page (*A, a*), and *reading it!*

Most students who embark on this seldom get beyond the first page. Then they give up all attempts at learning words. Trying to learn new words in this way is virtually impossible. Besides, there are easier and more efficient ways. Like starting with this book.

WHICH DICTIONARY SHOULD YOU USE?

A dictionary is a dictionary, but like cars, not all of them have the same features.

Dictionaries can range from children's editions with lots of pictures to humongous unabridged dictionaries with lots of entries in tiny type. (By the way, *abridged* means *shortened*. An unabridged dictionary is one that includes almost every single word in the English language!) And then there's the twenty-volume *Oxford English Dictionary*.

For most people, however, a good college-edition dictionary is sufficient.

IF YOU'RE A STUDENT, YOU SHOULD CARRY A PORTABLE DICTIONARY WITH YOU

And maybe even if you're not a student.

Carrying around a large hardcover dictionary isn't very practical. So buy yourself a small paperback dictionary to carry with you wherever you go. That way, whenever you encounter a new word, you can look it up on the spot and increase the likelihood that you will retain it.

By the way, the definitions in even the best small paperback dictionaries are not always exact. It's a good idea to verify the definition of a word in a college dictionary when you have access to one.

WHAT FEATURES SHOULD A GOOD COLLEGE DICTIONARY HAVE?

We used several dictionaries in verifying the definitions and usages that appear in *Word Smart: The American Heritage Dictionary, Webster's Third New International Dictionary, Webster's Seventh New Collegiate Dictionary,* and *The Random House College Dictionary*. (A "college" dictionary is not for use in college only; the phrase "college dictionary" is simply a rough indication of the vocabulary level of the readers for whom the dictionary is appropriate.) Let's take a look at a sample entry from *The Random House College Dictionary:*

> a•bridge (ə brij'), *v.t.,* a•bridged, a•bridg•ing. 1. to shorten by condensation or omission while retaining the basic contents: *to abridge a long novel.* 2. To reduce or lessen in duration, scope, etc.; diminish, curtail. 3. to deprive; cut off [ME *abregge, abrigge* < MF *abreg(i)er* < LL *abbreviāre* to

shorten. See ABBREVIATE] —a•bridg'a•ble; *esp. Brit.,*
a•bridg'á•ble, *adj.*— a•bridg'ér, *n.* —Syn.**1.** condense, abstract. See **shorten. 2.** contract.

Some of us may have developed a fear of dictionaries at about the age
when we formed a fear of dentists. "Dad, what does *abridge* mean?" "Look
it up!" So you dutifully open the dictionary and scan the entries until you
find the one above. And that entry is supposed to *help* you understand what
the word means? No wonder we open the dictionary so infrequently.

A DICTIONARY REALLY CAN HELP

If you know how to decipher the entry. Let's examine the above entry part
by part:

a•bridge
The main entry. The dot separates the words into syllables.
Sometimes the main entry includes stress marks to tell you
which syllables to stress when pronouncing the word.

(ə brij')
The pronunciation. Every dictionary includes a pronunciation
key up front to explain symbols like the upside-down *e*.
(Known as a *schwa*, and pronounced "uh." Frankly, we wish
all dictionaries would drop symbols like the schwa and substitute phonetic spellings using the regular alphabet.) If a word
has more than one acceptable pronunciation, the entry will list
them.

Always observe the pronunciation of a word when you look
it up. If you know how to pronounce a word, you're more
likely to use it. (If you don't know how to pronounce a word,
you're more likely to embarrass yourself at cocktail parties
and the like.) And the more you use a word, the more you'll be
able to remember it.

v.t.
Part of speech. This abbreviation means that *abridge* is a verb,
specifically, a transitive verb.

A transitive verb is one that carries action from a subject to
a direct object. For example, in the sentence *The dog ate the
book,* the verb *ate* carries action from the dog to the book.
Similarly, in *The editor abridged the book,* the verb *abridged*
carries action from the editor to the book.

An example of an *in*transitive verb is *to sleep.* In *The dog
sleeps,* the verb does not carry any action from the subject
(dog) to anything.

a•bridged, a•bridg•ing
These entries let us know that we should note the spellings of

different forms of the word *abridge*. Notice, for example, that we drop the *e* before adding *ing*.

1. to shorten by condensation or omission while retaining the basic contents: *to abridge a long novel.*

The most common definition of the word. *The Random House College Dictionary* is one of the few that include helpful phrases or sentences to show you how to use the word *in context.*

This feature is quite useful. The example tells us that we would not use *abridge* this way: *The tailor abridged Susan's long skirt to make it a mini.*

2. to reduce or lessen in duration, scope, etc.; diminish, curtail. **3.** to deprive; cut off.

Other definitions, generally in order of importance. Sometimes a definition will include close synonyms.

[ME *abregge, abrigge* < MF *abreg(i)er* < LL *abreviāre* to shorten. See ABBREVIATE]

The etymology. Some dictionaries include the etymology before the definitions.

You don't have to be a linguist, but the word *abridge* developed from Late Latin to Middle French to Middle English:

abbreviāre (meaning "to shorten"), in Late Latin
   became
abreg(i)er in Middle French,
   which became
abregge or *abrigge* in Middle English,
   which finally became
abridge, today.

The etymology suggests that we look up *abbreviate.* If you have the time you should do so, since it will reinforce your understanding of *abridge.*

We will discuss etymology in more detail later, since it is a powerful *mnemonic.* (Look It Up!)

— **a•bridg′a•ble;** *esp. Brit.,* **a•bridge′á•ble,** *adj.* — **a•bridg′ér,** *n.*
Other parts of speech.

Syn. 1. condense, abstract. See **shorten. 2.** contract.

An abridged (!) list of synonyms. The numbers refer to the preceding order of definitions. The entry suggests that we look up *shorten.*

Again, this is a feature of *The Random House College Dictionary.* Not all dictionaries include it.

Don't Stop with the Definition

The editors of the dictionary advise us to look up *shorten* if we want a better understanding of *abridge*, so let's do just that:

> **shorten** (shôr'tən), *v.t.*, **1.** to make short or shorter. **2.** to reduce, decrease, take in, etc.: *to shorten sail.* **3.** to make (pastry, bread, etc.) short, as with butter or other fat. —*v.i.* **4.** to become short or shorter. **5.** (of odds) to decrease. — **short'en**, *n.* —**Syn.** **1.** condense, lessen, limit, restrict. SHORTEN, ABBREVIATE, ABRIDGE, CURTAIL mean to make shorter or briefer. SHORTEN is a general word meaning to make less in extent or duration: *to shorten a dress, a prisoner's sentence.* The other three words suggest methods of shortening. To ABBREVIATE is to make shorter by omission or contraction: *to abbreviate a word.* To ABRIDGE is to reduce in length or size by condensing, summarizing, and the like: *to abridge a document.* CURTAIL suggests deprivation and lack of completeness because of cutting off part: *to curtail an explanation.* **2.** lessen.

This entry distinguishes *shorten* from a number of synonyms, including *abridge*. The digression took another minute or so, but we've come away with a better understanding of the meanings and their *nuances* (LIU!). We will consider synonyms in detail when we discuss how to use a thesaurus.

Why Aren't Entries in *Word Smart* Like Dictionary Entries?

In the first place because this isn't a dictionary. We've tried to make *Word Smart* easier to read and understand than a big dictionary.

Don't get us wrong. We use dictionaries, we rely on dictionaries, but sometimes we wish that lexicographers (those fun-loving people who write dictionaries) would communicate in basic English.

We aren't as sophisticated as lexicographers. So for each word in *Word Smart*, we give you a basic definition. Sometimes a close synonym is enough. Then we give you—and this is important—a sentence or two so that you can see how to use the word. Our entry for *abridge* reads:

> **ABRIDGE** (uh BRIJ) *v* to shorten; to condense
> The thoughtful editor had *abridged* the massive book by removing the boring parts.
> An *abridged* dictionary is one that has been shortened to keep it from crushing desks and people's laps.

The problem with most dictionaries is that they don't tell you how to use the word. You can always spot someone who has learned new words almost exclusively through the dictionary rather than through general reading supplemented with a dictionary. When you ask such people the definition of a word, it's almost as if they fall into a trance—their eyes glaze over as they rattle off the definition almost word for word from a dictionary.

Use a dictionary, but don't become a slave to it.

YOU DON'T UNDERSTAND A MEANING UNLESS YOU CAN DEFINE IT IN YOUR OWN WORDS

To understand a word completely, to make a word yours, you should try to define it in your own words. Don't settle for the dictionary definition. For that matter, don't settle for our definition.

Make up your own definition. You'll understand the meaning better. What's more, you'll be more likely to remember it.

DON'T CLOSE THAT DICTIONARY UNTIL YOU'VE *MEMORIZED* THE DEFINITION!

How many times have you looked up the definition of a certain word? Ideally, you shouldn't have to look up the definition of a word more than once—that is, if you memorize the definition.

Many students look up words only to forget them a week later. We try to get our students to form the habit of never shutting the dictionary until they have satisfied themselves that they have permanently memorized the definition of a word.

How can you memorize words? We'll show you how shortly. First we need to discuss a companion to the dictionary: the thesaurus.

THESAURUSES: DON'T MISUSE, ABUSE, EXPLOIT, CORRUPT, MISAPPLY, OR MISEMPLOY THEM

A thesaurus is a dictionary-like reference book that lists synonyms for many words. A thesaurus can be another useful tool in your word-building campaign, but only if you use it properly. Many people don't.

Thesaurus abuse is very common. Students very often try to make their vocabularies seem bigger than they actually are by using a thesaurus to beef up the papers they write. (*Neophytes chronically endeavor to induce their parlance to portend more magisterially by employing a lexicon of synonyms to amplify the theses they inscribe.*) They write their papers in their own words, then plug in big words from a thesaurus. That's what we did with the silly-sounding sentence in the parentheses above. You'd be surprised how many students actually compose their papers that way.

Good teachers are never fooled by this. The big words culled from the thesaurus usually tend to be the wrong words—words that have lots of syllables but that don't mean quite what the student thinks they do. A "thesaurusized" sentence is very often incomprehensible—or unintentionally silly.

STILL, A THESAURUS DOES HAVE USES, FUNCTIONS, PURPOSES, AND APPLICATIONS

Despite these cautions, we do believe that a thesaurus can be very helpful—if you use it properly.

The best way to use a thesaurus is as a supplement to your dictionary, as a reference work that can help you find the word that expresses precisely what you are trying to say. A good thesaurus is intended to help a speaker or writer distinguish the shades of difference between words of similar meaning.

HOW TO USE THE THESAURUS: AN EXAMPLE

Let's say you're trying to describe Randolph, someone who never lends money to anyone. Randolph examines his monthly bank statement with a calculator to make sure that his interest has been properly computed to the penny. Randolph is someone who, like Jack Benny, would have to think long and hard if a mugger presented him with the dilemma "Your money or your life."

Let's say that the first word that comes to mind in describing Randolph is *cheap*. Now, being the careful writer you are, you decide to see if *cheap* is the most precise word you can come up with. After all, *cheap* can describe Randolph or the clothes he wears.

Looking up *cheap* in *The Random House Thesaurus* (College Edition), you find the following entry:

> **cheap** *adj.* **1.** *Chicken is not as cheap as it was:* inexpensive, low-priced, economical, reasonable. **2.** *Talk is cheap:* effortless, costless, easy. **3.** *The coat may be expensive but it looks cheap:* shoddy, shabby, inferior, worthless, poor, second-rate, trashy, meager, paltry, gimcrack, flashy, gaudy, in bad taste, tawdry, tacky, common, inelegant. **4.** *Spreading gossip is a cheap thing to do:* contemptible, petty, despicable, sordid, ignoble, wretched, mean, base. *Slang* two-bit; vulgar, immoral, indecent. **5.** *He's too cheap to pick up the check:* tight, stingy, miserly, penurious, tightfisted, close. **Ant. 1.** expensive, costly, high-priced, high, overpriced. **2.** worthwhile, valuable; difficult, troublesome. **3.** superior, good, fine, first-rate, worthy; in good taste, tasteful, high-class, classy, elegant, chic, smart. **4.** admirable, commendable; moral, decent. **5.** generous, charitable, openhanded.

The entry *cheap* lists five primary meanings, each preceded by an illustrative sentence. You scan the sentences until you find the one you want: the last one. Now you examine the synonyms:

> *tight:* Okay, but perhaps too informal or colloquial. Might be confused with other definitions of the word *tight*. Forget this one.

stingy: A possibility.

miserly: Let's say you're not exactly sure what this one means. You decide to look this one up in the regular dictionary.

penurious: Better look this one up, too.

tightfisted: A little better than *tight,* though perhaps still too slangy. You'll think about it.

close: Nope. Too many other definitions.

Before leaving the thesaurus, however, you decide to check out the listing for *miserly* and come up with the following additional words:

parsimonious: Look it up.

avaricious: Look it up.

mean: Too many other definitions.

grasping: More a synonym of *greedy.* Randolph isn't precisely greedy. He doesn't want to accumulate a lot; he just wants to hold on to what he has. Forget this one.

scrimping: Doesn't sound right. Forget this one.

pinching: Nope.

penny-pinching: Better than *pinching* alone, but colloquial. Maybe.

frugal: Look it up.

illiberal: Too vague.

closehanded: Nah.

closefisted: Similar to *tightfisted* and *penny-pinching,* but not as good. Drop.

selfish: Too general. Randolph is selfish only with money.

ungenerous: Nope. Randolph isn't generous, but you want to say what he *is* rather than what he is *not.*

greedy: You ruled this out earlier.

niggardly: Look it up.

near: Nope.

meager: Look it up.

grudging: Not precisely what you mean.

You decide you have enough synonyms to work with. Now you have to look up and verify definitions.

Next, the Dictionary

You are left with three synonyms you know (*stingy, tightfisted,* and *penny-pinching*) and seven you don't know. Just to be orderly, you look up the seven words alphabetically in *The Random House College Dictionary:*

avaricious characterized by avarice (insatiable greed for riches; inordinate desire to gain and hoard wealth); covetous

Nope, you don't mean *greedy. Avaricious* is out.

frugal 1. economical in use or expenditure; prudently saving or sparing. **2.** entailing little expense; requiring few resources; meager, scanty.

The first definition means careful with money. *Economical* and *prudent* both have positive connotations, but Randolph's obsession with money is not something good. The second definition is not the one we want. Out.

meager 1. deficient in quantity or quality; lacking fullness or richness; poor; scanty. **2.** having little flesh; lean; thin. **3.** maigre.

Nope. None of these seems to convey the meaning you want.

miserly of, like, or befitting a miser (one who lives in wretched circumstances in order to save and hoard money); penurious; niggardly.

Well, this might be right. You have to think about Randolph a little more. What are his circumstances like? Is he willing to live in wretched circumstances?

niggardly reluctant to give or spend; stingy. —**Syn. 1.** penurious, miserly.

Possible. Let's take a look at the last few before you decide.

parsimonious characterized by or showing parsimony; sparing or frugal, esp. to excess.

Now you have established that *parsimonious* means stingier than frugal. This seems to hit the mark.

penurious 1. extremely stingy. **2.** extremely poor; indigent. **3.** poorly or inadequately supplied.

The first definition works, but the second definition seems to imply a stinginess perhaps resulting from poverty. The third definition does not apply. Now you have to think again about Randolph. Is he poor as well as cheap? If so this is the right word.

So Which Is the Right Word?

You're still left with *stingy, tightfisted, penny-pinching, miserly, niggardly, parsimonious,* and *penurious.* Oh, and there's still the blunt, if unassuming, *cheap,* which you started with. Which word is the right word?

Stingy is the right word if you want to use a simple, no-nonsense word.

Tightfisted is the right phrase if you want something a little more slangy and graphic.

Penny-pinching is the right phrase if you want the image to be a little more literal than tightfisted.

Miserly is the right word, depending on Randolph's living circumstances.

Niggardly is the right word if Randolph is merely reluctant to spend money. If he's more than reluctant, this isn't the right word.

Parsimonious is the right word if you want a multisyllabic synonym for *cheap* or *stingy.* From the definitions, *parsimonious* seems more extreme than *stingy.*

Penurious is the right word if Randolph is poor as well as stingy.

To decide which word is the right word, you must give more thought to precisely what aspect of Randolph you're trying to capture and convey.

The Right Word Is Not Merely the Accurate Word with the Proper Connotations

We don't want to get into writing style, but other considerations to keep in mind when choosing the right word are:

Rhythm, or Cadence
Which word best fits in with the overall flow of the sentence and paragraph? Perhaps you want to achieve alliteration *(Randolph is a pretentious, penny-pinching poet)* or a certain rhyme *(Alimony drove Randolph to parsimony).*

Part of Speech
Miserly seems okay as an adjective, but *miserliness* seems a little awkward as a noun.

Vocabulary Level
Who will be reading your description of Randolph? Your word choice may be limited by your potential reader or audience. Other things being equal, the simple word is invariably the better word.

Variety
If you've used *cheap* several times already in the same piece of writing, you may want to use a different word for spice.

Repetition

On the other hand, repeating the same word may have a powerful effect.

Dramatic Effect

A simple word in an academic setting, or an academic word in a simple setting, can have a dramatic effect. Comic effects can also be achieved by using a word in an inappropriate or incongruous context.

ALL THAT FOR ONE LITTLE WORD?

After our little excursions in the thesaurus and dictionary, you are probably wondering why we went to so much trouble about one little word—*cheap.*

First, your journey through the thesaurus and dictionary taught you the definitions of several new words. Perhaps more important, you were forced to *think.*

To think? Sure. You had to think more about what precisely you wanted to say about Randolph and whom you were saying it to.

EDITING IS MORE THAN CHOOSING THE RIGHT WORD

Word Smart is a book on words rather than on writing. Still, we want to note in passing that good editing is more than simply reviewing the words you use.

Editing means refining your ideas. Editing means deciding on the ordering and presentation of your ideas. Editing means deciding which ideas you're going to present at all.

WHICH THESAURUS SHOULD I USE?

There are a lot of thesauruses out there. The granddaddy thesaurus is *Roget's International Thesaurus.* It's the oldest and perhaps the best known. In our opinion it is also the most difficult to use. *Roget's* bills itself as a dictionary of ideas. Words are not listed alphabetically, but by some unwieldy Dewey decimal–type classification system that we've never been able to understand.

We recommend that the thesaurus you use be one that lists words alphabetically in the text itself. Ideally, the thesaurus should include sample sentences that distinguish at least some of the different shades of meanings.

We like *The Random House Thesaurus* (College Edition). Another good book is *Webster's New Collegiate Dictionary of Synonyms.*

READING THIS BOOK

Reading widely—with the help of a dictionary and perhaps also a thesaurus—is a great way to build a vocabulary. But it's also a very slow way. Which words you encounter in your reading depends on which words the writers happen to use.

That's where we come in. The main section of *Word Smart* is a concentrated source of the words you want to know—the words you need to help you build an educated vocabulary.

To get as much out of this book as possible, you need to use it correctly. In working with thousands of students over the years, we've learned quite a bit about which methods work and which ones don't.

BEFORE WE BEGIN, A WARNING

Learning new words is like losing weight—there is no truly easy way to do it.

If you want to lose weight, you have to eat less and exercise more. Thinking good thoughts and taking little blue pills won't do it, at least not in the long run.

If you want to build an educated vocabulary, you have to work, too. We have had a great deal of success with our methods, and we think they're more successful than other methods. But there's nothing magical about them. You'll just have to roll up your sleeves and get to work.

THE BEST METHOD TO MEMORIZE WORDS IS THE METHOD THAT WORKS BEST FOR YOU

Over the years, we have discovered that our students seem to have more success with some methods of learning new words than with others. We'll describe these methods in a moment. Then, at the end of this chapter, we'll outline an effective general regimen for learning new words permanently and for incorporating them into your life.

As you work through this book, you'll undoubtedly find that you need to tailor your approach to the way you think and learn best. You may discover that for a particular word one method works best, and that for another word another method works best. That's fine.

We'll show you the methods we have found to be the most successful for our students. Use the one or ones that suit you best.

Basic Method No. 1: TRICKS AND MNEMONICS

A mnemonic is a device or trick that helps you remember something specific. Grade schoolers are sometimes taught to remember the spelling of *arithmetic* by using the following mnemonic: *A Rat In The House Might Eat Tom's Ice Cream.* The first letter in each word in this silly sentence stands for the letters in *arithmetic.* Remember the sentence and you remember how to spell the word.

Mnemonics can appeal to our ears, too. How about the history mnemonic: *In fourteen hundred and ninety-two, Columbus sailed the ocean blue . . . ?* Or the spelling mnemonic: *"i" before "e" except after "c," and in words that say "a," as in "neighbor" and "weigh."*

You Already Know How to Use Mnemonics

Whether you realize it or not, you use mnemonics all the time. When you make up a little game to remember your locker combination or a friend's birthday, you're using a mnemonic.

How Do Mnemonics Work?

All mnemonics work in the same way: by forcing you to associate what you're trying to remember with something that you already know, or with something that is easier to memorize. Patterns and rhymes are easy to memorize, which explains why so many mnemonics involve one of them.

Incidentally, it may also explain why rhyming became a part of poetry. The earliest poets and balladeers didn't write down their compositions, because they didn't know how to write. Instead, they kept them in their heads. Among other things, the rhymes at the ends of the lines made them easier to remember.

There's a Science to Mnemonics

Even though we all use mnemonics every day, you may not be aware that some very clever systems of mnemonics have been developed to enable people to memorize just about anything.

The undisputed mnemonic champ is Harry Lorayne, who as a trick used to memorize telephone directories! We're talking about names, phone numbers, and addresses!

Lorayne's best book is *The Page-a-Minute Memory Book*, which we recommend highly.

Basic Method No. 2: SEEING IS REMEMBERING

Letting a new word suggest a vivid mental image to you is a powerful and effective way to remember that word. Mental images are really mnemonics, too. They help you remember. The emphasis here is on suggestive mental pictures rather than on tricky abbreviations or coincidences of spelling.

Let's look at an example. We'll start with a word we've already used in this chapter: *abridge*. As you know, to abridge is to shorten or condense.

What image pops into your mind when you think of the word *abridge*? That's easy: a bridge. Now you need to picture something happening on or to that bridge that will help you remember the meaning of the word *abridge*. Your goal is to create such a vivid and memorable image in your mind that the next time you encounter *abridge* in your reading, you'll instantly remember what it means.

To be useful, your image must have something to do with the meaning of the word rather than merely with the way it sounds or looks. If you merely think of a bridge when you see *abridge*, you won't be helping yourself remember what you want to remember.

What you need is an image that suggests shortening or condensing. A dinosaur taking a big bite out of the middle of a bridge? A bomb exploding on a bridge? The image you choose is up to you.

How About Another Example?

Another useful word on the *Word Smart* master list is *gregarious*, which means sociable; enjoying the company of others. What image springs to mind? Really think now.

Can't think of an image? Be creative. A party animal is *gregarious*. How about imagining a party animal named Greg Arious. Don't stop with

his name. You need a picture. So give Greg a funny hat, a noisemaker, and some polka-dot dancing shoes. Or put a lampshade on his head. Think of something that will make you think of sociability the next time you see Greg Arious's name in a book or a magazine you're reading. The more real you make Greg Arious seem in your imagination the less trouble you'll have remembering the meaning of *gregarious.*

The Crazier the Mental Image, the Better

When it comes to mental images, crazy is better than normal. Normal is bland. Normal is boring. If you could easily remember boring things, you wouldn't have any trouble learning new words. Normal is harder to remember than crazy.

Crazy is dramatic. Crazy leaps out at you. You remember crazy. And remember this: anything goes when you're learning new words.

Memory Aids Have to Be Personal

Sometimes we'll give you a mnemonic for the listings in *Word Smart,* but we won't do this very often. Memory aids work best when you have to struggle a little to come up with them.

If you come up with your own memory aid, if it really means something to you, it will become a permanent part of your memory.

The very effort you take in devising a mental image or mnemonic is a large part of what enables you to remember it. This is why we take issue with those vocabulary books that provide ready-made memory aids for every word. These ready-made memory aids may help the authors of these books remember the meanings of the words in them, but they probably won't help you much.

What If You Can't Come up with a Mnemonic?

One of our students once told us that he had tried and tried to come up with an image for the word *proselytize,* but he hadn't been able to think of one.

We asked him what the word meant. He said, "To try to convert someone to a religion or a point of view." We just smiled and looked at him.

Suddenly, he started laughing. He had tried so hard to devise a mnemonic that he had memorized the word without realizing it.

Harry Lorayne makes this same point in his book: The beauty of a mnemonic is that even if you can't devise one, you may have memorized the word anyway!

Basic Method No. 3: ETYMOLOGICAL CLUES

Although the English language contains hundreds of thousands of words, you will discover that many groups of words are related in meaning because they developed from a common root. When you recognize that a group of words shares a similar root, you will more easily remember the entire group.

For example, take the word *mnemonic.* You know now, if you hadn't known it already, that a mnemonic is a device that helps you remember something. We're going to show you two other words that are related to it.

mnemonic: device to help you remember something
amnesty: a general pardon for offenses against a government (an official "forgetting")
amnesia: loss of memory

Pretty neat, eh? How about words from another common root:

chronological: in order according to time
syn**chron**ize: to put on the same timetable
ana**chron**ism: something out of place in time or history
chronic: continuing over a long time
chronicle: chronological record of events
chronometer: device to measure time

Sometimes it is easier to learn a whole cluster of related words than to come up with mnemonics for them individually.

The Advantages of Etymology
The principal virtues of using etymology to remember a definition are that the etymology actually relates to the word's meaning (as opposed to the image approach) and that the same etymology may be shared by lots of words. Another advantage of etymology is that it may get you interested in words. Etymology gets you involved in a story—the story of a word through the centuries of history.

In Chapter Six you will find our list of the most important roots with numerous examples following each. We collected all the etymologically related words in the back of the book because we thought that was easier and more efficient than providing the etymology of each word with its entry.

The Dangers of Etymology
Many vocabulary books claim that etymology helps you decipher the meanings of words. That's true sometimes, but etymology can lead you astray.

The etymology of a word will tell you something about the word, but it will rarely give you the definition. And it's easy to be mistaken about the etymology of a word.

For example, on a certain SAT, many clever students got a question wrong because they thought that the word *verdant* was etymologically related to words like *verify, verdict, verisimilitude,* and *veritable. Verdant* must have something to do with the concept of truth or reality, they reasoned.

Clever, but wrong. *Verdant* comes from a different family of words. It comes from the same old root as does the French word *vert,* which means green. If those same clever students had recognized that connection, they might have realized that *verdant* means green with vegetation, as in *a verdant forest.*

Similarly, a lot of words that begin with *ped* have something to do with foot: *pedestrian, pedal, pedestal, pedometer, impede, expedite.* A *pediatri-*

cian, however, is *not* a foot doctor. A pediatrician is a doctor for children. A *podiatrist* is a foot doctor. (The word *pediatrician* is, however, related to the word meaning a strict teacher of children: *pedagogue.*)

Etymology is a powerful tool to remember words that you already know, but it is a dangerous tool to determine the meaning of words you don't know.

Basic Method No. 4: WRITING ON YOUR BRAIN

Many people find that they can learn new information more readily if they write it down. The physical act of writing seems to plant the information more firmly in their minds. Perhaps the explanation is that by writing you are bringing another sense into play (you've seen the word, you've said and heard the word, and now you're *feeling* the word).

You may find it useful to spend some time writing down phrases or sentences incorporating each new word. This is a good way to practice and strengthen your spelling as well.

You'll probably have more luck if you don't merely write down the word and its definition over and over again. If you've hit upon a good mnemonic or mental image to help you remember it, or you liked the etymology, write it down. You can even draw a picture or a diagram.

Basic Method No. 5: PUTTING IT ALL TOGETHER WITH FLASH CARDS AND A NOTEBOOK

A flash card is a simple piece of paper or cardboard with a word on one side and a definition on the other. You may have used flash cards when you were first learning to read, or when you were first tackling a foreign language. Used in the proper spirit, flash cards can turn learning into a game.

Most of our students find it useful to make flash cards out of three-by-five index cards. They write or type a Hit Parade word on one side and the definition on the other. (You should also indicate the pronunciation if you aren't sure you'll remember it.) Then they can quiz one another or practice by themselves during spare moments.

Here's a basic flash card, front and back:

Front

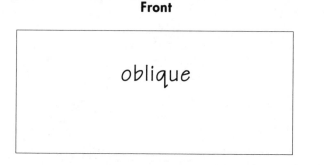

Back

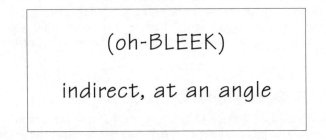

You'll learn even more if you use your imagination to make the backs of your flash cards a bit more elaborate. For example, you might decorate the back of this card with a diagram of oblique lines—that is, lines that are neither parallel nor perpendicular to each other:

Back

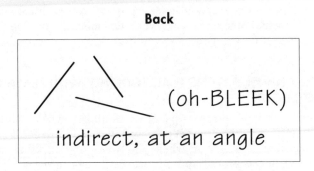

Your diagram now gives you a mental image that can help you remember the word. You'll probably think of your own mental image, one that means something to you. You could even use the word itself to create a picture that conveys the meaning of the word and that will stick in your mind to help you remember it.

Here's one possibility. We've divided the word into two parts and written them on two different lines that—surprise!—are at an oblique angle to each other:

Back

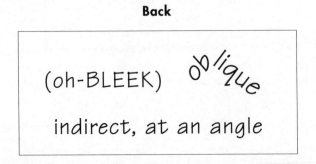

Practicing with flash cards can be a lot of fun. Parents and siblings sometimes lend a hand and discover that they are learning new words, too. And every time you look at the back of the card, you'll be reminded of the mnemonic, trick, or mental image you've devised to keep the word firmly in your memory.

Never an Idle Moment

Many of our students even tuck a few of their flash cards into a pocket when they head out the door in the morning. They can then work on them in spare moments—while riding on a bus or while listening to the radio. The more often you flash through your flash cards, the faster you'll build your vocabulary.

Ahem

Reading your flash cards isn't enough, of course. You also need to make an effort to use the words on them. Using the words, much more than reading the cards, makes the definitions sink in and take hold.

For many of our students, the most effective method is to make a few new flash cards each day, study them in spare moments throughout the day, and make an effort to use the new words in their conversations and in their writing.

A Notebook, Too

We also encourage students to compile notebooks with the new words they learn. Every time they learn new words, they record them in their notebooks. If you devote an entire page to each new word, the notebook will give you room to practice "writing on your brain." It will also give you plenty of space to doodle or jot down images that come to mind.

Even better, you can use your notebook as a place to record actual uses of new words that you discover in your own reading. If, while reading a magazine, you come across one of the words you're working on, you can copy the sentence into your notebook, giving you a brand-new example of the word in context.

Students who keep notebooks report a sense of accomplishment when they look back through their notebooks at the hundreds of new words they have learned. A notebook gives you tangible (a good word) evidence of the progress you're making.

Some People Don't Use Flash Cards and Vocabulary Notebooks

Some authorities do not believe in flash cards or vocabulary notebooks. They claim that if students forced themselves to use a mnemonic to memorize the word in the first place, they wouldn't have to use flash cards or notebooks.

There may be something to this position, but we're not going to quibble. If a student likes to use flash cards and notebooks, great. Why should we tell a student to throw away his flash cards and use only mnemonics if the student is learning lots of words?

Remember: anything goes when memorizing words. There are no rules.

OVERVIEW: A MEMORIZATION GAME PLAN

Here, pulling it all together, is our step-by-step approach to memorizing new words permanently:

Step 1:   Try to deduce the word's meaning from context.
Step 2:   Look it up!
Step 3:   Note the spelling.
Step 4:   Say the word out loud.
Step 5:   Read the main definition. Scan the secondary definitions.
Step 6:   (If you have time) Compare the definition with the definitions and usages of its synonyms.
Step 7:   Define the word using your own words.
Step 8:   Use it in a sentence.
Step 9:   Attach the word to a mnemonic, mental image, or other memory aid.
Step 10: Fill out a flash card and make a new entry in your notebook.
Step 11: Use the new word every chance you get.

Let's take a look at each of these steps.

Step 1: TRY TO DEDUCE THE WORD'S MEANING FROM CONTEXT

Context will often lead you astray, but doing a bit of detective work is a good way to sharpen your mind and hone your reading comprehension skills. And who knows? You might even guess the right meaning.

Step 2: LOOK IT UP!

Most people try to skip this step. Don't you dare! You won't know whether you're correct about the meaning of a new word until you've made sure by looking it up.

No one can learn new words without a dictionary. If you don't have one, get one now. Even good dictionaries aren't terribly expensive.

LIU!

Step 3: NOTE THE SPELLING

Look at the spelling. Close your eyes and try to reconstruct the spelling. If you have trouble visualizing, test yourself by writing out the spelling on scrap paper and checking it against the dictionary.

Also, compare the spelling variations with other spelling variations you know. This is a nice trick that helps you recognize words that you think you don't know.

For example, *sober* is an adjective; the noun form is *sobriety.* Okay, with that as a clue, the noun *propriety* relates to what adjective? *Proper. Propriety* means what is socially proper or acceptable.

Here's another example: Do you know what *incisive* means? Give up? Well, you know what *decisive* means, don't you? *Decisive* relates to what word you know? *Decision,* of course. Now, what noun do you think *incisive* relates to? *Incision. Incisive* means *sharp* or *cutting,* as in an *incisive remark,* or an *incisive observation.*

Step 4: SAY THE WORD OUT LOUD

Say the word. No, saying it to yourself is not good enough. *Out loud.* Hearing the word will bring another sense into play and help you remember the word. And as we noted earlier, you don't want to make a fool of yourself by mispronouncing words.

Our Pronunciation Key

We've never liked the pronunciation keys most dictionaries use. This may offend pedants and lexicographers, but we have decided to use a simplified pronunciation key. Our key is based on consistent phonetic sounds, so you don't have to memorize it. Still, it would be a good idea to take a few minutes now and familiarize yourself with it (especially the *e* and the *i*):

The letter(s)	is (are) pronounced like the letter(s)	in the word(s)
a	a	bat, can
ah	o	con, on
aw	aw	paw, straw
ay	a	skate, rake
e	e	stem, hem, err
ee	ea	steam, clean
i	i	rim, chin, hint
ing	ing	sing, ring
oh	o	row, tow
oo	oo	room, boom
ow	ow	cow, brow
oy	oy	boy, toy
u, uh	u	run, bun
y (ye, eye)	i	climb, time
ch	ch	chair, chin
f	f, ph	film, phony
g	g	go, goon
j	j	join, jungle
k	c	cool, cat
s	s	solid, wisp
sh	sh	shoe, wish
z	z	zoo, razor
zh	s	measure
uh	a	abridge

All other consonants are pronounced as you would expect. Capitalized letters are accented.

Step 5: READ THE MAIN DEFINITION; READ OR SCAN THE SECONDARY DEFINITIONS

Most dictionaries list the definitions in order of importance. That does not mean, of course, that the first definition is the one you are looking for. Read all the definitions; each will add to your understanding of the word.

Step 6: COMPARE THE DEFINITIONS WITH THE DEFINITIONS AND USAGES OF THE WORD'S SYNONYMS

As we showed you with the earlier examples, this step takes a little extra time, but believe us when we say that it is time well spent. Again, seeing how a word is similar to or different from synonyms or related words enhances your understanding of all of them.

Step 7: DEFINE THE WORD USING YOUR OWN WORDS

We said it before, and we'll say it again: you don't truly know what a word means unless you can define it yourself in your own way.

Step 8: USE IT IN A SENTENCE

Now that you know what the word means and what it doesn't mean, use it. Make up a sentence.

It helps to use the word in a sentence that includes a person or thing or event you know and that creates a concrete feeling or image. For example, the sentence *They are gregarious* is not as good as *Greg, Gertrude,* and *Gretchen* are *gregarious.* Which sentence do you think will help you remember what *gregarious* means?

Step 9: FIX THE WORD WITH A MNEMONIC, MENTAL IMAGE, OR OTHER MEMORY AID

With all that you've done with the word in the previous steps, you may already have memorized it. The only way to be sure, however, is to fix the word with a mnemonic.

Step 10: FILL OUT A FLASH CARD AND MAKE A NEW ENTRY IN YOUR NOTEBOOK

The paperwork is very important, particularly if you're trying to learn a lot of new words in a short period of time.

Step 11: USE THE NEW WORD EVERY CHANCE YOU GET

Dare to be repetitious. If you don't keep new knowledge in shape, you won't keep it at all.

TWO FINAL WORDS OF ADVICE: BE SUSPICIOUS

You already know some of the words in the book. You may know quite a few of them. Naturally, you don't need to drill yourself on words you already know and use.

But be careful. Before skipping a word, make certain you really do know what it means. Some of the most embarrassing vocabulary mistakes occur when a person confidently uses familiar words incorrectly.

GET TO WORK

Now on to the words. Remember that you'll retain more (and have more fun) if you tackle this book a little at a time.

CHAPTER **2**

THE
WORDS

A

ABASH (uh BASH) *v* to make ashamed; to embarrass

Meredith felt *abashed* by her inability to remember her lines in the school chorus of "Old McDonald Had a Farm."

To do something without shame or embarrassment is to do it *unabashedly*. Ken handed in a term paper that he had *unabashedly* copied from the *National Enquirer*.

ABATE (uh BAYT) *v* to subside; to reduce

George spilled a pot of hot coffee on his leg. It hurt quite a bit. Then, gradually, the agony *abated*.

Bad weather *abates* when good weather begins to return. A rain storm that does not let up continues *unabated*.

A tax *abatement* is a reduction in taxes. Businesses are sometimes given tax *abatements* in return for building factories in places where there is a particular need for jobs.

ABDICATE (AB duh kayt) *v* to step down from a position of power or responsibility

When King Edward VIII of England decided he would rather be married to Wallis Warfield Simpson, an American divorcée, than be king of England, he turned in his crown and *abdicated*.

Even people who aren't monarchs can *abdicate* duties and responsibilities. Mary *abdicated* her responsibility as a baby-sitter by locking the five-year-old in a closet and flying to the Bahamas.

ABERRATION (ab uh RAY shun) *n* something not typical; a deviation from the standard

Tom's bad behavior was an *aberration*. So was Harry's good behavior. That is, Tom was usually good and Harry was usually bad.

A snowstorm in June is an *aberration*; snow doesn't normally fall in June.

The chef at this restaurant is dreadful; the good meal we just had was an *aberration*.

An *aberration* is an *aberrant* (uh BER unt) occurrence. Tom's behavior was *aberrant*. The summer snowstorm was *aberrant*.

Note carefully the pronunciation of these words.

ABHOR (ab HOR) *v* to hate very, very much; to detest

To *abhor* something is to view it with horror. Hating a person is almost friendly in comparison with *abhorring* him or her.

Emanuel *abhorred* having anvils dropped on his head.

To *abhor* raw chicken livers is to have an *abhorrence* of them or to find them *abhorrent*.

ABJECT (AB jekt) *adj* hopeless; extremely sad and servile; defeated; utterly bummed out

An *abject* person is one who is crushed and without hope. A slave would be *abject,* in all likelihood.

Perhaps 90 percent of the time, when you encounter this word it will be followed by the word *poverty. Abject poverty* is hopeless, desperate poverty. The phrase "abject poverty" is overused. Writers use it because they are too lazy to think of anything more novel.

ABNEGATE (AB nuh gayt) *v* to deny oneself things; to reject; to renounce

Samantha *abnegated* desserts for one month after getting on the scale.

Self-abnegation is giving up oneself, usually for some higher cause. Ascetics practice *self-abnegation* because they believe it will bring them closer to spiritual purity.

ABORTIVE (uh BOR tiv) *adj* unsuccessful

Mary and Elisabeth made an *abortive* effort to bake a birthday cake; that is, their effort did not result in a birthday cake.

Fred's attempt to climb the mountain was *abortive;* he fell off when he was halfway up.

To *abort* something is to end it before it is completed. An *aborted* pregnancy, called an *abortion,* is one that is ended before the baby is born. An *abortion* in this sense doesn't have to be the result of a controversial medical procedure.

ABRIDGE (uh BRIJ) *v* to shorten; to condense

The thoughtful editor had *abridged* the massive book by removing the boring parts.

An *abridged* dictionary is one that has been shortened to keep it from crushing desks and people's laps.

An *abridgment* is a shortened or condensed work.

ABSOLUTE (AB suh loot) *adj* total; unlimited; perfect

An *absolute* ruler is one who is ruled by no one else. An *absolute* mess is a total mess. An *absolute* rule is one that has no exceptions and that you must follow, no two ways about it.

Absolute is also a noun. It means something that is total, unlimited, or perfect. Death, for living things, is an *absolute.* There just isn't any way around it.

ABSOLVE (ab ZOLV) *v* to forgive or free from blame; to free from sin; to free from an obligation

The priest *absolved* the sinner who had come to church to confess his sin.

Tom's admission of guilt *absolved* Dick, who had originally been accused of the crime.

It is also possible to *absolve* someone of a responsibility. Bill *absolved* Mary of her obligation to go to the prom with him. That is, he told her it was all right if she went with the captain of the football team instead.

The act of *absolving* is called *absolution* (ab suh LOO shun).

Q•U•I•C•K • Q•U•I•Z #1

Match each word in the first column with its definition in the second column. Check your answers in the back of the book.

1. abash   a. step down from power
2. abate   b. hopeless
3. abdicate   c. unsuccessful
4. aberration   d. forgive
5. abhor   e. total
6. abject   f. subside
7. abnegate   g. detest
8. abortive   h. shorten
9. abridge   i. deviation
10. absolute   j. embarrass
11. absolve   k. renounce

ABSTINENT (AB stuh nunt) *adj* abstaining; voluntarily not doing something, especially something pleasant that is bad for you or has a bad reputation

Beulah used to be a chain-smoker; now she's *abstinent* (it was just too hard to get those chains lit).

Cynthia, who was dieting, tried to be *abstinent,* but when she saw the chocolate cake she realized that she would probably have to eat the entire thing.

A person who *abstains* from something is an *abstainer.*

ABSTRACT (AB strakt) *adj* theoretical; impersonal

To like something in the *abstract* is to like the idea of it. He liked oysters in the *abstract,* but when he actually tried one he became nauseated.

ABSTRUSE (ab STROOS) *adj* hard to understand

The professor's article, on the meaning of meaning, was very *abstruse.* Michael couldn't even pronounce the words in it.

Nuclear physics is a subject that is too *abstruse* for most people.

ABYSMAL (uh BIZ mul) *adj* extremely hopeless or wretched; bottomless

An *abyss* (uh BIS) is a bottomless pit, or something so deep that it seems bottomless. *Abysmal* despair is despair so deep that no hope seems possible.

The nation's debt crisis was *abysmal;* there seemed to be no possible solution to it.

Abysmal is often used somewhat sloppily to mean very bad. You might hear a losing baseball team's performance referred to as *abysmal*. This isn't strictly correct, but many people do it.

ACCOLADE (AK uh layd) n an award; an honor

This word is generally used in the plural. The first break-dancing troupe to perform in Carnegie Hall, the Teflon Toughs, received the *accolades* of the critics as well as of the fans.

ACCOST (uh KAWST) v to approach and speak to someone

Amanda karate chopped the stranger who *accosted* her in the street and was embarrassed to find he was an old blind man.

ACERBIC (uh SUR bik) adj bitter; sour; severe

Barry sat silently as our teacher read aloud her *acerbic* comments on his paper.

Acerb and *acerbic* are synonyms. *Acerbity* is bitterness.

ACQUIESCE (ak wee ES) v to comply passively; to accept; to assent; to agree

To *acquiesce* is to do something without objection—to do it *quietly*. As the similarity of their spellings indicates, the words *acquiesce* and *quiet* are closely related. They are both based on Latin words meaning rest or be quiet.

The pirates asked Pete to walk the plank; he took one look at their swords and then *acquiesced*.

Acquiesce is sometimes used sloppily as a simple synonym for *agree* in situations where it isn't really appropriate. For example, it isn't really possible to *acquiesce* noisily, enthusiastically, or eagerly. Don't forget the *quiet* in the middle.

To *acquiesce* is to exhibit *acquiescence*.

ACRID (AK rid) adj harsh; like acid

The chili we had at the party had an *acrid* taste; it was harsh and unpleasant.

Long after the fire had been put out, we could feel the *acrid* sting of smoke in our nostrils.

Acrid is used most often with tastes and smells, but it can be used more broadly to describe anything that is offensive in a similar way. A comment that stung like acid could be called *acrid*. So could a harsh personality.

ACRIMONIOUS (ak ruh MOH nee us) adj full of spite; bitter; nasty

George and Elizabeth's discussion turned *acrimonious* when Elizabeth introduced the subject of George's perennial, incorrigible stupidity.

Relations between the competing candidates were so *acrimonious* that each refused to acknowledge the presence of the other.

ACUMEN (AK yoo mun) n keenness of judgment; mental sharpness

A woman who knows how to turn a dollar into a million dollars overnight might be said to have a lot of business *acumen*.

Ernie's near-total lack of *acumen* led him to invest all his money in a company that had already gone out of business.

Note carefully the pronunciation of this word.

Q•U•I•C•K • Q•U•I•Z #2

Match each word in the first column with its definition in the second column. Check your answers in the back of the book.

1. abstinent b
2. abstract h
3. abstruse a
4. abysmal c
5. accolade i
6. accost j
7. acerbic d
8. acquiesce e
9. acrid f
10. acrimonious d
11. acumen g

a. hard to understand
b. voluntarily avoiding
c. wretched
d. bitter (2)
e. comply
f. harsh
g. mental sharpness
h. theoretical
i. award
j. approach someone

ACUTE (uh KYOOT) *adj* sharp; shrewd

If your eyesight is *acute,* you can see things that other people can't. You have visual *acuity* (uh KYOO uh tee). An *acute* mind is a quick, intelligent one. You have mental *acuity.* An *acute* pain is a sharp pain.

Acute means sharp only in a figurative sense. A knife, which is sharp enough to *cut,* is never said to be *acute.*

Acute is a word doctors throw around quite a bit. An *acute* disease is one that reaches its greatest intensity very quickly and then goes away. What could a disease be if it isn't *acute?* See *chronic.*

ADAMANT (AD uh munt) *adj* stubborn; unyielding; completely inflexible

Candice was *adamant:* she would never go out with Paul again.

A very hard substance, like a diamond, is also *adamant.*

Adamantine (ad uh MAN teen) and *adamant* are synonyms. *Adamancy* is being *adamant.*

ADDRESS (uh DRES) *v* to speak to; to direct one's attention to

To *address* a convention is to give a speech to the convention. To *address* a problem is to face it and set about solving it. Ernie *addressed* the problem of *addressing* the convention by sitting down and writing his speech.

ADHERENT (ad HEER unt) *n* follower; supporter; believer

The king's *adherents* threw a big birthday party for him, just to show how much they liked him.

To *adhere* to something is to stick to it. *Adherents* are people who *adhere* to, or stick to, something or someone. Following someone or something, especially rules or laws, is *adherence.*

A religion could be said to have *adherents,* assuming there are people who believe in it. Governments, causes, ideas, people, philoso-

phies, and many other things can have *adherents,* too.
Note carefully the pronunciation of this word.

ADMONISH (ad MAHN ish) *v* to scold gently; to warn

The boys' mother *admonished* them not to eat the pie she had just baked. When they did so anyway, she *admonished* them for doing it. In the first sentence *admonish* means warn; in the second it means scold gently. Consider yourself *admonished* not to misuse this word.

The noun is *admonition* (ad muh NISH un) and the adjective is *admonitory* (ad MAHN i tor ee).

ADROIT (uh DROYT) *adj* skillful; dexterous; clever; shrewd; socially at ease

Adroit comes from *droit,* which is the French word for *right* (the opposite of *left*). *Dexterous,* which means pretty much the same thing as *adroit,* comes from *dexter,* which is the Latin word for *right* (the opposite of *left*). Right-handed people were once thought to be more *dexterous* and *adroit* than left-handed people. In fact, left-handed people were once thought to be downright evil, or *sinister,* which is the Latin word for *left* (the opposite of *right*). To say nowadays that right-handed people are better than left-handed people would be considered *gauche,* which means graceless, crude, socially awkward, or clumsy. *Gauche* (gohsh) is the French word for *left* (the opposite of *right*). A synonym for *gauche* is *maladroit.*

Got all that? Here it is again. It would be *gauche* to go to the ball wearing your right shoe on your left foot and your left shoe on your right foot. It would also be hard to dance *adroitly* with your shoes that way. If you were sufficiently *dexterous,* you might be able to switch and retie your shoes while you were dancing, but your dancing partner might think you were up to something *sinister* down there and ask you to keep both your right hand and your left hand to yourself.

ADULATION (aj uh LAY shun) *n* wild or excessive admiration; flattery

The boss thrived on the *adulation* of his scheming secretary.
The rock star grew to abhor the *adulation* of his fans.
There is a note of insincerity in *adulation,* as there is in *flattery.*
The verb is *adulate* (AJ uh layt).

Q•U•I•C•K • Q•U•I•Z #3

Match each word in the first column with its definition in the second column. Check your answers in the back of the book.

1. acute a
2. adulation h
3. adamant g
4. address e
5. adherent B
6. admonish d
7. adroit f
8. dexterous f
9. gauche c

    a. sharp
    b. follower
    c. socially awkward
    d. scold gently
    e. speak to
    f. skillful (2)
    g. unyielding
    h. wild admiration

ADULTERATE (uh DUL tuh rayt) *v* to contaminate; to make impure

We discovered that our orange juice had radioactive waste in it; we discovered, in other words, that our orange juice had been *adulterated*.

Vegetarians do not like their foods *adulterated* with animal fats.

Unadulterated means pure. *Unadulterated* joy is joy untainted by sadness.

ADVERSE (ad VURS) *adj* unfavorable; antagonistic

Airplanes often don't fly in *adverse* weather.

We had to play our soccer match under *adverse* conditions: it was snowing and only three members of our team had bothered to show up.

An airplane that took off in bad weather and reached its destination safely would be said to have overcome *adversity*. *Adversity* means misfortune or unfavorable circumstances. To do something "in the face of *adversity*" is to undertake a task despite obstacles. Some people are at their best in *adversity*, because they rise to the occasion.

A word often confused with *adverse* is *averse* (uh VURS). The two are related but they don't mean quite the same thing. A person who is *averse* to doing something is a person who doesn't want to do it. To be *averse* to something is to be opposed to doing it—to have an *aversion* to doing it.

AESTHETIC (es THET ik) *adj* having to do with artistic beauty; artistic

Our art professor had a highly developed *aesthetic* sense; he found things to admire in paintings that, to us, looked like garbage.

Someone who admires beautiful things greatly can be called an *aesthete* (ES theet). *Aesthetics* is the study of beauty or principles of beauty.

AFFABLE (AF uh bul) *adj* easy to talk to; friendly

Susan was an *affable* girl; she could strike up a pleasant conversation with almost anyone.

The Jeffersons' dog was big but *affable;* it liked to lick little children on the nose.

The noun is *affability.*

AFFECTATION (af ek TAY shun) *n* unnatural or artificial behavior, usually intended to impress

Bucky's English accent is an *affectation.* He spent only a week in England, and that was several years ago.

Elizabeth had somehow acquired the absurd *affectation* of pretending that she didn't know how to turn on a television set.

A person with an *affectation* is said to be *affected.*

To *affect* a characteristic or habit is to adopt it consciously, usually in the hope of impressing other people. Edward *affected* to be more of an artist than he really was. Everyone hated him for it.

AFFINITY (uh FIN uh tee) *n* sympathy; attraction; kinship; similarity

Ducks have an *affinity* for water; that is, they like to be in it.

Children have an *affinity* for trouble; that is, they often find themselves in it.

Magnets and iron have an *affinity* for each other; that is, each is attracted to the other.

Affinity also means similarity or resemblance. There is an *affinity* between snow and sleet.

AFFLUENT (AF loo unt) *adj* rich; prosperous

A person can be *affluent;* all it takes is money. A country can be *affluent,* too, if it's full of *affluent* people.

Affluence means the same thing as wealth or prosperity.

Note carefully the pronunciation of this word.

AGENDA (uh JEN duh) *n* program; the things to be done

What's on the *agenda* for the board meeting? A little gossip, then lunch.

A politician is often said to have an *agenda.* The politician's *agenda* consists of the things he or she wishes to accomplish.

An *agenda,* such as that for a meeting, is often written down, but it doesn't have to be. A person who has sneaky ambitions or plans is often said to have a secret or hidden *agenda.*

AGRARIAN (uh GRAR ee un) *adj* relating to land; relating to the management or farming of land

Agrarian usually has to do with farming. Think of agriculture. Politics in this country often pit the rural, *agrarian* interests against the urban interests.

AGGREGATE (AG ruh gut) *n* sum total; a collection of separate things
mixed together

Chili is an *aggregate* of meat and beans.

Aggregate (AG ruh gayt) can also be a verb or an adjective. You
would make chili by *aggregating* meat and beans. Chili is an *aggregate* (AG ruh gut) food.

Similar and related words include *congregate, segregate,* and *integrate.* To *aggregate* is to bring together, to *congregate* is to get together, to *segregate* is to keep apart (or separate), to *integrate* is to unite.

A church's *congregation* is the group of people that gets together
inside it on Sunday.

Racial *segregation* is the separation of different races. School systems in which blacks and whites attend different schools are called
segregated.

The act of opening those schools to members of all races is called
integration.

AGNOSTIC (ag NAHS tik) *n* one who believes that the existence of a
god can be neither proven nor disproven

An *atheist* is someone who does not believe in a god. An *agnostic,*
on the other hand, isn't sure. He doesn't believe but he doesn't *not*
believe, either.

The noun is *agnosticism* (ag NAHS tuh siz um).

ALACRITY (uh LAK ri tee) *n* cheerful eagerness or readiness to respond

David could hardly wait for his parents to leave; he carried their
luggage out to the car with great *alacrity.*

Note carefully the pronunciation of this word.

ALLEGE (uh LEJ) *v* to assert without proof

If I say, "Bill *alleges* that I stole his hat," I am saying two things:
1. Bill says I stole his hat.

2. I say I didn't do it.

To *allege* something is to assert it without proving it. Such an assertion is called an *allegation* (al uh GAY shun).

The adjective is *alleged* (uh LEJD). If the police accuse someone of having committed a crime, newspapers will usually refer to that person as an *alleged* criminal. The police have *alleged* that he or she committed the crime, but a jury hasn't made a decision yet.

ALLEVIATE (uh LEE vee ayt) *v* to relieve, usually temporarily or incompletely; to make bearable; to lessen

Aspirin *alleviates* headache pain. When your headache comes back, take some more aspirin.

Visiting the charming pet cemetery *alleviated* the woman's grief over the death of her canary.

ALLOCATE (AL uh kayt) *v* to distribute; to assign; to allot

The long car trip had been a big failure, and David, Doug, and Jan spent several hours attempting to *allocate* the blame. In the end, they decided it had all been Jan's fault.

The office manager had *allocated* just seven paper clips for our entire department.

ALLOY (AL oy) *n* a combination of two or more things, usually metals

Brass is an *alloy* of copper and zinc. That is, you make brass by combining copper and zinc.

Alloy (uh LOY) is often used as a verb. To *alloy* two things is to mix them together. There is usually an implication that the mixture is less than the sum of the parts. That is, there is often something undesirable or debased about an *alloy* (as opposed to a pure substance).

Unalloyed means undiluted or pure. *Unalloyed* dislike is dislike undiminished by any positive feelings; *unalloyed* love is love undiminished by any negative feelings.

Q•U•I•C•K • Q•U•I•Z #5

Match each word in the first column with its definition in the second column. Check your answers in the back of the book.

1. aggregate
2. congregate
3. segregate
4. integrate
5. agnostic
6. alacrity
7. allege
8. alleviate
9. allocate
10. alloy

a. get together
b. unite
c. someone unconvinced about the existence of a god
d. relieve
e. keep apart
f. combination of metals
g. sum total
h. distribute
i. assert
j. cheerful eagerness

ALLUSION (uh LOO zhun) *n* an indirect reference (often to a literary work); a hint

To *allude* to something is to refer to it indirectly. When Ralph said, "I sometimes wonder whether to be or not to be," he was *alluding* to a famous line in *Hamlet*. If Ralph had said, "As Hamlet said, 'To be or not to be, that is the question,'" his statement would have been a direct reference, not an *allusion*.

An *allusion* is an *allusion* only if the source isn't identified directly. Anything else is a reference or a quotation.

If Andrea says, "I enjoyed your birthday party," she isn't *alluding* to the birthday party; she's referring to it, or mentioning it. But if she says, "I like the way you blow out candles," she is *alluding* to the party.

ALOOF (uh LOOF) *adj* uninvolved; standing off; keeping one's distance

Al, on the roof, felt very *aloof*.

To stand *aloof* from a touch-football game is to stand on the sidelines and not take part.

Cats are often said to be *aloof* because they usually mind their own business and don't crave the affection of people.

ALTRUISM (AL troo iz um) *n* selflessness; generosity; devotion to the interests of others

The private foundation depended on the *altruism* of the extremely rich old man. When he decided to start spending his money on his new eighteen-year-old girlfriend instead, the foundation went out of business.

To be *altruistic* is to help others without expectation of personal gain. Giving money to charity is an act of *altruism*. The *altruist* does it just to be nice, although he'll probably also remember to take a tax deduction.

An *altruistic* act is also an act of *philanthropy*, which means almost the same thing.

AMBIENCE (AM bee uns) *n* atmosphere; mood; feeling

By decorating their house with plastic beach balls and Popsicle sticks, the Cramers created a playful *ambience* that delighted young children.

A restaurant's *ambience* is the look, mood, and feel of the place. People sometimes say that a restaurant has "an atmosphere of *ambience*." To do so is redundant—*atmosphere* and *ambience* mean the same thing.

Ambience is a French word that can also be pronounced "ahm BYAHNS." The adjective *ambient* (AM bee unt) means surrounding or circulating.

AMBIGUOUS (am BIG yoo us) *adj* unclear in meaning; confusing; capable of being interpreted in different ways

We listened to the weather report, but the forecast was *ambiguous*; we couldn't tell if the day was going to be rainy or sunny.

The poem we read in English class was *ambiguous;* no one had any idea what the poet was trying to say.

The noun is *ambiguity* (am buh GYOO uh tee).

AMBIVALENT (am BIV uh lunt) *adj* undecided; neutral; wishy-washy

Susan felt *ambivalent* about George as a boyfriend. Her frequent desire to break up with him reflected this *ambivalence.*

Q•U•I•C•K • Q•U•I•Z #6

Match each word in the first column with its definition in the second column. Check your answers in the back of the book.

1. allusion *e*
2. aloof *b*
3. altruism *d*
4. ambience *a*
5. ambiguous *c*
6. ambivalent *e*

    a. atmosphere
    b. standoffish
    c. confusing
    d. generosity
    e. indirect reference
    f. undecided

AMELIORATE (uh MEEL yuh rayt) *v* to make better or more tolerable

The condition of the prisoners was *ameliorated* when the warden gave them color television sets and keys to their cells.

My great-uncle's gift of several million dollars considerably *ameliorated* my financial condition.

AMENABLE (uh MEE nuh bul) *adj* obedient; willing to give in to the wishes of another; agreeable

I suggested that Bert pay for my lunch as well as for his own and, to my surprise, he was *amenable.*

The plumber was *amenable* to my paying my bill with jelly beans, which was lucky, because I had more jelly beans than money.

Note carefully the pronunciation of this word.

AMENITY (uh MEN i tee) *adj* pleasantness; attractive or comfortable feature

The *amenities* at the local club include a swimming pool, a golf course, and a fallout shelter.

If an older guest at your house asks you where the *amenities* are, he or she is probably asking for directions to the bathroom. Provide them.

Those little bars of soap and bottles of shampoo found in hotel rooms are known in the hotel business as *amenities.* They are meant to increase your comfort. People like them because people like almost anything that is free (although, of course, the cost of providing such *amenities* is simply added to the price of hotel rooms).

AMIABLE (AY mee uh bul) *adj* friendly; agreeable

Our *amiable* guide made us feel right at home in what would otherwise have been a cold and forbidding museum.

The drama critic was so *amiable* in person that even the subjects of negative reviews found it impossible not to like her.

Amicable is a similar and related word. Two not very *amiable* people might nonetheless make an *amicable* agreement. *Amicable* means politely friendly, or not hostile. Two countries might trade *amicably* with each other even while technically remaining enemies. Jeff and Clarissa had a surprisingly *amicable* divorce and remained good friends even after paying their lawyers' fees.

AMNESTY (AM nuh stee) *n* an official pardon for a group of people who have violated a law or policy

Amnesty comes from the same root as *amnesia*, the condition that causes characters in movies to forget everything except how to speak English and drive their cars.

An *amnesty* is an official forgetting. When a state government declares a tax *amnesty*, it is saying that if people pay the taxes they owe, the government will officially "forget" that they broke the law by not paying them in the first place.

The word *amnesty* always refers to a pardon given to a group or class of people. A pardon granted to a single person is simply a pardon.

AMORAL (ay MOR ul) *adj* lacking a sense of right and wrong; neither good nor bad, neither moral nor immoral; without moral feelings

Very young children are *amoral;* when they cry, they aren't being bad or good, they're merely doing what they have to do.

A *moral* person does right; an *immoral* person does wrong; an *amoral* person simply does.

AMOROUS (AM ur us) *adj* feeling loving, especially in a sexual sense; in love; relating to love

The *amorous* couple made quite a scene at the movie. The movie they were watching, *Love Story*, was pretty *amorous* itself. It was about an *amorous* couple, one of whom died.

AMORPHOUS (uh MOR fus) *adj* shapeless; without a regular or stable shape; bloblike

Ed's teacher said that his term paper was *amorphous;* she said that it was as shapeless and disorganized as a cloud.

The sleepy little town was engulfed by an *amorphous* blob of glowing protoplasm—a higher intelligence from outer space.

To say that something has an "*amorphous* shape" is a contradiction. How can a shape be shapeless?

ANACHRONISM (uh NAK ruh niz um) *n* something out of place in time or history; an incongruity

In this day of impersonal hospitals, a family doctor who will visit you at home seems like an *anachronism*.

In these modern, liberated times, some women disdain the *anachronistic* practice of a man's holding open a door for a woman.

ANALOGY (uh NAL uh jee) *n* a comparison of one thing to another; similarity

To say having an allergy feels like being bitten by an alligator would be to make or draw an *analogy* between an allergy and an alligator bite. *Analogy* usually refers to similarities between things that are not otherwise very similar. If you don't think an allergy is at all like an alligator bite, you might say, "That *analogy* doesn't hold up." To say that there is no *analogy* between an allergy and an alligator bite is to say that they are not *analogous* (uh NAL uh gus).

Something similar in a particular respect to something else is its *analog* (AN uh lawg), sometimes spelled *analogue*.

Q•U•I•C•K • Q•U•I•Z #7

Match each word in the first column with its definition in the second column. Check your answers in the back of the book.

1. ameliorate	a. pleasantness
2. amenable	b. comparison
3. amenity	c. obedient
4. amiable	d. without moral feeling
5. amicable	e. feeling loving
6. amnesty	f. make better
7. amoral	g. shapeless
8. amorous	h. politely friendly
9. amorphous	i. official pardon
10. anachronism	j. friendly
11. analogy	k. incongruity

ANARCHY (AN ur kee) *n* absence of government or control; lawlessness; disorder

The country fell into a state of *anarchy* after the rebels kidnapped the president and locked the legislature inside the Capitol.

The word doesn't have to be used in its strict political meaning. You could say that there was *anarchy* in the kindergarten when the teacher stepped out of the door for a moment. You could say it, and you would probably be right.

The words *anarchy* and *monarchy* are closely related. *Anarchy* means no leader; *monarchy*, a government headed by a king or queen, means one leader.

ANECDOTE (AN ik doht) *n* a short account of a humorous or revealing incident

The old lady kept the motorcycle gang thoroughly amused with *anecdote* after *anecdote* about her cute little dog.

Fred told an *anecdote* about the time Sally got her big toe stuck in a bowling ball.

The vice president set the crowd at ease with an *anecdote* about his childhood desire to become a vice president.

To say that the evidence of life on other planets is merely *anecdotal* is to say that we haven't captured any aliens, but simply heard a lot of stories from people who claimed to have been kidnapped by flying saucers.

ANGUISH (ANG gwish) *n* agonizing physical or mental pain

Theresa had been a nurse in the emergency room for twenty years, but she had never gotten used to the *anguish* of accident victims.

ANIMOSITY (an uh MAHS uh tee) *n* resentment; hostility; ill will

Loulou hates Eric so much that she would like to stuff him in a mail sack and throw him out of an airplane. Loulou is full of *animosity*.

A person whose look could kill is a person whose *animosity* is evident.

The rivals for the state championship felt great *animosity* toward each other. Whenever they ran into each other, they snarled.

ANOMALY (uh NAHM uh lee) *n* an aberration; an irregularity; a deviation

A snowy winter day is not an *anomaly*, but a snowy July day is.

A house without a roof is an *anomaly*—a cold, wet *anomaly*. A roofless house could be said to be *anomalous*. Something that is *anomalous* is something that is not normal or regular.

ANTECEDENT (an tuh SEED unt) *n* someone or something that went before; something that provides a model for something that came after it

Your parents and grandparents could be said to be your *antecedents;* they came before you.

The horse-drawn wagon is an *antecedent* of the modern automobile.

Antecedent can also be used as an adjective. The oil lamp was *antecedent* to the light bulb.

In grammar, the *antecedent* of a pronoun is the person, place, or thing to which it refers. In the previous sentence, the *antecedent* of *it* is *antecedent*. In the sentence "Bill and Harry were walking together, and then he hit him," it is impossible to determine what the *antecedents* of the pronouns (*he* and *him*) are.

Antecedent is related to a word that is similar in meaning: *precedent*.

ANTIPATHY (an TIP uh thee) *n* firm dislike; a dislike

I feel *antipathy* toward bananas wrapped in ham. I do not want them for dinner. I also feel a certain amount of *antipathy* toward the cook who keeps trying to force me to eat them. My feelings on these matters are quite *antipathetic* (an tip uh THET ik).

I could also say that ham-wrapped bananas and the cooks who serve them are among my *antipathies*. My *antipathies* are the things I don't like.

Note carefully the pronunciation of this word.

ANTITHESIS (an TITH uh sis) *n* the direct opposite

Erin is the *antithesis* of Erika: Erin is bright and beautiful; Erika is dull and plain.

Note carefully the pronunciation of this word.

APARTHEID (uh PAHRT hayt) *n* the abhorrent policy of racial segregation and oppression in the Republic of South Africa

The word *apartheid* is related to the word *apart*. Under *apartheid* in South Africa, blacks are kept apart from whites and denied all rights.

The word *apartheid* is sometimes applied to less radical forms of racial injustice and to other kinds of separation. Critics have sometimes accused American public schools of practicing educational *apartheid*, by providing substandard schooling for nonwhites.

This word can also be pronounced "uh PAHRT hyte."

Q•U•I•C•K • Q•U•I•Z #8

Match each word in the first column with its definition in the second column. Check your answers in the back of the book.

1. anarchy
2. monarchy
3. anecdote
4. anguish
5. animosity
6. anomaly
7. antecedent
8. antipathy
9. antithesis
10. apartheid

a. resentment
b. racial oppression
c. firm dislike
d. irregularity
e. what went before
f. agonizing pain
g. amusing account
h. government by king or queen
i. lawlessness
j. direct opposite

APATHY (AP uh thee) *n* lack of interest; lack of feeling

The members of the student council accused the senior class of *apathy* because none of the seniors had bothered to sign up for the big annual bake sale.

Jill didn't care one bit about current events; she was entirely *apathetic.*

APHORISM (AF uh riz um) *n* a brief, often witty saying; a proverb

Benjamin Franklin was fond of *aphorisms.* He was frequently *aphoristic.*

APOCALYPSE (uh PAHK uh lips) *n* a prophetic revelation, especially one concerning the end of the world

In strict usage, *apocalypse* refers to specific Judeo-Christian writings from ancient times, but most people use it more generally in connection with predictions of things like nuclear war, the destruction of the ozone layer, and the spread of fast-food restaurants to every corner of the universe. To make such predictions, or to be deeply pessimistic, is to be *apocalyptic* (uh pahk uh LIP tik).

APOCRYPHAL (uh POK ruh ful) *n* of dubious authenticity; fictitious; spurious

An *apocryphal* story is one whose truth is not proven or whose falsehood is strongly suspected. Like *apocalypse,* this word has a religious origin. The *Apocrypha* are a number of "extra" books of the Old Testament that Protestants and Jews don't include in their Bibles because they don't think they're authentic.

APOTHEOSIS (uh pahth ee OH sis) *n* elevation to divine status; the perfect example of something

Some people think that the Corvette is the *apotheosis* of American car making. They think it's the ideal.

Geoffrey is unbearable to be with. He thinks he's the *apotheosis* of masculinity.

APPEASE (uh PEEZ) *v* to soothe; to pacify by giving in to

Larry *appeased* his angry mother by promising to make his bed every morning without fail until the end of time.

The trembling farmer handed over all his grain, but still the emperor was not *appeased.*

We *appeased* the angry juvenile delinquents by permitting them to slash the tires of Jerry's father's car.

The noun is *appeasement.*

APPRECIATE (uh PREE shee ayt) *v* to increase in value

The Browns bought their house twenty years ago for a hundred dollars, but it has *appreciated* considerably since then; today it's worth almost a million dollars.

Harry bought Joe's collection of old chewing-tobacco tins as an investment. His hope was that the tins would *appreciate* over the next few years, enabling him to turn a profit by selling them to someone else.

The opposite of *appreciate* is *depreciate.* When a new car loses value over time, we say it has *depreciated.*

APPREHENSIVE (ap ruh HEN siv) *adj* worried; anxious

The *apprehensive* child clung to his father's leg as the two of them walked into the main circus tent to watch the lion tamer.

Bill was *apprehensive* about the exam, because he had forgotten to go to class for several months. As it turned out, his *apprehensions* were justified. He couldn't answer a single question on the test.

A *misapprehension* is a misunderstanding. Bill had no *misapprehensions* about his lack of preparation; he knew perfectly well he would fail abysmally.

Q•U•I•C•K • Q•U•I•Z #9

Match each word in the first column with its definition in the second column. Check your answers in the back of the book.

1. apathy	a. of dubious authenticity
2. aphorism	b. misunderstanding
3. apocalypse	c. increase in value
4. apocryphal	d. lack of interest
5. apotheosis	e. soothe
6. appease	f. prophetic revelation
7. appreciate	g. decrease in value
8. depreciate	h. the perfect example
9. apprehensive	i. witty saying
10. misapprehension	j. worried

APPROBATION (ap ruh BAY shun) *n* approval; praise

The crowd expressed its *approbation* of what the team had done by gleefully covering the field with chicken carcasses.

The ambassador's actions met with the *approbation* of his commander in chief.

Approbation is a fancy word for *approval,* to which it is closely related. *Disapprobation* is disapproval.

APPROPRIATE (uh PROH pree ayt) *v* to take without permission; to set aside for a particular use

Nick *appropriated* my lunch; he grabbed it out of my hands and ate it. So I *appropriated* Ed's.

The deer and raccoons *appropriated* the vegetables in our garden last summer. This year we'll build a better fence.

Don't confuse the pronunciation of the verb *to appropriate* with the pronunciation of the adjective *appropriate* (uh PROH pree it). When Congress decides to buy some new submarines, it *appropriates* money for them. That is, it sets some money aside. The money thus set aside is called an *appropriation.*

When an elected official takes money that was supposed to be spent on submarines and spends it on a Rolls-Royce and a few mink coats, he is said to have *misappropriated* the money.

When the government decides to build a highway through your backyard, it *expropriates* your property for this purpose. That is, it uses its official authority to take possession of your property.

APTITUDE (AP tuh tood) *n* capacity for learning; natural ability

Princeton Review students have a marked *aptitude* for taking the Scholastic Aptitude Test. They earn high scores.

I tried to repair my car, but as I sat on the floor of my garage surrounded by mysterious parts, I realized that I had no *aptitude* for automobile repair.

The opposite of *aptitude* is *ineptitude*.

ARBITER (AHR buh tur) *n* one who decides; a judge

A judge is an *arbiter*.

An *arbiter* of fashion is someone who determines what other people will wear by wearing it herself.

An *arbiter arbitrates*, or weighs opposing viewpoints and makes decisions. The words *arbiter* and *arbitrator* mean the same thing. An *arbiter* presides over an *arbitration*, which is a formal meeting to settle a dispute.

ARBITRARY (AHR buh trer ee) *adj* random; capricious

The grades Mr. Simone gave his English students appeared to be *arbitrary;* they didn't seem to be related to anything the students had done in class.

The old judge was *arbitrary* in sentencing criminals; there was no sensible pattern to the sentences he handed down.

ARCANE (ahr KAYN) *adj* mysterious; known only to a select few

The rites of the secret cult were *arcane;* no one outside the cult knew what they were.

The *arcane* formula for the cocktail was scrawled in blood on a faded scrap of paper.

We could make out only a little of the *arcane* inscription on the old trunk.

ARCHAIC (ahr KAY ik) *adj* extremely old; ancient; outdated

The tribe's traditions are *archaic*. They have been in force for thousands of years.

Archaic civilizations are ones that disappeared a long time ago.

An *archaic* meaning of a word is one that isn't used anymore.

Q•U•I•C•K • Q•U•I•Z #10

Match each word in the first column with its definition in the second column. Check your answers in the back of the book.

1. approbation
2. appropriate
3. misappropriate
4. expropriate
5. aptitude
6. arbiter
7. arbitrate
8. arbitrary
9. arcane
10. archaic

a. misuse public money
b. extremely old
c. take without permission
d. weigh opposing views
e. mysterious
f. approval
g. random
h. take property officially
i. judge
j. natural ability

ARCHETYPE (AHR kuh type) *n* an original model or pattern

An *archetype* is similar to a *prototype*. A *prototype* is a first, tentative model that is made but that will be improved in later versions. Henry Ford built a *prototype* of his Model T in his basement. His mother kicked him out, so he had no choice but to start a motor car company.

An *archetype* is usually something that precedes something else. Plato is the *archetype* of all philosophers.

An *archetype* is *archetypal* or *archetypical*.

Note carefully the pronunciation of this word.

ARDENT (AHR dunt) *adj* passionate

Larry's *ardent* wooing finally got on Cynthia's nerves, and she told him to get lost.

Blanche happily stuffed badgers from morning to night. She was an *ardent* taxidermist.

To be *ardent* is to have *ardor*. The young lovers were oblivious to everything except their *ardor* for each other.

ARDUOUS (AHR joo us) *adj* hard; difficult

Climbing the mountain was *arduous*. We were so exhausted when we got to the top that we forgot to enjoy the view.

The *arduous* car trip was made even more difficult by the fact that all four tires went flat, one after another.

ARISTOCRATIC (uh ris tuh KRAT ik) *adj* of noble birth; snobbish

Prince Charles is *aristocratic*. He is a member of the British *aristocracy,* a small class of privileged people.

Polo, which Prince Charles enjoys, is often said to be an *aristocratic* sport, because it is typically played by dukes, marquises, and other privileged people.

It is possible to be an *aristocrat* (uh RIS tuh krat) without being rich, although *aristocrats* tend to be quite wealthy. There is nothing you can do to become an *aristocrat,* short of being born into a family of them.

People who act as though they think they are better than everyone else are often said to be *aristocratic*. A person with an "*aristocratic* bearing" is a person who keeps his or her nose in the air and looks down on everyone else.

ARTFUL (AHRT ful) *adj* crafty; wily; sly

After dinner, the *artful* counselor told the campers that there was a madman loose in the woods, thus causing them to lie quietly in the tent.

The *Artful* Dodger is a sly con man in Charles Dickens's *Oliver Twist*.

Someone who is *artless,* on the other hand, is simple and honest. Young children are charmingly *artless*.

ARTIFICE (AHRT uh fus) *n* a clever trick; cunning

The Trojan Horse was an *artifice* designed to get the soldiers inside the walls.

Mrs. Baker had to resort to *artifice* to get her children to take their baths: she told them that the bathtub was filled with sugar syrup and that they could drink it if they would take off their clothes and climb in.

Artifice and *artificial* are related words.

ASCENDANCY (uh SEN dun see) n supremacy; domination

Small computers have been in *ascendancy* for the past few years.

The *ascendancy* of the new regime had been a great boon for the economy of the tiny tropical kingdom.

When something is in *ascendancy,* it is *ascendant.*

ASCETIC (uh SET ik) adj hermitlike; practicing self-denial

The college professor's apartment, which contained no furniture except a single tattered mattress, was uncomfortably *ascetic.*

In his effort to save money, Roy led an *ascetic* existence: he never went out, he never ate anything but soup, and he never had any fun.

Ascetic can also be a noun. A person who leads an *ascetic* existence is an *ascetic.* An *ascetic* is someone who practices *asceticism.*

A similar-sounding word with a very different meaning is *aesthetic* (es THET ik). Don't be confused.

ASSIDUOUS (uh SIJ oo us) adj hardworking; busy; quite diligent

The workmen were *assiduous* in their effort to get nothing done; instead of working, they drank coffee all day long.

Wendell was the only *assiduous* student in the entire math class; all the other students had to copy their homework from him.

Q•U•I•C•K • Q•U•I•Z #11

Match each word in the first column with its definition in the second column. Check your answers in the back of the book.

1. archetype	a. passionate
2. ardent	b. of noble birth
3. arduous	c. supremacy
4. aristocratic	d. hardworking
5. artful	e. difficult
6. artifice	f. trickery
7. ascendancy	g. hermitlike
8. ascetic	h. crafty
9. assiduous	i. original model

ASSIMILATE (uh SIM uh layt) v to take in; to absorb; to learn thoroughly

To *assimilate* an idea is to take it in as thoroughly as if you had eaten it. (Your body *assimilates* nutrients from the food you eat.) To *assimilate* knowledge is to absorb it, to let it soak in.

People can be *assimilated,* too. Margaret didn't have any friends when she first went to the new school, but she was gradually *assimilated*—she became part of the new community. When she was chosen for the cheerleading squad, her *assimilation* was complete.

ASSUAGE (uh SWAYJ) v to soothe; to pacify; to ease the pain of; to relieve

Beth was extremely angry, but I *assuaged* her by promising to leave the house and never return.

The thunderstorm made the baby cry, but I *assuaged* her fears by singing her a lullaby.

Note carefully the pronunciation of this word.

ASTUTE (uh STOOT) adj shrewd; keen in judgment

Morris was an *astute* judge of character; he was very good at seeing what people are really like.

Amanda, who notices everything that is important and many things that other people don't see, is an *astute* observer.

ATTRITION (uh TRISH un) n gradual wearing away, weakening, or loss; a natural or expected decrease in numbers or size

Mr. Gregory did not have the heart to fire his workers even though his company was losing millions each year. He altruistically preferred to lose workers through *attrition* when they moved away, retired, or decided to change jobs.

AUDACITY (aw DAS uh tee) n boldness; reckless daring; impertinence

Edgar's soaring leap off the top of the building was an act of great *audacity.*

Ivan had the *audacity* to tell that nice old lady to shut up.

A person with *audacity* is said to be *audacious.* Bert made the *audacious* decision to climb Mt. Everest in bowling shoes.

AUGMENT (awg MENT) v to make bigger; to add to; to increase

The army *augmented* its attack by sending in a few thousand more soldiers.

To *augment* a record collection is to add more records to it.

Adding another example to this definition would *augment* it.

The act of *augmenting* is called *augmentation.*

AUSPICIOUS (aw SPISH us) adj favorable; promising; pointing to a good result

A clear sky in the morning is an *auspicious* sign on the day of a picnic.

The first quarter of the football game was not *auspicious;* the home team was outscored by seventy points.

AUSTERE (aw STEER) adj unadorned; stern; forbidding; without excess

The Smiths' house was very *austere;* there was no furniture in it, and there was nothing hanging on the walls.

Quentin, with his *austere* personality, didn't make many friends.

Most people were too intimidated by him to introduce themselves and say hello.

The noun *austerity* (aw STER uh tee) is generally used to mean roughly the same thing as poverty. To live in *austerity* is to live without comforts. Conditions in Austria were very *austere* after the war.

AUTOCRATIC (aw tuh KRAT ik) *adj* ruling with absolute authority; extremely bossy

The ruthless dictator's *autocratic* reign ended when the rebels blew up his palace with a few thousand pounds of plastic explosive.

A two-year-old can be very *autocratic*—he wants what he wants when he wants it.

No one at our office liked the *autocratic* manager. He always insisted on having his own way, and he never let anyone make a decision without consulting him.

An *autocrat* is an absolute ruler. *Autocracy* (aw TAHK ruh see), a system of government headed by an *autocrat,* is not democratic—the people don't get a say.

Note carefully the pronunciation of these words.

Q•U•I•C•K • Q•U•I•Z #12

Match each word in the first column with its definition in the second column. Check your answers in the back of the book.

1. assimilate	a. shrewd
2. assuage	b. boldness
3. astute	c. favorable
4. attrition	d. make bigger
5. audacity	e. soothe
6. augment	f. extremely bossy
7. auspicious	g. absorb
8. austere	h. unadorned
9. autocratic	i. gradual wearing away

AUTONOMOUS (aw TAHN uh mus) *adj* acting independently

The West Coast office of the law firm was quite *autonomous;* it never asked the East Coast office for permission before it did anything.

An *autonomous* nation is one that is independent—it governs itself. It is said to have *autonomy.*

To act *autonomously* is to act on your own authority. If something happens *autonomously,* it happens all by itself.

AVARICE (AV ur is) *n* greed; excessive love of riches

The rich man's *avarice* was annoying to everyone who wanted to lay hands on some of his money.

Avarice is the opposite of generosity or philanthropy.

To be *avaricious* is to love wealth above all else and not to share it with other people.

AVOW (uh VOW) *v* to claim; to declare boldly; to admit

At the age of twenty-five, Louis finally *avowed* that he couldn't stand his mother's apple pie.

To *avow* something is to declare or admit something that most people are reluctant to declare or admit. Mr. Smith *avowed* on television that he had never paid any income tax. Shortly after this *avowal*, he received a lengthy letter from the Internal Revenue Service.

An *avowed* criminal is one who admits he is a criminal. To *disavow* is to deny or repudiate someone else's claim. The mayor *disavowed* the allegation that he had embezzled campaign contributions.

AVUNCULAR (uh VUNG kyuh lur) *adj* like an uncle, especially a nice uncle

What's an uncle like? Kind, helpful, generous, understanding, and so on, in an uncle-y sort of way. This is a fun word to use, although it's usually hard to find occasions to use it.

Note carefully the pronunciation of this word.

AWRY (uh RYE) *adj* off course; twisted to one side

The hunter's bullet went *awry*. Instead of hitting the bear, it hit another hunter.

When we couldn't find a restaurant, our dinner plans went *awry*.

The old man's hat was *awry;* it had dipped in front of his left eye.

AXIOM (AK see um) *n* a self-evident rule or truth; a widely accepted saying

"Everything that is living dies" is an *axiom*.

An *axiom* in geometry is a rule that doesn't have to be proved, because its truth is accepted as obvious, self-evident, or unprovable.

That the rich get richer is an *axiom*. It is unquestionable; it is *axiomatic*.

Q•U•I•C•K • Q•U•I•Z #13

Match each word in the first column with its definition in the second column. Check your answers in the back of the book.

1. autonomous	a. greed
2. avarice	b. like an uncle
3. avow	c. self-evident truth
4. avuncular	d. acting independently
5. awry	e. claim
6. axiom	f. off course

B

BANAL (buh NAL) *adj* unoriginal; ordinary

The dinner conversation was so *banal* that Amanda fell asleep in her dessert dish.

A *banal* statement is a boring, trite, and uncreative statement. It is a *banality*.

What made Amanda fall asleep was the *banality* of the dinner conversation.

This word can also be pronounced "BANE ul."

BANE (bayn) *n* poison; torment; cause of harm

Bane means poison (wolfbane is a kind of poisonous plant), but the word is usually used figuratively. To say that someone is the *bane* of your existence is to say that that person poisons your enjoyment of life.

Baneful means harmful.

BASTION (BAS chun) *n* stronghold; fortress; fortified place

Mrs. Garnett's classroom is a *bastion* of banality; that is, it's a place where originality seldom if ever makes its way inside.

The robbers terrorized the village for several weeks, then escaped to their *bastion* high in the treacherous mountains.

BEGET (bi GET) *v* to give birth to; to create; to lead to; to cause

Those who lie should be creative and have good memories, since one lie often *begets* another lie, which *begets* another.

BELABOR (bi LAY bur) *v* to go over repeatedly or to an absurd extent

For more than an hour, the boring speaker *belabored* his point about the challenge of foreign competition.

Mr. Irving spent the entire period *belaboring* the obvious; he made the same dumb observation over and over again.

BELEAGUER (bi LEE gur) *v* to surround; to besiege; to harass

No one could leave the *beleaguered* city; the attacking army had closed off all the exits.

Oscar felt *beleaguered* at work. He was months behind in his assignments, and he had little hope of catching up.

The *beleaguered* president seldom emerged from the Oval Office as he struggled to deal with the growing scandal.

BELIE (bi LYE) *v* to give a false impression of; to contradict

Melvin's smile *belied* the grief he was feeling; despite his happy expression he was terribly sad inside.

The messy appearance of the banquet table *belied* the huge effort that had gone into setting it up.

A word that is sometimes confused with *belie* is *betray*. To rework the first example above: Melvin was smiling, but a small tear in one eye *betrayed* the grief he was feeling.

BELITTLE (bi LIT ul) *v* to make to seem little; to put someone down
  We worked hard to put out the fire, but the fire chief *belittled* our
efforts by saying he wished he had brought some marshmallows.
  The chairman's *belittling* comments made everyone feel small.

Q•U•I•C•K • Q•U•I•Z #14

*Match each word in the first column with its definition in the
second column. Check your answers in the back of the book.*

1. banal	a. make to seem little
2. bane	b. unoriginal
3. bastion	c. go over repeatedly
4. beget	d. stronghold
5. belabor	e. poison
6. beleaguer	f. give a false impression
7. belie	g. surround
8. belittle	h. give birth to

BELLIGERENT (buh LIJ ur unt) *adj* combative; quarrelsome; waging war
  A bully is *belligerent*. To be *belligerent* is to push other people
around, to be noisy and argumentative, to threaten other people, and
generally to make a nuisance of oneself.
  Al was so *belligerent* that the convention had the feel of a boxing
match.
  Opposing armies in a war are referred to as *belligerents*. Sometimes
one *belligerent* in a conflict is more *belligerent* than the other.

BEMUSED (bi MYOOZD) *adj* confused; bewildered
  To *muse* is to think about or ponder things. To be *bemused,* then, is
to have been thinking about things to the point of confusion.
  The two stood *bemused* in the middle of the parking lot at
Disneyland, trying to remember where they had parked their car.
  Ralph was *bemused* when all lights and appliances in his house
began switching on and off for no apparent reason.
  People often use the word *bemused* when they really mean amused,
but *bemusement* is no laughing matter. *Bemused* means confused.

BENEFACTOR (BEN uh fak tur) *n* one who provides help, especially in
the form of a gift or donation
  To give benefits is to be a *benefactor*. To receive benefits is to be
a *beneficiary*. People very, very often confuse these two words. It
would be to their benefit to keep them straight.
  If your next-door neighbor rewrites his life insurance policy so that
you will receive all his millions when he dies, then you become the
beneficiary of the policy. If your neighbor dies, he is your *benefactor*.
  A *malefactor* (MAL uh fak tur) is a person who does bad things.
Batman and Robin made life hell for *malefactors* in Gotham City.

BENEVOLENT (buh NEV uh lunt) *adj* generous; kind; doing good deeds

Giving money to the poor is a *benevolent* act. To be *benevolent* is to bestow benefits. The United Way, like any charity, is a *benevolent* organization.

Malevolent (muh LEV uh lunt) means evil, or wishing to do harm.

BENIGN (bi NYNE) *adj* gentle; not harmful; kind; mild

Betty has a *benign* personality; she is not at all unpleasant to be with.

The threat of revolution turned out to be *benign;* nothing much came of it.

Charlie was worried that he had cancer, but the lump on his leg turned out to be *benign.*

The difference between a *benign* person and a *benevolent* (see separate entry) one is that the *benevolent* one is actively kind and generous while the *benign* one is more passive. *Benevolence* is usually active generosity or kindness, while *benignancy* tends to mean simply not causing harm.

The opposite of a *benign* tumor is a *malignant* one. This is a tumor that can kill you. A *malignant* personality is one you wish a surgeon would remove. *Malignant* means nasty, evil, full of ill will. The word *malignant* also conveys a sense that evil is spreading, as with a cancer. An adjective that means the same thing is *malign.*

As a verb, *malign* has a different meaning. To *malign* someone is to say unfairly bad things about that person, to injure that person by telling evil lies about him or her. *Slander* and *malign* are synonyms.

Q•U•I•C•K • Q•U•I•Z #15

Match each word in the first column with its definition in the second column. Check your answers in the back of the book.

1. belligerent	a. intending harm
2. bemused	b. donor
3. benefactor	c. not harmful
4. beneficiary	d. deadly
5. benevolent	e. confused
6. benign	f. generous
7. malignant	g. combative
8. malign	h. injure with lies
9. malevolent	i. one who receives benefits
10. malefactor	j. evildoer

BEQUEST (bi KWEST) *n* something left to someone in a will

If your next-door neighbor leaves you all his millions in a will, the money is a *bequest* from him to you. It is not polite to request a *bequest.* Just keep smiling and hope for the best.

To leave something to someone in a will is to *bequeath* it. A *bequest* is something that has been *bequeathed*.

BEREAVED (buh REEVD) *adj* deprived or left desolate, especially through death

The new widow was still *bereaved* when we saw her. Every time anyone mentioned her dead husband's name, she burst into tears.

The children were *bereaved* by the death of their pet. Then they got a new pet.

Bereft (buh REFT) means the same thing as *bereaved*.

BESET (bi SET) *v* to harass; to surround

The bereaved widow was *beset* by grief.

Problems *beset* the expedition almost from the beginning, and the mountain climbers soon returned to their base camp.

The little town was *beset* by robberies, but the police could do nothing.

BLASPHEMY (BLAS fuh mee) *n* irreverence; an insult to something held sacred; profanity

In the strictest sense, to commit *blasphemy* is to say nasty, insulting things about God. The word is used more broadly, though, to cover a wide range of nasty, insulting comments.

To *blaspheme* (blas FEEM) is to use swear words or say deeply irreverent things. A person who says such things is *blasphemous*.

BLATANT (BLAYT unt) *adj* unpleasantly or offensively noisy; glaring

David was *blatantly* critical of our efforts; that is, he was noisy and obnoxious in making his criticisms.

Blatant is often confused with *flagrant*, since both words mean glaring. A *blatant* act is usually also a *flagrant* one, but a *flagrant* act isn't necessarily *blatant*. You might want to refer to the listing for *flagrant*.

Q•U•I•C•K • Q•U•I•Z #16

Match each word in the first column with its definition in the second column. Check your answers in the back of the book.

1. bequest	a. left desolate
2. bequeath	b. something left in a will
3. bereaved	c. harass
4. beset	d. offensively noisy
5. blasphemy	e. leaving in a will
6. blatant	f. irreverence

BLIGHT (blyte) *n* a disease in plants; anything that injures or destroys

An early frost proved a *blight* to the citrus crops last year, so we had no orange juice for breakfast.

BLITHE (blythe) *adj* carefree; cheerful
The *blithe* birds in the garden were making so much noise that Paul began to think about the shotgun in the attic.
The children were playing *blithely* in the hazardous-waste dump. While they played, they were *blithely* unaware that they were doing something dangerous.
To be *blithely* ignorant is to be happily unaware.
Note carefully the pronunciation of this word.

BOURGEOIS (boor ZHWAH) *adj* middle class, usually in a pejorative sense; boringly conventional
The original *bourgeoisie* (boor zhwaw ZEE) were simply people who lived in cities, an innovation at the time. They weren't farmers and they weren't nobles. They were members of a new class—the middle class. Now the word is used mostly in making fun of or sneering at people who seem to think about nothing but their possessions and other comforts and about conforming with other people who share those concerns.
A hip young city dweller might reject life in the suburbs as being too *bourgeois*. A person whose dream is to have a swimming pool in his backyard might be called *bourgeois* by someone who thinks there are more important things in life. Golf is often referred to as a *bourgeois* sport.
Note carefully the pronunciation of these words.

BOVINE (BOH vyne) *adj* cow related; cowlike
Cows are *bovine*, obviously. Eating grass is a *bovine* concern.
A fat or mooing person might be said to be *bovine*, too.
The woman's *bovine* figure made her very unpopular with the man sitting next to her on the airplane.
There are a number of similar words based on other animals:
canine (KAY nyne): dogs
equine (EE kyne): horses
feline (FEE lyne): cats
piscine (PIS yne): fish
porcine (POR syne): pigs
ursine (UR syne): bears

BREVITY (BREV i tee) *n* briefness
The audience was deeply grateful for the *brevity* of the after-dinner speaker's remarks.
The reader of this book may be grateful for the *brevity* of this example.
Brevity is related to the word *abbreviate*.

BROACH (brohch) *v* to open up a subject for discussion, often a delicate subject
Henrietta was proud of her new dress, so no one knew how to *broach* the subject with her of how silly grandmothers look in leather.

BUCOLIC (byoo KAHL ik) *adj* charmingly rural; rustic; countrylike

The changing of the autumn leaves, old stone walls, distant views, and horses grazing in green meadows are examples of *bucolic* splendor.

The *bucolic* scene didn't do much for the city child, who preferred screaming fire engines and honking horns to the sounds of a babbling brook.

BUREAUCRACY (byoo RAHK ruh see) *n* a system of government administration consisting of numerous bureaus or offices, especially one run according to inflexible and inefficient rules; any large administrative system characterized by inefficiency, lots of rules, and red tape

The Department of Motor Vehicles is a *bureaucracy*. Every clerk you speak with hands you a printed form and tells you to stand in line somewhere else. No one can answer all of your questions. At lunchtime, when the lines are longest, half the clerks disappear. The forms you have to fill out all request unnecessary information. After you finally get everything all filled out and handed in, you don't hear another word from the department for many months.

The people who work in a *bureaucracy* are called *bureaucrats*. These people and the inefficient procedures they follow might be called *bureaucratic*. Administrative systems outside the government can be *bureaucratic*, too. A high school principal who required teachers and students to fill out forms for everything might be called *bureaucratic*.

BURGEON (BUR jun) *v* to expand; to flourish

The *burgeoning* weeds in our yard soon overwhelmed the grass.

Note carefully the pronunciation of this word.

BURLESQUE (bur LESK) *n* a ludicrous, mocking, or exaggerated imitation

Vaudeville actors frequently performed *burlesque* works on the stage.

Burlesque, parody, lampoon, and *caricature* share similar meanings.

Q•U•I•C•K • Q•U•I•Z #17

Match each word in the first column with its definition in the second column. Check your answers in the back of the book.

1. blight
2. blithe
3. bourgeois
4. bovine
5. canine
6. feline
7. equine
8. piscine
9. porcine
10. ursine
11. brevity
12. broach
13. bucolic
14. bureaucracy
15. burgeon
16. burlesque

a. flourish
b. bearlike
c. carefree
d. catlike
e. cowlike
f. charmingly rural
g. middle class
h. horselike
i. briefness
j. piglike
k. inflexible administration
l. fishlike
m. doglike
n. plant disease
o. open a subject
p. ludicrous imitation

C

CACOPHONY (kuh KAHF uh nee) *n* harsh-sounding mixture of words, voices, or sounds

A *cacophony* isn't just a lot of noise—it's a lot of noise that doesn't sound good together. A steam whistle blowing isn't a *cacophony*. But a high school orchestra that had never rehearsed together might very well produce a *cacophony*. The roar of engines, horns, and sirens arising from a busy city street would be a *cacophony*. A lot of people all shouting at once would produce a *cacophony*.

Euphony is the opposite of *cacophony*. *Euphony* is pleasing sound.

CADENCE (KAYD uns) *n* rhythm; the rise and fall of sounds

We wished the tone of Irwin's words would have a more pleasing *cadence,* but he spoke in a dull monotone.

CAJOLE (kuh JOHL) *v* to persuade someone to do something he or she doesn't want to do

I didn't want to give the speech, but Joel *cajoled* me into doing it by telling me what a good speaker I am. As it turned out, he simply hadn't been able to find anyone else.

CALLOW (KAL oh) *adj* immature

To be *callow* is to be youthfully naive, inexperienced, and unsophisticated.

A teenager might show *callow* disregard for the feelings of adults. Driving fast cars and hanging out in the parking lot at the 7-Eleven are *callow* pursuits.

The patient was alarmed by the *callowness* of the medical staff. The doctors looked too young to have graduated from high school, much less from medical school.

CANDOR (KAN dur) *n* truthfulness; sincere honesty

My best friend exhibited *candor* when he told me that for many years now he has believed me to be a jerk.

Teddy appreciated Ross's *candor;* Teddy was glad to know that Ross thought Teddy's sideburns looked stupid.

To show *candor* is to be *candid*. What is *candid* about the camera on *Candid Camera*? The camera is *candid* because it is truthful in showing what people do when they can't turn off the coffee machine in the office where they're applying for a job. *Candid* does *not* mean concealed or hidden, even though the camera on *Candid Camera* is concealed. To be *candid* is to speak frankly.

CAPITALISM (KAP uh tuh liz um) *n* free enterprise; an economic system in which businesses are owned by private citizens (not by the government) and in which the resulting products and services are sold with relatively little government control

The American economy is *capitalistic*. If you wanted to start a company to sell signed photographs of yourself, you could. You, and not the government, would decide how much you would charge for the pictures. Your success or failure would depend on how many people decided to buy your pictures.

CAPITULATE (kuh PICH uh layt) *v* to surrender; to give up or give in

I urged him and urged him to take off his cap; when I threatened to knock his head off, he *capitulated*.

On the twentieth day of the strike, the workers *capitulated* and went back to work without a new contract.

To *recapitulate* is not to *capitulate* again. To *recapitulate* is to summarize.

So few students paid attention to Mr. Jones that he had to *recapitulate* his major points at the end of the class.

CAPRICIOUS (kuh PRISH us) *adj* unpredictable; likely to change at any moment

Bill was very *capricious*. One minute he said his favorite car was a Chevy Caprice; the next minute he said it was a Camaro.

The weather is often said to be *capricious*. One minute it's snowing, the next minute it's 120 degrees in the shade.

A *caprice* (kuh PREES) is a whim.

Penny attempted a quadruple somersault off the ten-meter diving board as a *caprice*. It was a painful *caprice*.
Note carefully the pronunciation of this word.

CARICATURE (KAR uh kuh chur) *n* a portrait or description that is purposely distorted or exaggerated, often to prove some point about its subject

Editorial cartoonists often draw *caricatures*. Big noses, enormous glasses, floppy ears, and other distortions are common in such drawings. A politician who has been convicted of bribery might be depicted in a prison uniform or with a ball and chain around his ankle. If the politician has big ears to begin with, the ears might be drawn vastly bigger.

A *caricature* uses exaggeration to bring out the hidden character of its subject.

The word can also be used as a verb. To *caricature* someone is to create such a distorted portrait.

CASTIGATE (KAS tuh gayt) *v* to criticize severely; to chastise

Jim's mother-in-law *castigated* him for forgetting to pick her up at the airport.

CATALYST (KAT uh list) *n* in chemistry, something that changes the rate of a chemical reaction without itself being changed; anyone or anything that makes something happen without being directly involved in it

When the mad scientist dropped a few grains of the *catalyst* into his test tube, the bubbling liquid began to boil furiously.

This word is often used outside the laboratory as well. The launching of Sputnik by the Russians provided the *catalyst* for the creation of the modern American space program.

The tragic hijacking provided the *catalyst* for Congress's new antiterrorist legislation.

Q•U•I•C•K • Q•U•I•Z #18

Match each word in the first column with its definition in the second column. Check your answers in the back of the book.

1. cacophony	a. truthfulness
2. cadence	b. harsh mixture of sounds
3. cajole	c. surrender
4. callow	d. distorted portrait
5. candor	e. unpredictable
6. capitalism	f. immature
7. capitulate	g. free enterprise
8. recapitulate	h. it makes things happen
9. capricious	i. summarize
10. caricature	j. persuade deceptively
11. castigate	k. criticize severely
12. catalyst	l. rhythm

CATEGORICAL (kat uh GOR uh kul) *adj* unconditional; absolute

A *categorical* denial is one without exceptions—it covers every *category*. Crooked politicians often make *categorical* denials of various charges against them. Then they go to jail.

I *categorically* refuse to do anything whatsoever at any time, in any place, with anyone.

CATHARSIS (kuh THAR sis) *n* purification that brings emotional relief or renewal

To someone with psychological problems, talking to a psychiatrist can lead to a *catharsis*. A *catharsis* is a sometimes traumatic event after which one feels better.

A *catharsis* is *cathartic*. Some people find emotional movies *cathartic*—watching one often allows them to release buried emotions. *Cathartic* can also be a noun. Young Teddy swallowed the contents of a bottle of shoe polish, so his mother gave him a raw egg as a *cathartic* to make him vomit.

CATHOLIC (KATH lik) *adj* universal; embracing everything

Catholic with a small *c* means universal. Da Vinci was a *catholic* genius who excelled at everything he did. *Parochial* means narrow-minded, so *parochial* and *catholic* are almost opposites.

CAUSTIC (KAW stik) *adj* like acid; corrosive

Paint remover is a *caustic* substance; if you spill it on your skin, your skin will burn.

The *caustic* detergent ate right through Henry's laundry.

Caustic can be used figuratively as well. A *caustic* comment is one that is so nasty or insulting that it seems to sting or burn the person to whom it is directed. The teacher's *caustic* criticism of Sally's term paper left her in tears.

CELIBACY (SEL uh buh see) *n* abstinence from sex

People who practice *celibacy* don't practice sex.

Celibacy is one of the requirements for Catholic priesthood.

To practice *celibacy* is to be *celibate*. You will look a very long time in Hollywood before you find a *celibate* celebrity.

CENSURE (SEN shur) *v* to condemn severely for doing something bad

The Senate sometimes *censures* senators for breaking laws or engaging in behavior unbecoming to an elected official.

Censure can also be a noun. The clumsy physician feared the *censure* of his fellow doctors, so he stopped treating anything more complicated than the common cold.

A Senate that made a habit of *censuring* senators might be said to be *censorious*. To be *censorious* is to be highly critical—to do a lot of *censuring*.

CEREBRAL (suh REE brul) *adj* brainy; intellectually refined

Your *cerebrum* is the biggest part of your brain. To be *cerebral* is to do and care about things that really smart people do and care about.

A *cerebral* discussion is one that is filled with big words and concerns abstruse matters that ordinary people can't understand.

Bill was too *cerebral* to be a baseball announcer; he kept talking about the existentialism of the outfield.

This word can also be pronounced "SER uh brul."

CHAGRIN (shuh GRIN) n humiliation; embarrassed disappointment

Much to my *chagrin*, I began to giggle during the eulogy at the funeral.

Doug was filled with *chagrin* when he lost the race because he had put his shoes on the wrong feet.

The word *chagrin* is sometimes used incorrectly to mean surprise. There is, however, a definite note of shame in *chagrin*.

To be *chagrined* is to feel humiliated or mortified.

CHARISMA (kuh RIZ muh) n a magical-seeming ability to attract followers or inspire loyalty

The glamorous presidential candidate had a lot of *charisma*; voters didn't seem to support him so much as be entranced by him.

The evangelist's undeniable *charisma* enabled him to bring in millions and millions of dollars in donations to his television show.

To have *charisma* is to be *charismatic*.

Q•U•I•C•K • Q•U•I•Z #19

Match each word in the first column with its definition in the second column. Check your answers in the back of the book.

1. categorical	a. unconditional
2. catharsis	b. relieving purification
3. catholic	c. abstinence from sex
4. caustic	d. brainy
5. celibacy	e. humiliation
6. censure	f. magical attractiveness
7. cerebral	g. corrosive
8. chagrin	h. condemn severely
9. charisma	i. universal

CHARLATAN (SHAR luh tun) n fraud; quack; con man

Buck was selling what he claimed was a cure for cancer, but he was just a *charlatan* (the pills were jelly beans).

The flea market usually attracts a lot of *charlatans* who sell phony products that don't do what they claim they will.

CHASM (KAZ um) n a deep, gaping hole; a gorge

Bill was so stupid that his girlfriend wondered whether there wasn't a *chasm* where his brain should be.

The bad guys were gaining, so the hero grabbed the heroine and swung across the *chasm* on a slender vine.

Note carefully the pronunciation of this word.

CHASTISE (chas TYZE) v to inflict punishment on; to discipline

Mother *chastised* us for firing our bottle rockets through the living-room window.

Chastising the dog for sleeping in the fireplace never seemed to do any good; the minute we turned our backs, he'd curl up in the ashes again.

CHICANERY (shi KAY nuh ree) n trickery; deceitfulness; artifice, especially legal or political

Political news would be dull were it not for the *chicanery* of our elected officials.

Note carefully the pronunciation of this word.

CHIMERA (kye MEER uh) n an illusion; a foolish fancy

Susan's dream of becoming a movie star was just a *chimera*.

Could you take a picture of a *chimera* with a camera? No, of course not. It wouldn't show up on the film.

Be careful not to mispronounce this word. Its apparent similarity to *chimney* is just a *chimera*.

Note carefully the pronunciation of this word.

CHOLERIC (KAHL ur ik) adj hot-tempered; quick to anger

The *choleric* watchdog would sink his teeth into anyone who came within biting distance of his doghouse.

When the grumpy old man was in one of his *choleric* moods, the children refused to go near him.

The *choleric* administrator kept all the secretaries in a state of terror.

CHRONIC (KRAHN ik) adj constant; lasting a long time; inveterate

Someone who always comes in last could be called a *chronic* loser.

Chronic is usually associated with something negative or undesirable: *chronic* illness, *chronic* failure, *chronic* depression. You would be much less likely to encounter a reference to *chronic* success or *chronic* happiness, unless the writer or speaker was being ironic.

A *chronic* disease is one that lingers for a long time, doesn't go away, or keeps coming back. The opposite of a *chronic* disease is an *acute* disease. An *acute* disease is one that comes and goes very quickly. It may be severe, but it doesn't last forever.

CHRONICLE (KRAHN uh kul) n a record of events in order of time; a history

Sally's diary provided her mother with a detailed *chronicle* of her daughter's extracurricular activities.

Chronicle can also be used as a verb. The reporter *chronicled* all the events of the revolution. *Chronology* and *chronicle* are nearly synonyms: both provide a *chronological* list of events. *Chronological* means in order of time.

Q•U•I•C•K • Q•U•I•Z #20

Match each word in the first column with its definition in the second column. Check your answers in the back of the book.

1. charlatan	a. in order of occurrence
2. chasm	b. constant
3. chastise	c. hot-tempered
4. chicanery	d. punish
5. chimera	e. account of past times
6. chivalrous	f. list in time order
7. choleric	g. illusion
8. chronic	h. fraud
9. chronological	i. gallant
10. chronology	j. gaping hole
11. chronicle	k. trickery

CIRCUITOUS (sur KYOO uh tus) *adj* roundabout; not following a direct path

The *circuitous* bus route between the two cities went here, there, and everywhere, and it took an extremely long time to get anywhere.

The salesman's route was *circuitous*—it wound aimlessly through many small towns.

A *circuitous* argument is one that rambles around for quite a while before making its point.

A *circuitous* argument is very similar to a *circular* argument, which is one that ends up where it begins or attempts to prove something without offering any new information. To say "A majority is that which exists when there is a majority" is to give a circular, or tautological, definition of the word *majority*.

CIRCUMLOCUTION (sur kum loh KYOO shun) *n* an indirect expression; use of wordy or evasive language

The lawyer's *circumlocution* left everyone in the courtroom wondering what had been said.

The indicted executive evaded the reporters' questions by resorting to *circumlocution*.

To use a lot of big, vague words and to speak in a disorganized way is to be *circumlocutory*.

CIRCUMSCRIBE (SUR kum skrybe) *v* to draw a line around; to set the limits; to define; to restrict

The Constitution clearly *circumscribes* the restrictions that can be placed on our personal freedoms.

A barbed-wire fence and armed guards *circumscribed* the movement of the prisoners.

CIRCUMSPECT (SUR kum spekt) *adj* cautious

As a public speaker, Nick was extremely *circumspect;* he always took great care not to say the wrong thing or give offense.

The *circumspect* general did everything he could not to put his soldiers at unnecessary risk.

The word *circumspect* comes from Greek roots meaning around and look (as do the words *circle* and *inspect*). To be *circumspect* is to look around carefully before doing something.

CIRCUMVENT (sur kum VENT) *v* to frustrate as though by surrounding

Our hopes for an early end of the meeting were *circumvented* by the chairperson's refusal to deal with the items on the agenda.

The angry school board *circumvented* the students' effort to install color television sets in every classroom.

CIVIL (SIV ul) *adj* polite; civilized; courteous

Our dinner guests conducted themselves *civilly* when we told them we weren't going to serve them dinner after all. They didn't bang their cups on the table or throw their plates to the floor.

The word *civil* also has other meanings. *Civil* rights are rights established by law. *Civil* service is government service. Consult your dictionary for the numerous shades of meaning.

CLEMENCY (KLEM un see) *n* mercy; forgiveness; mildness

The judge displayed *clemency* in giving the student a suspended sentence for shooting Mr. Reed, his dreadful math teacher.

The governor committed an act of *clemency* when he released all the convicts from the state penitentiary.

Mild weather is called *clement* weather; bad weather is called *inclement*. You should wear a coat and carry an umbrella in *inclement* weather.

CLICHÉ (klee SHAY) *n* an overused saying or idea

The expression "You can't judge a book by its cover" is a *cliché;* it's been used so many times its freshness has been worn away.

Clichés are usually true. That's why they've been repeated often enough to become overused. But they are boring. A writer who uses a lot of *clichés*—referring to a foreign country as "a land of contrasts," describing spring as "a time of renewal," saying that a snowfall is "a blanket of white"—is not interesting to read, because there is nothing new about his observations.

Note carefully the pronunciation of this French word.

CLIQUE (kleek) *n* an exclusive group bound together by some shared quality or interest

The high school newspaper staff was a real *clique;* they all hung out together and wouldn't talk to anyone else. It's hard to have fun at that school if you aren't a member of the right *clique.*

The cheerleaders were *cliquish* as well.

Note carefully the pronunciation of this word.

Q•U•I•C•K • Q•U•I•Z #21

Match each word in the first column with its definition in the second column. Check your answers in the back of the book.

1. circuitous	a. cautious
2. circumlocution	b. draw a line around
3. circumscribe	c. mercy
4. circumspect	d. polite
5. circumvent	e. roundabout
6. civil	f. frustrate
7. clique	g. overused saying
8. clemency	h. indirect expression
9. inclement	i. exclusive group
10. cliché	j. bad, as in weather

COALESCE (koh uh LES) *v* to come together as one; to fuse; to unite

When the dough *coalesced* into a big black blob, we began to wonder whether the cookies would be good to eat.

The people in our neighborhood *coalesced* into a powerful force for change in the community.

A *coalition* is a group of people that has come together for some purpose, often a political one. Coal miners and cola bottlers might *coalesce* into a *coalition* for the purpose of persuading coal mine owners to provide cola machines in coal mines.

The southern *coalition* in Congress is the group of representatives from southern states who often vote the same way.

COERCE (koh URS) *v* to force someone to do or not to do something

Darth Vader tried flattery, Darth Vader tried gifts, Darth Vader even tried to *coerce,* but Darth Vader was never able to make Han Solo reveal the hidden rebel base.

The noun is *coercion* (koh UR shun).

COGENT (KOH junt) *adj* powerfully convincing

Cogent reasons are extremely persuasive ones.

Kojak was *cogent* in explaining why he needed another lollipop, so we gave him one.

The lawyer's argument in his client's behalf was not *cogent,* so the jury convicted his client. The jury was persuaded by the *cogency* of the district attorney's argument.

COGNITIVE (KAHG nu tiv) *adj* dealing with how we know the world around us through our senses; mental

Scientists study the *cognitive* apparatus of human beings to pattern how computers should gather information about the world.

Cognition is knowing.

COGNIZANT (KAHG nu zunt) *adj* aware; conscious

To be *cognizant* of your responsibilities is to know what your responsibilities are.

Al was *cognizant* of the dangers of sword swallowing, but he tried it anyway and hurt himself quite badly.

COHERENT (koh HEER unt) *adj* holding together; making sense

A *coherent* wad of cotton balls is one that holds together.

A *coherent* explanation is an explanation that makes sense; the explanation holds together.

To hold together is to *cohere*.

COLLOQUIAL (kul OH kwee ul) *adj* conversational; informal in language

A writer with a *colloquial* style is a writer who uses ordinary words and whose writing seems as informal as common speech.

"The way I figure it" is a *colloquial* expression, or a *colloquialism:* people often say it but it isn't used in formal prose.

A *colloquy* (KAHL uh kwee) is a conversation or conference.

COLLUSION (kuh LOO zhun) *n* conspiracy; secret cooperation

The increase in oil prices was the result of *collusion* by the oil-producing nations.

There was *collusion* among the owners of the baseball teams; they agreed secretly not to sign any expensive free agents.

If the baseball owners were in *collusion,* then you could say that they had *colluded.* To *collude* is to conspire.

COMMENSURATE (kuh MEN sur it) *adj* equal; proportionate

Ernie's salary is *commensurate* with his abilities; like his abilities, his salary is small.

The number of touchdowns scored by the team and the number of its victories were *commensurate* (both zero).

COMPELLING (kum PEL ing) *adj* forceful; causing to yield

A *compelling* argument for buying a videocassette recorder is one that makes you go out and buy a videocassette recorder.

The recruiter's speech was so *compelling* that nearly everyone in the auditorium enlisted in the army when it was over.

To *compel* someone to do something is to force him or her to do it. Our consciences *compelled* us to turn the money we had found over to the authorities.

The noun is *compulsion,* which also means an irresistible impulse to do something irrational.

COMPENDIUM (kum PEN dee um) *n* a summary; an abridgment

A yearbook often contains a *compendium* of the offenses, foibles, and crimes of the members of the senior class.

Q•U•I•C•K • Q•U•I•Z #22

Match each word in the first column with its definition in the second column. Check your answers in the back of the book.

1. coalesce	a. perceptive
2. coalition	b. unite
3. coerce	c. conversational
4. cogent	d. force someone to do
5. cognitive	something
6. cognizant	e. proportionate
7. coherent	f. making sense
8. colloquial	g. group with a purpose
9. collusion	h. powerfully convincing
10. commensurate	i. summary
11. compelling	j. forceful
12. compendium	k. conspiracy
	l. dealing with how we know
	our environment

COMPLACENT (kum PLAY sunt) *adj* self-satisfied; overly pleased with oneself; contented to a fault

The *complacent* camper paid no attention to the bear prowling around his campsite, and the bear ate him up.

The football team won so many games that it became *complacent*, and the worst team in the league snuck up and beat it.

To fall into *complacency* is to become comfortably uncaring about the world around you.

The president of the student council was appalled by the *complacency* of his classmates; not one of the seniors seemed to care whether the theme of the prom was "You Light up My Life" or "Color My World."

Don't confuse *complacent* with *complaisant* (kum PLAY zunt), which means eager to please.

COMPLEMENT (KAHM pluh munt) *v* to complete or fill up; to be the perfect counterpart

This word is often confused with *compliment*, which means to praise. It's easy to tell them apart. *Complement* is spelled like *complete*. The flower arrangement *complemented* the table decorations.

Complement can also be a noun. Fish-flavored ice cream was a perfect *complement* to the seafood dinner.

COMPLICITY (kum PLIS uh tee) *n* participation in wrongdoing; the act of being an accomplice

There was *complicity* between the bank robber and the dishonest

teller. The teller neglected to turn on the alarm, and the robber rewarded him by sharing the loot.

Complicity among the students made it impossible to find out which
of them had set fire to the Spanish teacher.

COMPREHENSIVE (kahm pruh HEN siv) *adj* covering or including everything

The insurance policy was *comprehensive;* it covered all possible
losses.

A *comprehensive* examination is one that covers everything in the
course, or everything in a particular field of knowledge.

Mabel's knowledge of English was *comprehensive;* she even understood what *comprehensive* means.

COMPRISE (kum PRYZE) *v* to consist of

A football team *comprises* eleven players on offense and eleven
players on defense.

A company *comprises* employees.

This word is very often misused. Be careful. Players do *not* "comprise" a football team, and employees do *not* "comprise" a company.
Nor can a football team be said to be "*comprised* of" players, or a
company to be "*comprised* of" employees. These are very common
mistakes. Instead, you can say that players *constitute* or *compose* a
team, and that employees *constitute* or *compose* a company. You can
also say that a team *consists* of players or a company *consists* of
employees.

CONCILIATORY (kun SIL ee uh tor ee) *adj* making peace; attempting to resolve a dispute through goodwill

To be *conciliatory* is to kiss and make up. Come on—be *conciliatory!*

The formerly warring countries were *conciliatory* at the treaty conference.

After dinner at the all-you-can-eat pancake house, the divorced
couple began to feel *conciliatory,* so they flew to Las Vegas and were
remarried.

When peace has been made, we say that the warring parties have
come to a *reconciliation* (rek un sil ee AY shun). To *reconcile*
(REK un syle) is to bring two things into agreement. The accountant
managed to *reconcile* the company books with the cash on hand only
with great creativity.

CONCISE (kun SYSE) *adj* brief and to the point; succinct

The scientist's explanation was *concise;* it was brief and it helped
us understand the difficult concept.

To be *concise* is to say much with few words.

A *concise* speaker is one who speaks *concisely,* or who speaks with
concision.

Q•U•I•C•K • Q•U•I•Z #23

Match each word in the first column with its definition in the second column. Check your answers in the back of the book.

1. complacent
2. complement
3. complicity
4. comprehensive
5. comprise
6. compose
7. constitute
8. conciliatory
9. concise

a. covering everything
b. complete
c. consist of
d. make up (2)
e. brief and to the point
f. making peace
g. participation in wrongdoing
h. self-satisfied

CONCORD (KAHN kord) *n* harmony; agreement

Nations that live in *concord* are nations that live together in peace.

The war between the neighboring tribes ended thirty years of *concord*.

The faculty meeting was marked by *concord*; no one yelled at anyone else.

Discord is the opposite of *concord*. A faculty meeting where everyone yelled at one another would be a faculty meeting marked by *discord*. It would be a *discordant* meeting.

An *accord* is a formal agreement, usually reached after a dispute.

CONCURRENT (kun KUR unt) *adj* happening at the same time; parallel

The criminal was sentenced to two *concurrent* fifteen-year sentences; the sentences will run at the same time, and he will be out of jail in fifteen years.

High prices, falling demand, and poor weather were three *concurrent* trends that made life especially difficult for popcorn farmers last month.

To *concur* means to agree. The assistant wanted to keep his job, so he always *concurred* with his boss.

CONDESCEND (KAHN duh send) *v* to stoop to someone else's level, usually in an offensive way; to patronize

I was surprised that the president of the company had *condescended* to talk with me, a mere temporary employee.

Many grown-ups make the mistake of *condescending* to young children, who usually prefer to be treated as equals, or at least as rational beings.

CONDONE (kun DOHN) *v* to overlook; to permit to happen

To *condone* what someone does is to look the other way while it happens, or to permit it to happen by not doing anything about it.

The principal *condoned* the hoods' smoking in the bathroom; he simply ignored it.

CONDUCIVE (kun DOO siv) *adj* promoting

The chairs in the library are *conducive* to sleep. If you sit in them to study, you will fall asleep.

The foul weather was not *conducive* to our having a picnic.

The teacher's easygoing manner was *conducive* to chaos in the classroom.

CONFLUENCE (KAHN floo uns) *n* a flowing together, especially of rivers; the place where they begin to flow together

The *confluence* of the Missouri and Mississippi rivers is at St. Louis; that's the place where they join together.

There is a remarkable *confluence* in our thoughts: we think the same way about almost everything.

A *confluence* of many factors (no ice, bad food, terrible music) made it inevitable that the party would be a big flop.

CONGENIAL (kun JEEN yul) *adj* agreeably suitable; pleasant

The little cabin in the woods was *congenial* to the writer; he was able to get a lot of writing done there.

The new restaurant has a *congenial* atmosphere. We enjoy just sitting there playing with the ice in our water glasses.

When people get along together at a restaurant, and don't throw food at one another, they are being *congenial.*

Genial and *congenial* share similar meanings. *Genial* means pleasing, kind, sympathetic, or helpful. You can be pleased by a *genial* manner or by a *genial* climate.

CONGENITAL (kun JEN uh tul) *adj* a trait or condition acquired between conception and birth; innate

A *congenital* birth defect is one that is present at birth but was not caused by one's genes.

The word is also used more loosely to describe any (usually bad) trait or behavior that is so firmly fixed it seems to be a part of a person's nature.

A *congenital* liar is a natural liar, a person who can't help but lie.

Q•U•I•C•K • Q•U•I•Z #24

Match each word in the first column with its definition in the second column. Check your answers in the back of the book.

1. concord	a. agreeably suitable
2. discord	b. innate
3. concurrent	c. harmony
4. condescend	d. flowing together
5. condone	e. promoting
6. conducive	f. stoop or patronize
7. confluence	g. overlook
8. congenial	h. happening at the same time
9. congenital	i. disharmony

CONJECTURE (kun JEK chur) v to guess; to deduce or infer on slight evidence

If forced to *conjecture*, I would say the volcano will erupt in twenty-four hours.

Conjecture can also be a noun. The divorce lawyer for Mr. Davis argued that the putative cause of the lipstick on his collar was mere *conjecture*.

A *conjecture* is *conjectural*.

CONJURE (KAHN jur) v to summon or bring into being as if by magic

The chef *conjured* (or *conjured* up) a fabulous gourmet meal using nothing more than the meager ingredients in Lucy's kitchen.

The wizard *conjured* (or *conjured* up) an evil spirit by mumbling some magic words and throwing a little powdered eye of newt into the fire.

CONNOISSEUR (kahn uh SUR) n an expert, particularly in matters of art or taste

The artist's work was very popular, but *connoisseurs* rejected it as amateurish.

Frank was a *connoisseur* of bad movies. He had seen them all and knew which ones were genuinely dreadful and which ones were merely poorly made.

The meal was exquisite enough to impress a *connoisseur*.

I like sculpture, but I'm no *connoisseur*; I couldn't tell you why one statue is better than another.

CONSECRATE (KAHN suh krayt) v to make or declare sacred

The Veterans Day speaker said that the battlefield had been *consecrated* by the blood of the soldiers who had died there.

The priest *consecrated* the building by sprinkling holy water on it.

The college chaplain delivered a sermon at the *consecration* (kahn suh KRAY shun) ceremony for the new chapel.

The opposite of *consecrate* is *desecrate* (DES uh krayt), which means to treat irreverently. The vandals *desecrated* the cemetery by knocking down all the tombstones. Their act of vandalism was a *desecration.*

Desecrate can also be applied to areas outside religion.

Doodling in a book *desecrates* the book, even if the book isn't a Bible.

The wife *desecrated* a photograph of her husband by drawing a mustache on it.

The graffiti on the front door of the school is a *desecration.*

CONSENSUS (kun SEN sus) *n* unanimity or general agreement

When there is a *consensus,* everybody feels the same way.

Contrary to how the word is often used, *consensus* implies more than just a rough agreement or a majority opinion. Election results don't reflect a *consensus* unless everyone or nearly everyone votes for the same candidate.

CONSONANT (KAHN suh nunt) *adj* harmonious; in agreement

Our desires were *consonant* with theirs; we all wanted the same thing.

The decision to construct a new gymnasium was *consonant* with the superintendent's belief in physical education.

The opposite of *consonant* is *dissonant* (DIS uh nunt), which means inharmonious. *Dissonant* voices are voices that don't sound good together.

Q•U•I•C•K • Q•U•I•Z #25

Match each word in the first column with its definition in the second column. Check your answers in the back of the book.

1. conjecture	a. incompatible
2. conjure	b. harmonious
3. connoisseur	c. make sacred
4. consecrate	d. unanimity
5. desecrate	e. summon as if by magic
6. consensus	f. treat irreverently
7. consonant	g. artistic expert
8. dissonant	h. guess

CONSTRUE (kun STROO) *v* to interpret

The meaning of the poem, as I *construed* it, had to do with the love of a man for his dog.

Mickey *construed* his contract as giving him the right to do anything he wanted.

The law had always been *construed* as permitting the behavior for which Joe had been arrested.

To *misconstrue* is to misinterpret. Hank *misconstrued* Pamela's smile, but he certainly did not *misconstrue* the slap she gave him.

CONSUMMATE (kun SUM it) *adj* perfect; complete; supremely skillful
A *consummate* pianist is an extremely good one. Nothing is lacking in the way he or she plays.
Consummate (KAHN suh mayt) is also a verb. Notice the different pronunciation. To *consummate* something is to finish it or make it complete. Signing a contract would *consummate* an agreement.
Note carefully the pronunciation of both parts of speech.

CONTENTIOUS (kun TEN shus) *adj* argumentative; quarrelsome
A person looking for a fight is *contentious*.
Two people having a fight are *contentious*.
To be *contentious* in a discussion is to make a lot of noisy objections.
A *contender* is a fighter. To *contend* is to fight or argue for something. Someone who breaks the law may have to *contend* with the law.

CONTIGUOUS (kun TIG yoo us) *adj* side by side; adjoining
Two countries that share a border are *contiguous*. So are two events that happened one right after the other.
If two countries are *contiguous*, the territory they cover is continuous. That is, it spreads or continues across both countries without any interruption.

CONTINGENT (kun TIN junt) *adj* dependent; possible
Our agreement to buy their house is *contingent* upon the sellers' finding another house to move into. That is, they won't sell their house to us unless they can find another house to buy.
My happiness is *contingent* on yours; if you're unhappy, I'm unhappy.
A *contingency* is a possibility or something that may happen but is at least as likely not to happen. Several *contingencies* stand between us and the successful completion of our business; several things could happen to screw it up.
The Joneses were prepared for any *contingency*. Their front hall closet contained a first-aid kit, a fire extinguisher, a life raft, a parachute, and a pack of sled dogs.

CONTRITE (kun TRYTE) *adj* admitting guilt; especially feeling remorseful
To be *contrite* is to admit whatever terrible thing you did.
Sally was *contrite* about her mistake, so we forgave her.
A criminal who won't confess his crime is not *contrite*.
Saying that you're sorry is an act of *contrition*.

CONTRIVED (kun TRYVED) *adj* artificial; labored
Sam's acting was *contrived*: no one in the audience believed his character or enjoyed his performance.
The artist was widely admired for his originality, but his paintings seemed *contrived* to me.

No one laughed at Sue's *contrived* attempt at humor.

A *contrivance* is a mechanical device, usually something rigged up.

CONVENTIONAL (kun VEN shun nul) *adj* common; customary; unexceptional

The architect's *conventional* designs didn't win him awards for originality.

Tipping the waiter in a restaurant is a *conventional* courtesy.

Conventional wisdom is what everyone thinks. The bland politician maintained his popularity by never straying far from the *conventional* wisdom about any topic.

CONVIVIAL (kun VIV ee ul) *adj* fond of partying; festive

A *convivial* gathering is one in which the people present enjoy eating, drinking, and being together.

To be *convivial* is to be an eager but generally well-behaved party animal.

A *convivial* person is the opposite of an antisocial person.

Note carefully the pronunciation of this word.

COPIOUS (KOH pee us) *adj* abundant; plentiful

The champagne at the wedding reception was *copious* but not very good.

Harry had a *copious* supply of nails in his workshop. Everywhere you stepped, it seemed, there was a pile of nails.

We ate *copiously* at the banquet and went home feeling quite sick.

Q•U•I•C•K • Q•U•I•Z #26

Match each word in the first column with its definition in the second column. Check your answers in the back of the book.

1. construe	a. admitting guilt
2. consummate	b. interpret
3. contentious	c. perfect
4. contiguous	d. labored
5. contingent	e. dependent
6. contrite	f. abundant
7. contrived	g. adjoining
8. conventional	h. argumentative
9. convivial	i. festive
10. copious	j. common

COROLLARY (KOR uh ler ee) *n* something that follows; a natural consequence

In mathematics, a *corollary* is a law that can be deduced without further proof from a law that has already been proven.

Bloodshed and death are *corollaries* of any declaration of war.

Higher prices were a *corollary* of the two companies' agreement not to compete.

CORROBORATE (kuh ROB uh rayt) *v* to confirm; to back up with evidence

I knew my statement was correct when my colleague *corroborated* it.

Henny Penny's contention that the sky was falling could not be *corroborated*. That is, no one was able to find any fallen sky.

The police could find no evidence of theft and thus could not *corroborate* Bill's claim that he had been robbed.

Note carefully the pronunciation of this word.

COSMOPOLITAN (kahz muh PAHL uh tun) *adj* at home in many places or situations; internationally sophisticated

Huey's interests were *cosmopolitan*—he liked Greek wine, German beer, Dutch cheese, Japanese cars, and French fries.

A truly *cosmopolitan* traveler never feels like a foreigner anywhere on earth.

New York is a *cosmopolitan* city; you can hear nearly every language in the world spoken there.

COUNTENANCE (KOWN tuh nuns) *n* face; facial expression, especially an encouraging one

His father's confident *countenance* gave Lou the courage to persevere.

Ed's harsh words belied his *countenance,* which was kind and encouraging.

Countenance can also be a verb. To *countenance* something is to condone it or tolerate it.

Dad *countenanced* our backyard rock fights even though he didn't really approve of them.

COUP (koo) *n* a brilliant victory or accomplishment; the violent overthrow of a government by a small internal group

Winning a gold medal at the Olympics was a real *coup* for the skinny, sick, fifty-year-old man.

The student council's great *coup* was persuading the Rolling Stones to play at our prom.

In the attempted *coup* in the Philippines, some army officers tried to take over the government. The full name for this type of *coup* is *coup d'état* (koo day TAH). A *coup de grace* (koo duh GRAHS) is a final blow or concluding event.

Note carefully the pronunciation of these words.

COVENANT (KUV uh nunt) *n* a solemn agreement; a contract; a pledge

The warring tribes made a *covenant* in which they agreed not to fight each other anymore.

We signed a *covenant* in which we promised never to drive Harry's father's car into the Murphys' living room again.

COVERT (KUV urt) *adj* secret; hidden

To be *covert* is to be covered.

Covert activities are secret activities.

A *covert* military operation is one the public knows nothing about.

Most of the activities of spies are *covert*.

This word can also be pronounced "KOH vurt."

The opposite of *covert* is *overt*. *Overt* (OH vurt) means open or unconcealed.

COVET (KUV it) *v* to wish for enviously

To *covet* thy neighbor's wife is to want thy neighbor's wife for thyself.

Billy *coveted* Bobby's bicycle and very nearly decided to steal it.

To be *covetous* is to be envious.

Q•U•I•C•K • Q•U•I•Z   #27

Match each word in the first column with its definition in the second column. Check your answers in the back of the book.

1. corollary
2. corroborate
3. cosmopolitan
4. countenance
5. coup
6. covenant
7. covert
8. covet

a. worldly and sophisticated
b. face
c. wish for enviously
d. confirm
e. solemn agreement
f. brilliant victory
g. natural consequence
h. secret

CREDULOUS (KREJ uh lus) *adj* eager to believe; gullible

The *credulous* postal patron believed that he had won a million dollars from Publishers Clearing House.

Paula was so *credulous* that she simply nodded happily when Ralph told her he could teach her how to fly. Paula's *credulity* (kri DYOOL uh tee) was limitless.

Credulous should not be confused with *credible*. To be *credible* is to be believable.

Almost anything, however *incredible*, is *credible* to a *credulous* person.

Larry's implausible story of heroism was not *credible*. Still, *credulous* old Louis believed it.

A story that cannot be believed is *incredible*. If you don't believe that story someone just told you, you are *incredulous*.

If something is *credible*, it may gain *credence* (KREED uns), which means belief or intellectual acceptance. The chemist's sound techniques inspired *credence* in the scientific world.

No one could prove Frank's theory, but his standing at the university helped it gain *credence*.

Another similar word is *creditable,* which means worthy of credit or praise. Frances made a *creditable* effort to play on the boys' football team, even though she was ultimately forced to sit on the bench.

Our record in raising money was very *creditable;* we raised several thousand dollars every year.

CRITERION (krye TEER ee un) *n* standard; basis for judgment

When Garfield judges a meal, he has only one *criterion:* is it edible?

In choosing among the linemen, the most important *criterion* was quickness.

The plural of *criterion* is *criteria.* You can't have one *criteria;* you can only have one *criterion.* If you have two or more, you have *criteria.* There is no such thing as *criterions* and no such thing as a *criteria.*

CRYPTIC (KRIP tik) *adj* mysterious; mystifying

Elaine's remarks were *cryptic;* everyone was baffled by what she said.

A *cryptic* statement is one in which something important remains hidden. The ghost made *cryptic* comments about the *crypt* from which he had just emerged; that is, no one could figure out what the ghost meant.

CULINARY (KYOO luh ner ee) *adj* relating to cooking or the kitchen

A cooking school is sometimes called a *culinary* institute. Stan pursued his *culinary* interests by attending the *culinary* institute. His first meal, which was burned beyond recognition, was a *culinary* disaster.

Note carefully the pronunciation of this word.

CULMINATE (KUL muh nayt) *v* to climax; to reach full effect

Susan's years of practice *culminated* in a great victory at the international blow ball championship.

The masked ball was the *culmination* of our fund-raising efforts.

Q•U•I•C•K • Q•U•I•Z #28

Match each word in the first column with its definition in the second column. Check your answers in the back of the book.

1. credulous	a. related to cooking
2. credible	b. believable
3. incredible	c. believability
4. incredulous	d. worthy of praise
5. credence	e. eager to believe
6. creditable	f. unbelieving
7. criterion	g. unbelievable
8. cryptic	h. climax
9. culinary	i. standard
10. culminate	j. mysterious

CULPABLE (KUL puh bul) *adj* deserving blame; guilty

A person who is *culpable* (a *culprit*) is one who can be blamed for doing something.

The accountant's failure to spot the errors made him *culpable* in the tax-fraud case.

We all felt *culpable* when the homeless old man died in the doorway of our apartment building.

To decide that a person is not *culpable* after all is to *exculpate* (EK skul payt) that person. Lou's confession didn't *exculpate* Bob, because one of the things that Lou confessed was that Bob had helped him do it. The opposite of *exculpate* is *inculpate*. To *inculpate* is to accuse someone of something.

CURSORY (KUR suh ree) *adj* hasty; superficial

To give a book a *cursory* reading is to skim it quickly without comprehending much.

To make a *cursory* attempt at learning French is to memorize a couple of easy words and then say "the heck with it."

The *cursor* on Dave's computer made a *cursory* sweep across the data as he scrolled down the page.

CURTAIL (kur TAYL) *v* to shorten; to cut short

The vet *curtailed* his effort to cut the cat's tail with the lawn mower. That is, he stopped trying.

To *curtail* a tale is to cut it short.

CYNIC (SIN ik) *n* one who deeply distrusts human nature; one who believes humans are motivated only by selfishness

When the rich man gave a million dollars to the museum, *cynics* said he was merely trying to buy himself a reputation as a cultured person.

To be cynical is to be extremely suspicious of the motivations of other people.

Cynicism is general grumpiness and pessimism about human nature.

Q•U•I•C•K • Q•U•I•Z #29

Match each word in the first column with its definition in the second column. Check your answers in the back of the book.

1. culpable
2. exculpate
3. cursory
4. curtail
5. cynic

a. free from guilt
b. shorten
c. one who distrusts humanity
d. hasty
e. guilty

D

DAUNT (dawnt) v to make fearful; to intimidate

The steepness of the mountain *daunted* the team of amateur climbers, who hadn't realized what they were in for.

The size of the players on the visiting team was *daunting;* the players on the home team began to perspire nervously.

To be *dauntless* or *undaunted* is to be fearless or unintimidated. The rescue crew was *undaunted* by the flames and ran into the burning house to look for survivors. They were *dauntless* in their effort to save the people inside.

DEARTH (durth) n lack; scarcity

There is no *dearth* of comedy at a convention of clowns.

When there is a *dearth* of food, many people may starve.

There was a *dearth* of gaiety at the boring Christmas party.

DEBACLE (di BAHK ul) n violent breakdown; sudden overthrow; overwhelming defeat

A football game can turn into a *debacle* if one team is suddenly being clobbered.

A political debate would become a *debacle* if the candidates began screaming and throwing dinner rolls at each other.

The government fell as a result of a *debacle* instigated by a scheming general.

This word can also be pronounced "day BAHK ul."

DEBAUCHERY (di BAW chuh ree) n wild living; excessive intemperance

Debauchery can be expensive; fortunately for William, his wallet matched his appetite for extravagant pleasures. He died a poor, albeit happy, man.

To *debauch* is to seduce or corrupt. Someone who is *debauched* has been seduced or corrupted.

DEBILITATE (di BIL uh tayt) v to weaken; to cripple

Hank *debilitated* Stu by hitting him on the head with a skillet.

The football player's career was ended by a *debilitating* injury to his knee.

To become *debilitated* is to suffer a *debility*, which is the opposite of an ability. A surgeon who becomes *debilitated* is one who has lost the ability to operate on the *debilities* of other people.

DECADENT (DEK uh dunt) adj decaying or decayed, especially in terms of morals

A person who engages in *decadent* behavior is a person whose morals have decayed or fallen into ruin.

Carousing in local bars instead of going to class is *decadent*.

Decadent behavior is often an affectation of bored young people.

The noun is *decadence*.

DECIMATE (DES uh mayt) v to kill or destroy a large part of

To *decimate* an army is to come close to wiping it out.

When locusts attack a crop, they sometimes *decimate* it, leaving very little that's fit for human consumption.

You might say in jest that your family had *decimated* its turkey dinner on Thanksgiving, leaving nothing but a few crumbs and a pile of bones.

The noun is *decimation*.

DECOROUS (DEK ur us) adj proper; in good taste; orderly

Decorous behavior is good, polite, orderly behavior.

To be *decorous* is to be sober and tasteful.

The New Year's Eve crowd was relatively *decorous* until midnight, when they went wild.

To behave *decorously* is to behave with *decorum* (di KOR um).

DEDUCE (di DOOS) v to conclude from the evidence; to infer

To *deduce* something is to conclude it without being told it directly.

From the footprints on the ground, the detective *deduced* that the criminal had feet.

Nancy *deduced* from the gun in Sluggo's hand that all was not well with their relationship.

Daffy *deduced* from the shape of its bill that the duck was really a chicken.

That the duck was really a chicken was Daffy's *deduction*.

DEFAME (di FAYM) v to libel or slander; to ruin the good name of

To *defame* someone is to make accusations that harm the person's reputation.

The local businessman accused the newspaper of *defaming* him by publishing an article that said his company was poorly managed.

To *defame* is to take away fame, to take away a good name.

To suffer such a loss of reputation is to suffer *defamation*. The businessman who believed he had been *defamed* by the newspaper sued the paper's publisher for *defamation*.

Q•U•I•C•K • Q•U•I•Z #30

Match each word in the first column with its definition in the second column. Check your answers in the back of the book.

1. daunt		a. conclude from evidence
2. dearth		b. lack
3. debacle		c. kill a large part of
4. debauchery		d. libel or slander
5. debilitate		e. make fearful
6. decadent		f. decaying or decayed
7. decimate		g. proper
8. decorous		h. weaken
9. deduce		i. violent breakdown
10. defame		j. wild living

DEFERENCE (DEF ur uns) *n* submission to another's will; respect; courtesy

To show *deference* to another is to place that person's wishes ahead of your own.

The young man showed *deference* to his grandfather: he let the old man have first dibs on the birthday cake.

Herbie stopped yodeling at the dinner table in *deference* to the wishes of his mother.

To show *deference* to another is to *defer* to that person. Joe was supposed to go first, but he *deferred* to Steve, who had been waiting longer.

To show *deference* is also to be *deferential* (def uh REN shul). Joe was being *deferential* when he allowed Steve to go first.

DEFINITIVE (di FIN uh tiv) *adj* conclusive; providing the last word

Walter wrote the *definitive* biography of Keats; nothing more could have been added by another book.

The army completely wiped out the invaders; its victory was *definitive*.

No one could find anything to object to in Cindy's *definitive* explanation of how the meteorite had gotten into the bathtub.

DEGENERATE (di JEN uh rayt) *v* to break down; to deteriorate

The discussion quickly *degenerated* into an argument.

Over the years, the nice old neighborhood had *degenerated* into a terrible slum.

The fans' behavior *degenerated* as the game went on.

A person whose behavior has *degenerated* can be referred to as a *degenerate* (di JEN ur it). The mood of the party was spoiled when a drunken *degenerate* wandered in from off the street.

Degenerate (di JEN ur it) can also be an adjective, meaning *degenerated*. The slum neighborhood was *degenerate*. The fans' *degenerate* behavior prompted the police to make several arrests.

Note carefully the pronunciation of the various parts of speech.

DELETERIOUS (del uh TIR ee us) *adj* harmful

Smoking cigarettes is *deleterious* to your health. So is brushing your teeth with oven cleaner or washing your hair with gasoline.

Is watching *Family Feud deleterious?* Of course not.

DELINEATE (di LIN ee ayt) *v* to describe accurately; to draw in outline

After Jack had *delineated* his plan, we had no doubt about what he intended to do.

Sharon's peculiar feelings about her pet gorilla were *delineated* in the newspaper article about her.

The portrait artist *delineated* Sarah's features, then filled in the shading.

The noun is *delineation.*

DELUDE (di LOOD) *v* to deceive

The con man *deluded* us into thinking that he would make us rich. Instead, he tricked us into giving him several hundred dollars.

The *deluded* mental patient believed that he was a chicken sandwich.

Betty is so persuasive that she was able to *delude* Henrietta into thinking she was a countess.

To be *deluded* is to suffer from a *delusion.* That he was a great poet was the *delusion* of the English teacher, who could scarcely write two complete sentences in a row.

Bert, the well-known jerk, suffered from the *delusion* that he was a very great man.

DELUGE (DEL yooj) *n* a flood; an inundation

A *deluge* is a flood, but the word is often used figuratively. The $1 million reward for the lost poodle brought in a *deluge* of hot leads. The distraught owner was *deluged* by phone calls all week.

Note carefully the pronunciation of this word.

DEMAGOGUE (DEM uh gawg) *n* a leader of the people, but more a rabble rouser

A *demagogue* is a leader, but not in a good sense of the word. He manipulates the public to support his aims, but he is little different from a dictator. A *demagogue* is often a despot.

This word can also be spelled *demagog.* The methods a *demagogue* uses are *demagoguery* (DEM uh gahg uh ree) or *demagogy* (DEM uh gahg ee).

DENIZEN (DEN i zun) *n* inhabitant

To be a *denizen* of a country is to live there. A citizen of a country is usually also a *denizen*.

To be a *denizen* of a restaurant is to go there often—so often that people begin to wonder whether you live there.

Fish are sometimes referred to as "*denizens* of the deep." Don't refer to them this way yourself; the expression is a cliché.

DEPRAVITY (di PRAV uh tee) *n* extreme wickedness or corruption

Mrs. Prudinkle wondered whether the *depravity* of her class of eight-year-olds was the result of their watching Saturday morning television.

To exhibit *depravity* is to be *depraved*.

DEPRECATE (DEP ruh kayt) *v* to express disapproval of

To *deprecate* a colleague's work is to risk making yourself unwelcome in your colleague's office.

"This stinks!" is a *deprecating* remark.

The critic's *deprecating* comments about my new novel put me in a bad mood for an entire month.

To be *self-deprecating* is to make little of one's own efforts, often in the hope that someone else will say, "No, you're swell!"

A very similar word is *depreciate* (di PREE shee ayt). To *depreciate* a colleague's work would be to represent it as being of little value.

For another meaning of *depreciate*, see *appreciate*.

DERIDE (di RYDE) *v* to ridicule; to laugh at contemptuously

Barry *derided* Barbara's driving ability after their hair-raising trip down the twisting mountain road.

Sportswriters *derided* Columbia's football team, which hadn't won a game in many years.

The boss *derided* his secretary mercilessly, so she poisoned him. She was someone who could not accept *derision* (di RIZH un).

Q•U•I•C•K • Q•U•I•Z #31

Match each word in the first column with its definition in the second column. Check your answers in the back of the book.

1. deference
2. definitive
3. degenerate
4. deleterious
5. delineate
6. delude
7. deluge
8. demagogue
9. denizen
10. depravity
11. deprecate
12. deride

a. deteriorate
b. ridicule
c. describe accurately
d. respect
e. conclusive
f. express disapproval of
g. harmful
h. inhabitant
i. deceive
j. flood
k. extreme wickedness
l. rabble-rousing leader

DEROGATORY (di RAHG uh tor ee) *adj* disapproving; degrading

Derogatory remarks are negative remarks expressing disapproval. They are nastier than merely critical remarks.

Oliver could never seem to think of anything nice to say about anyone; virtually all of his comments were *derogatory*.

DESICCATE (DES uh kayt) *v* to dry out

The hot wind *desiccated* the few grapes remaining on the vine; after a day or two, they looked like raisins.

After a week without water, the *desiccated* plant fell over and died.

Plums become prunes through a process of *desiccation*.

DESPONDENT (di SPAHN dunt) *adj* extremely depressed; full of despair

The cook became *despondent* when the wedding cake exploded fifteen minutes before the reception.

After the death of his wife, the man was *despondent* for many months.

The team fell into *despondency* after losing the state championship by a single point.

DESPOT (DES puht) *n* an absolute ruler; an autocrat

The manager of the office was a *despot*; workers who disagreed with him were fired.

The island kingdom was ruled by a ruthless *despot* who executed suspected rebels at noon each day in the village square.

To act like a *despot* is to be *despotic*. There was cheering in the street when the country's *despotic* government was overthrown.

DESTITUTE (DES tuh toot) *adj* extremely poor; utterly lacking

Destitute people are people without money or possessions, or with very little money and very few possessions.

To be left *destitute* is to be left without money or property.

The word can also be used figuratively. A teacher might accuse her students of being *destitute* of brains, or intellectually *destitute*.

DESULTORY (DES ul tor ee) *adj* without a plan or purpose; disconnected; random

Phil made a few *desultory* attempts to start a garden, but nothing came of them.

In his *desultory* address, Jake skipped from one topic to another and never came to the point.

The discussion at our meeting was *desultory;* no one's comments seemed to bear any relation to anyone else's.

Note carefully the pronunciation of this word.

DIALECTICAL (dye uh LEK ti kul) *adj* relating to discussions; relating to the rules and methods of reasoning; approaching truth in the middle of opposing extremes

The game of Twenty Questions is *dialectical,* in that the participants attempt to narrow down a chosen object by asking a series of ever more specific questions.

The noun is *dialectics.*

DICTUM (DIK tum) *n* an authoritative saying; an adage; a maxim; a proverb

"No pain, no gain" is a hackneyed *dictum* of sadistic coaches everywhere.

DIDACTIC (dye DAK tik) *adj* intended to teach; morally instructive; pedantic

Luther's seemingly amusing talk had a *didactic* purpose; he was trying to show his listeners the difference between right and wrong.

The priest's conversation was always *didactic.* He never said anything that wasn't intended to teach a lesson.

The new novel is painfully *didactic;* the author's aim is always to instruct and never to entertain.

DIFFIDENT (DIF i dunt) *adj* timid; lacking in self-confidence

The *diffident* student never made a single comment in class. *Diffident* and *confident* are opposites.

Mary's stammer made her *diffident* in conversation and shy in groups of strangers.

Amos's *diffidence* led many participants to believe he hadn't been present at the meeting, even though he had.

DIGRESS (dye GRES) *v* to stray from the main subject

Speaking metaphorically, to *digress* is to leave the main highway in order to travel aimlessly on back roads. When a speaker *digresses,* he departs from the main topic and tells a story only distantly related to it.

Such a story is called a *digression*. Sometimes a writer's or speaker's *digressions* are more interesting than his or her main points.

After a lengthy *digression*, the lecturer returned to his speech and brought it to a conclusion.

DILETTANTE (DIL uh tahnt) *n* someone with superficial knowledge of the arts; an amateur; a dabbler

To be a *dilettante* is to dabble in something rather than doing it in a serious way.

Reginald said he was an artist, but he was merely a *dilettante;* he didn't know a pencil from a paintbrush.

Helen dismissed the members of the ladies' sculpture club as nothing more than a bunch of *dilettantes.*

Q•U•I•C•K • Q•U•I•Z #32

Match each word in the first column with its definition in the second column. Check your answers in the back of the book.

1. derogatory	a. without purpose
2. desiccate	b. extremely depressed
3. despondent	c. amateur
4. despot	d. stray from main subject
5. destitute	e. extremely poor
6. desultory	f. timid
7. dialectical	g. dry out
8. dictum	h. disapproving
9. didactic	i. absolute ruler
10. diffident	j. intended to teach
11. digress	k. relating to discussions
12. dilettante	l. authoritative saying

DISCERN (di SURN) *v* to have insight; to see things clearly, to discriminate; to differentiate

To *discern* something is to perceive it clearly. A writer whose work demonstrates *discernment* is a writer who is a keen observer.

The ill-mannered people at Louise's party proved that she had little *discernment* when it came to choosing friends.

DISCREET (di SKREET) *adj* prudent; judiciously reserved

To make *discreet* inquiries is to ask around without letting the whole world know you're doing it.

The psychiatrist was very *discreet;* no matter how much we pestered him, he wouldn't gossip about the problems of his famous patients. He had *discretion* (di SKRESH un).

To be *indiscreet* is to be imprudent and especially to say or do things you shouldn't. It was *indiscreet* of Laura to tell Sally how much she hated Betty's new hairdo, because Sally always tells Betty everything.

When Laura told that to Sally, she committed an *indiscretion.*

DISCRETE (di SKREET) *adj* unconnected; separate; distinct

Do not confuse *discrete* with *discreet.* The twins were identical but their personalities were *discrete.*

The drop in the stock market was not the result of any single force but of many *discrete* trends.

When things are all jumbled up together, they are said to be *indiscrete,* which means not separated or sorted.

DISCRIMINATE (di SKRIM uh nayt) *v* to notice or point out the difference between two or more things; to discern; to differentiate

A person with a refined aesthetic sense is able to *discriminate* subtle differences where a less observant person would see nothing. Such a person is *discriminating.* This kind of *discrimination* is a good thing. To *discriminate* unfairly, though, is to dwell on differences that shouldn't make a difference. It is unfair—and illegal—to *discriminate* between black people and white people in selling a house. Such a practice is not *discriminating* (which is good), but *discriminatory* (which is wrong).

Indiscriminate means not *discriminating;* in other words, random or haphazard.

DISDAIN (dis DAYN) *n* arrogant scorn; contempt

Bertram viewed the hot dog with *disdain,* believing that to eat such a disgusting food was beneath him.

The millionaire looked upon the poor workers with evident *disdain.*

Disdain can also be a verb. The millionaire in the previous example could be said to have *disdained* those workers.

To be filled with *disdain* is to be *disdainful.*

DISINTERESTED (dis IN truh stid) *adj* not taking sides; unbiased

Disinterested should *not* be used to mean *uninterested.* If you don't care about knowing something, you are *uninterested,* not *disinterested.*

A referee should be *disinterested.* He or she should not be rooting for one of the competing teams.

A *disinterested* observer is one who has no personal stake in or attachment to what is being observed.

Agatha claimed that the accident had been Lester's fault, but several *disinterested* witnesses said that Agatha had actually bashed into his car after jumping the median and driving in the wrong lane for several miles.

DISPARAGE (di SPAR ij) *v* to belittle; to say uncomplimentary things about, usually in a somewhat indirect way

The mayor *disparaged* our efforts to beautify the town square by saying that the flower bed we had planted looked somewhat worse than the weeds it had replaced.

My guidance counselor *disparaged* my high school record by telling me that not everybody belongs in college.

Q•U•I•C•K • Q•U•I•Z #33

Match each word in the first column with its definition in the second column. Check your answers in the back of the book.

1. discern
2. discreet
3. discrete
4. indiscrete
5. discriminate
6. disdain
7. disinterested
8. disparage

a. insight
b. belittle
c. not separated
d. not taking sides
e. arrogant scorn
f. prudent
g. unconnected
h. differentiate

DISPARATE (DIS pur it) *adj* different; incompatible; unequal

Our interests were *disparate:* Cathy liked to play with dolls and I liked to throw her dolls out the window.

The *disparate* interest groups were united only by their intense dislike of the candidate.

The novel was difficult to read because the plot consisted of dozens of *disparate* threads that never came together.

The noun form of *disparate* is *disparity* (di SPAR i tee). *Disparity* means inequality. The opposite of *disparity* is *parity*.

Note carefully the pronunciation of this word.

DISSEMINATE (di SEM uh nayt) *v* to spread the seeds of something; to scatter; to make widely known

News is *disseminated* through many media: radio, television, newspapers, magazines, and gossips.

DISSIPATE (DIS uh payt) *v* to thin out, drift away, or dissolve; to cause to thin out, drift away, or dissolve; to waste or squander

The smoke *dissipated* as soon as we opened the windows.

Rex's anger *dissipated* as the day wore on and he gradually forgot what had upset him.

The police *dissipated* the riotous crowd by spraying the demonstrators with fire hoses and firing bullets over their heads.

Alex won the weekly lottery but *dissipated* the entire winnings in one abandoned, fun-filled weekend. We can also say that a person is *dissipated,* by which we mean that he indulges in wild living. Alex is *dissipated.*

DISSOLUTION (dis uh LOO shun) *n* the breaking up or dissolving of something into parts; disintegration

Nothing could prevent the *dissolution* of the Pee Wee Herman Fan Club after he retired to seek a political career.

A person who is *dissolute* has lived life in the fast lane too long. *Dissolute* and *dissipated* are synonyms in this sense.

DISTEND (di STEND) v to swell; to extend a great deal

The tire *distended* alarmingly as the forgetful gas station attendant kept pumping more and more air into it.

A *distended* belly is one symptom of malnutrition.

A swelling is a *distension.*

DISTINGUISH (di STING gwish) v to tell apart; to cause to stand out

The rodent expert's eyesight was so acute that he was able to *distinguish* between a shrew and a vole at more than a thousand paces.

I studied and studied but I was never able to *distinguish* between *discrete* and *discreet.*

His face had no *distinguishing* characteristics; there was nothing about his features that stuck in your memory.

Lou's uneventful career as a dogcatcher was not *distinguished* by adventure or excitement.

DOCILE (DAHS ul) adj easily taught; obedient; easy to handle

The *docile* students quietly memorized all the lies their teacher told them.

The baby raccoons appeared *docile* at first, but they were almost impossible to control.

Louise's *docility* fooled the professor into believing that she was incapable of thinking for herself.

Note carefully the pronunciation of both parts of speech.

DOCTRINAIRE (dahk truh NAYR) adj inflexibly committed to a doctrine or theory without regard to its practicality; dogmatic

A *doctrinaire* supporter of manned space flights to Pluto would be someone who supported such space flights even though it might be shown that such lengthy journeys could never be undertaken.

A *doctrinaire* opponent of fluoridation of water would be someone whose opposition could not be shaken by proof that fluoride is good for teeth and not bad for anything else.

A person with *doctrinaire* views can be called a *doctrinaire.*

DOGMATIC (dawg MAT ik) adj arrogantly assertive of unproven ideas; stubbornly claiming that something (often a system of beliefs) is beyond dispute

A *dogma* is a belief. A *dogmatic* person, however, is stubbornly convinced of his beliefs.

Marty is *dogmatic* on the subject of the creation of the world; he sneers at anyone whose views are not identical to his.

The philosophy professor became increasingly *dogmatic* as he grew older and became more firmly convinced of his strange theories.

The opinions or ideas *dogmatically* asserted by a *dogmatic* person are known collectively as *dogma.*

DOMESTIC (duh MES tik) adj having to do with the household or family; not foreign

A home that enjoys *domestic* tranquillity is a happy home.

A maid is sometimes referred to as a *domestic* engineer or simply as a *domestic*.

To be *domestic* is to enjoy being at home or to be skillful at doing things around the house.

Domestic wine is wine from this country, as opposed to wine imported from, say, France.

The *domestic* steel industry is the steel industry in this country.

A country that enjoys *domestic* tranquillity is a happy country.

Q•U•I•C•K • Q•U•I•Z #34

Match each word in the first column with its definition in the second column. Check your answers in the back of the book.

1. disparate	a. inharmonious
2. disseminate	b. committed to a theory
3. dissipate	c. thin out
4. dissolution	d. of the household
5. dissonant	e. firmly held system of ideas
6. distend	f. easily taught
7. distinguish	g. arrogantly assertive
8. docile	h. swell
9. doctrinaire	i. tell apart
10. dogmatic	j. incompatible
11. dogma	k. spread seeds
12. domestic	l. disintegration

DORMANT (DOR munt) *adj* inactive; as though asleep; asleep

Dormant, like *dormitory*, comes from a root meaning sleep.

The volcano erupted violently and then fell *dormant* for several hundred years.

Many plants remain *dormant* through the winter; that is, they stop growing until spring.

Frank's interest in playing the piano was *dormant* and, quite possibly, dead.

The snow fell silently over the *dormant* village, which became snarled in traffic jams the following morning.

The noun is *dormancy*.

DUBIOUS (DOO bee us) *adj* full of doubt; uncertain

I was fairly certain that I would be able to fly if I could merely flap my arms hard enough, but Mary was *dubious;* she said I'd better flap my legs as well.

We were *dubious* about the team's chance of success and, as it turned out, our *dubiety* (doo BYE uh tee) was justified: the team lost.

Dubious and *doubtful* don't mean exactly the same thing. A *dubious* person is a person who has doubts. A *doubtful* outcome is an outcome that isn't certain to occur.

Sam's chances of getting the job were *doubtful*, because the employer was *dubious* of his claim that he had been president of the United States while in high school.

Something beyond doubt is *indubitable*. A dogmatic person believes his opinions are *indubitable*.

DUPLICITY (doo PLIS uh tee) *n* the act of being two-faced; double-dealing; deception

Dave, in his *duplicity*, told us he wasn't going to rob the bank and then went right out and robbed it.

Liars engage in *duplicity* all the time; they say one thing and do another.

The *duplicitous* salesman sold the stuffed camel to someone else even though he had promised to sell it to us.

Q•U•I•C•K • Q•U•I•Z #35

Match each word in the first column with its definition in the second column. Check your answers in the back of the book.

1. dormant	a. uncertainty
2. dubiety	b. double-dealing
3. duplicity	c. inactive

E

EBULLIENT (i BUL yunt) *adj* boiling; bubbling with excitement; exuberant

A boiling liquid can be called *ebullient*. More often, though, this word describes excited or enthusiastic people.

The roaring crowd in a full stadium before the World Series might be said to be *ebullient*.

A person overflowing with enthusiasm might be said to be *ebullient*.

Mabel was *ebullient* when her fairy godmother said she could use one of her three wishes to wish for three more wishes.

Someone or something that is *ebullient* is characterized by *ebullience*.

Note carefully the pronunciation of this word.

ECCENTRIC (ek SEN trik) *adj* not conventional; a little kooky; irregular

The *eccentric* inventor spent all his waking hours fiddling with what he said was a time machine but was actually just an old telephone booth.

Fred's political views are *eccentric:* he believes that we should have kings instead of presidents and that the government should raise money by holding bake sales.

The rocket followed an *eccentric* course; first it veered in one direction, then it veered in another, then it crashed.

An *eccentric* person is a person who has *eccentricities* (ek sen TRIS uh teez).

ECLECTIC (i KLEK tik) *adj* choosing the best from many sources; drawn from many sources

Zeke's taste in art was *eclectic*. He liked the Old Masters, the Impressionists, and Walt Disney.

The *eclectic* menu included dishes from many different countries.

George's *eclectic* reading made him well rounded.

EDIFY (ED uh fye) *v* to enlighten; to instruct, especially in moral or religious matters

We found the pastor's sermon on the importance of not eating beans to be most *edifying*.

The teacher's goal was to *edify* her students, not to force a handful of facts down their throats.

We would have felt lost at the art show had not the excellent and informative programs been provided for our *edification*.

EFFACE (i FAYS) *v* to erase; to rub away the features of

The inscription on the tombstone had been *effaced* by centuries of weather.

The vandals *effaced* the delicate carving by rubbing it with sandpaper.

We tried to *efface* the dirty words that had been written on the front of our house, but nothing would remove them.

To be *self-effacing* is to be modest. Jennings is *self-effacing:* he won an Olympic gold medal and all he said was "Aw, shucks. I'm just a regular fella."

EFFUSION (i FYOO zhun) *n* a pouring forth

When the child was rescued from the well, there was an intense *effusion* of emotion from the crowd that had gathered around the hole.

The madman's writings consisted of a steady *effusion* of nonsense.

To be *effusive* is to be highly emotional. Sally's *effusive* thanks for our silly little present made us feel somewhat embarrassed, so we decided to move to a different city.

EGALITARIAN (i gal uh TAYR ee un) *adj* believing in the social and economic equality of all people

People often lose interest in *egalitarian* measures when such measures interfere with their own interests.

Egalitarian can also be used as a noun to characterize a person. An *egalitarian* advocates *egalitarianism*.

EGOCENTRIC (ee goh SEN trik) *adj* selfish; believing that one is the center of everything

Lou was so *egocentric* that he could never give anyone else credit for doing anything.

Egocentric Bill never read the newspaper unless there was something in it about him.

It never occurred to the *egocentric* musician that his audiences might like to hear someone else's songs every once in a while.

An *egoist* is an *egocentric* person. He believes the entire universe exists for his benefit.

An *egotist* is another type of *egocentric*. An *egotist* is an *egoist* who tells everyone how wonderful he is.

EGREGIOUS (i GREE jus) *adj* extremely bad; flagrant

Save this word for things that are worse than bad.

The mother's *egregious* neglect was responsible for her child's accidental cross-country ride on the freight train.

Stephen's manners were *egregious;* he ate his mashed potatoes with his fingers and slurped the peas right off his plate.

Q•U•I•C•K • Q•U•I•Z #36

Match each word in the first column with its definition in the second column. Check your answers in the back of the book.

1. ebullient	a. pouring forth
2. eccentric	b. self-obsessed person
3. eclectic	c. extremely bad
4. edify	d. not conventional
5. efface	e. drawn from many sources
6. effusion	f. bubbling with excitement
7. egalitarian	g. erase
8. egocentric	h. selfish
9. egotist	i. enlighten
10. egregious	j. believing in social equality

ELICIT (i LIS it) *v* to bring out; to call forth

The interviewer skillfully *elicited* our true feelings by asking us questions that got to the heart of the matter.

The defendant tried to *elicit* the sympathy of the jury by appearing at the trial in a wheelchair, but the jury convicted him anyway.

Don't confuse this word with *illicit*.

ELLIPTICAL (i LIP ti kul) *adj* oval; missing a word or words; obscure

This word has several meanings. Consult a dictionary if you are uncertain.

The orbit of the earth is not perfectly round; it is *elliptical*.

An egg may have an *elliptical* shape.

An *elliptical* statement is one that is hard or impossible to understand, either because something is missing from it or because the speaker or writer is trying to be hard to understand. The announcement from the State Department was purposely *elliptical*—the government didn't really want reporters to know what was going on.

ELUSIVE (i LOO siv) *adj* hard to pin down; evasive

To be *elusive* is to *elude*, which means to avoid, evade, or escape. The answer to the problem was *elusive*; every time the mathematician thought he was close, he discovered another error. (Or, one could say that the answer to the problem *eluded* the mathematician.)

The *elusive* criminal was next to impossible for the police to catch. (The criminal *eluded* the police.)

The team played hard, but victory was *elusive* and they suffered another defeat. (Victory *eluded* the hard-playing team.)

EMIGRATE (EM uh grayt) *v* to move to a new country; to move to a new place to live; to expatriate

At the heart of this word is the word *migrate*, which means to move from one place or country to another. *Emigrate* adds to migrate the sense of moving *out of* some place in particular. Pierre *emigrated* from France because he had grown tired of speaking French. Pierre became an *émigré* (EM uh gray).

The Soviet dissidents were persecuted by the secret police, so they sought permission to *emigrate*.

On the other end of every *emigration* is an *immigration*, or "in-migration." When Pierre *emigrated* from France, he *immigrated* to the United States.

To *emigrate* is to leave one country for another; to *immigrate* is to arrive in one country from another.

EMINENT (EM uh nunt) *adj* well-known and respected; standing out from all others in quality or accomplishment; outstanding

The visiting poet was so *eminent* that our English teacher fell to the ground before him and licked his shoes. Our English teacher thought the poet was *preeminent* in his field.

The entire audience fell silent when the *eminent* musician walked onto the stage and picked up his banjo and bongo drums.

Don't confuse this word with *imminent*.

EMPIRICAL (em PIR uh kul) *adj* relying on experience or observation; not merely theoretical

The apple-dropping experiment gave the scientists *empirical* evidence that gravity exists.

Huey's idea about the moon being made of pizza dough was not *empirical*.

We proved the pie's deliciousness *empirically*, by eating it.

Q•U•I•C•K • Q•U•I•Z #37

Match each word in the first column with its definition in the second column. Check your answers in the back of the book.

1. elicit   a. well-known
2. elliptical   b. bring out
3. elusive   c. hard to pin down
4. emigrate   d. relying on experience
5. immigration   e. move from a country
6. eminent   f. moving into a country
7. empirical   g. obscure

EMULATE (EM yuh layt) *v* to strive to equal or excel, usually through imitation

To *emulate* someone is to try to be just as good as, or better than, him or her.

The American company *emulated* its successful Japanese competitor but never quite managed to do as well.

Little Joey imitated his athletic older brother in the hope of one day *emulating* his success.

I got ahead by *emulating* those who had gone before me.

ENCROACH (en KROHCH) *v* to make gradual or stealthy inroads into; to trespass

As the city grew, it *encroached* on the countryside surrounding it.

With an *encroaching* sense of dread, I slowly pushed open the blood-spattered door.

My neighbor *encroached* on my yard by building his new stockade fence a few feet on my side of the property line.

ENDEMIC (en DEM ik) *adj* native; restricted to a particular region or era; indigenous

You won't find that kind of tree in California; it's *endemic* to our part of the country.

That peculiar strain of influenza was *endemic* to a small community in South Carolina; there were no cases anywhere else.

The writer Tom Wolfe coined the term "Me Decade" to describe the egocentricity *endemic* in the 1970s.

ENERVATE (EN ur vayt) *v* to reduce the strength or energy of, especially to do so gradually

Mark felt *enervated* by his long ordeal and couldn't make himself get out of bed.

Clinging to a flagpole for a month without food or water *enervated* me, and one day I fell asleep and fell off.

Life itself seemed to *enervate* the old man. He grew weaker and paler with every breath he drew.

ENFRANCHISE (en FRAN chyze) *v* to grant the privileges of citizenship, especially the right to vote

In the United States, citizens become *enfranchised* on their eighteenth birthdays. American women were not *enfranchised* until the adoption of the Nineteenth Amendment in 1920, which gave them the right to vote.

To *disfranchise* (or *disenfranchise*) someone is to take away the privileges of citizenship or take away the right to vote. One of the goals of the reform candidate was to *disfranchise* the bodies at the cemetery, which had had a habit of voting for the crooked mayor.

ENGENDER (en JEN dur) *v* to bring into existence; to create; to cause

My winning lottery ticket *engendered* a great deal of envy among my co-workers; they all wished that they had won.

Smiles *engender* smiles.

The bitter lieutenant *engendered* discontent among his troops.

ENIGMA (uh NIG muh) *n* a mystery

Hal is an *enigma;* he never does any homework but he always gets good grades.

The wizard spoke in riddles and *enigmas,* and no one could understand what he was saying.

An *enigma* is *enigmatic* (en ig MAT ik). Hal's good grades were *enigmatic.* So was the wizard's speech.

ENORMITY (i NOR muh tee) *n* extreme evil; a hideous offense; immensity

Hitler's soldiers stormed through the village, committing one *enormity* after another.

"Hugeness" or "great size" is not the main meaning of *enormity.* When you want to talk about the gigantic size of something, use *immensity* instead.

EPHEMERAL (i FEM ur al) *adj* lasting a very short time

Ephemeral comes from the Greek and means lasting a single day. The word is usually used more loosely to mean lasting a short time.

Youth and flowers are both *ephemeral.* They're gone before you know it.

Some friendships are *ephemeral.*

The tread on those used tires will probably turn out to be *ephemeral.*

Q•U•I•C•K • Q•U•I•Z #38

Match each word in the first column with its definition in the second column. Check your answers in the back of the book.

1. emulate
2. encroach
3. endemic
4. enervate
5. enfranchise
6. disfranchise
7. engender
8. enigma
9. enormity
10. ephemeral

a. cause to exist
b. mystery
c. remove voting rights
d. reduce the strength of
e. native
f. grant voting rights
g. strive to equal
h. lasting a very short time
i. extreme evil
j. trespass

EPIGRAM (EP uh gram) *n* a brief and usually witty or satirical saying

People often find it difficult to remember the difference between an *epigram* and an:

epigraph: an apt quotation placed at the beginning of a book or essay

epitaph: a commemorative inscription on a grave

epithet: a term used to characterize the nature of something; sometimes a disparaging term used to describe a person.

There. Now you know.

An *epigram* is *epigrammatic* (ep uh gruh MAT ik).

EPITOME (i PIT uh mee) *n* a brief summary that captures the meaning of the whole; the perfect example of something; a paradigm

The first paragraph of the new novel is an *epitome* of the entire book; you could read it and understand what the author was trying to get across. It *epitomized* the entire work.

Luke's freshman year was an *epitome* of the college experience. He made friends, missed classes, fell in love, and flunked out.

Eating corn dogs and drinking root beer is the *epitome* of the good life, as far as Wilson is concerned.

Note carefully the pronunciation of this word.

EQUANIMITY (ek wuh NIM uh tee) *n* composure; calm

The entire apartment building was crumbling, but Rachel faced the disaster with *equanimity*. She ducked out of the way of a falling beam and made herself a chocolate sundae.

The mother of twelve boys viewed the mudball fight with *equanimity;* at least they weren't shooting bullets at one another.

Note carefully the pronunciation of this word.

EQUITABLE (EK wuh tuh bul) *adj* fair

King Solomon's decision was certainly *equitable;* each mother would receive half the child.

The pirates distributed the loot *equitably* among themselves, so that each pirate received the same share as every other pirate.

The divorce settlement was quite *equitable.* Sheila got the right half of the house and Tom got the left half.

Equity is fairness; *inequity* is unfairness. *Iniquity* and *inequity* both mean unfair, but *iniquity* implies wickedness as well. By the way, *equity* has a meaning in business. See our Finance chapter at the end of the book.

EQUIVOCAL (i KWIV uh kul) *adj* ambiguous; intentionally confusing; capable of being interpreted in more than one way

Ambiguous means unclear. To be *equivocal* is to be intentionally ambiguous. Joe's response was *equivocal;* we couldn't tell whether he meant yes or no, which is precisely what Joe wanted.

The doctor's *equivocal* diagnosis made us think that he had no idea what Mrs. Johnson had.

To be *equivocal* is to *equivocate.* To *equivocate* is to mislead by saying confusing or ambiguous things. When we asked Harry whether that was his car that was parked in the middle of the hardware store, he *equivocated* and asked, "In which aisle?"

ERUDITE (ER yoo dyte) *adj* scholarly; deeply learned

The professor said things *erudite* that none of us had the slightest idea of what he was saying.

The *erudite* biologist was viewed by many of his colleagues as a likely winner of the Nobel Prize.

To be *erudite* is to possess *erudition* (er yoo DISH un), or extensive knowledge. Mr. Jones's vast library was an indication of his *erudition.*
Note carefully the pronunciation of both parts of speech.

Q•U•I•C•K • Q•U•I•Z #39

Match each word in the first column with its definition in the second column. Check your answers in the back of the book.

1. epigram	a. brief summary
2. epigraph	b. fair
3. epitaph	c. composure
4. epithet	d. intentionally confusing
5. epitome	e. apt quotation
6. equanimity	f. say confusing things
7. equitable	g. inscription on a grave
8. equivocal	h. scholarly
9. equivocate	i. brief, witty saying
10. erudite	j. characterizing term

ESOTERIC (es uh TER ik) *adj* hard to understand; understood by only a select few; peculiar

Chicken wrestling and underwater yodeling were just two of Bob's *esoteric* hobbies.

The author's books were so *esoteric* that no one except his mother ever bought any of them.

ESPOUSE (e SPOWZ) *v* to support; to advocate

The Mormons used to *espouse* bigamy, or marriage to more than one woman.

Bert *espoused* so many causes that he sometimes had trouble remembering which side he was on.

The candidate for governor *espoused* a program in which all taxes would be abolished and all the state's revenues would be supplied by income from bingo and horse racing.

ETHEREAL (i THIR ee ul) *adj* heavenly; as light and insubstantial as a gas or ether

The *ethereal* music we heard turned out to be not angels plucking on their harps but the wind blowing past our satellite-television antenna.

The *ethereal* mist on the hillside was delicate and beautiful.

EUPHEMISM (YOO fuh miz um) *n* a pleasant or inoffensive expression used in place of an unpleasant or offensive one

Aunt Gladys, who couldn't bring herself to say the word *death,* said that Uncle George had taken the big bus uptown. "Taking the big bus uptown" was her *euphemism* for dying.

The sex-education instructor wasn't very effective. She was so embarrassed by the subject that she could only bring herself to speak *euphemistically* about it.

EVANESCENT (ev uh NES unt) *adj* fleeting; vanishing; happening for only the briefest period

Meteors are *evanescent:* they last so briefly that it is hard to tell whether one has actually appeared.

EXACERBATE (ig ZAS ur bayt) *v* to make worse

Dipping Austin in lye *exacerbated* his skin condition.

The widow's grief was *exacerbated* by the minister's momentary inability to remember her dead husband's name.

The fender-bender was *exacerbated* when a line of twenty-five cars plowed into the back of Margaret's car.

EXACTING (ig ZAK ting) *adj* extremely demanding; difficult; requiring great skill or care

The *exacting* math teacher subtracted points for even the most unimportant errors.

Weaving cloth out of guinea-pig hair is an *exacting* occupation, because guinea pigs are small and their hair is short.

The surgeon's *exacting* task was to reconnect the patient's severed eyelashes.

EXALT (ig ZAWLT) *v* to raise high; to glorify
The manager decided to *exalt* the lowly batboy by asking him to pitch in the opening game of the World Series.

The adjective *exalted* is used frequently. Being queen of England is an *exalted* occupation.

Larry felt *exalted* when he woke up to discover that his great-uncle had left him $100 million.

Cleaning out a septic tank is not an *exalted* task.

Be careful not to confuse this word with *exult,* listed later.

EXASPERATE (ig ZAS puh rayt) *v* to annoy thoroughly; to make very angry; to try the patience of
The child's insistence on hopping backward on one foot *exasperated* his mother, who was in a hurry.

The algebra class's refusal to answer any questions was extremely *exasperating* to the substitute teacher.

EXEMPLIFY (ig ZEM pluh fye) *v* to illustrate by example; to serve as a good example
Fred participated in every class discussion and typed all of his papers. His teacher thought Fred *exemplified* the model student; Fred's classmates thought he was sycophantic.

An *exemplar* (ig ZEM plahr) is an ideal model or a paradigm. *Exemplary* (ig ZEM plur ee) means outstanding, or worthy of imitation.

EXHAUSTIVE (ig ZAWS tiv) *adj* thorough; rigorous; complete; painstaking
Before you use a parachute, you should examine it *exhaustively* for defects. Once you jump, your decision is irrevocable.

EXHORT (ig ZORT) *v* to urge strongly; to give a serious warning to
The coach used his bullhorn to *exhort* us to try harder.

The fearful forest ranger *exhorted* us not to go into the cave, but we did so anyway and became lost in the center of the earth.

The adjective is *hortatory* (HOR tuh tor ee).

Q•U•I•C•K • Q•U•I•Z #40

Match each word in the first column with its definition in the second column. Check your answers in the back of the book.

1. esoteric	a. peculiar
2. espouse	b. make worse
3. ethereal	c. extremely demanding
4. euphemism	d. raise high
5. evanescent	e. inoffensive substitute term
6. exacerbate	f. urge strongly
7. exacting	g. annoy thoroughly
8. exalt	h. heavenly
9. exasperate	i. advocate
10. exemplify	j. fleeting
11. exhaustive	k. illustrate by example
12. exhort	l. thorough

EXIGENCY (EK si jen see) *n* an emergency; an urgency

An academic *exigency:* you haven't opened a book all term and the final is tomorrow morning.

Exigent means urgent.

EXISTENTIAL (eg zis TEN shul) *adj* having to do with existence; having to do with the body of thought called existentialism, which basically holds that human beings are responsible for their own actions but is otherwise too complicated to summarize in a single sentence

This word is overused but under-understood by virtually all of the people who use it. Unless you have a very good reason for throwing it around, you should probably avoid it.

EXONERATE (ig ZAHN uh rayt) *v* to free completely from blame; to exculpate

The suspect was *exonerated* when the district attorney's finger-prints were found on the murder weapon.

The defendant, who had always claimed he wasn't guilty, expected to be *exonerated* by the testimony of his best friend.

Our dog was *exonerated* when we discovered that it was in fact the cat who had eaten all the chocolate-chip cookies.

EXPATRIATE (eks PAY tree ayt) *v* to throw (someone) out of his or her native land; to move away from one's native land; to emigrate

The rebels were *expatriated* by the nervous general, who feared that they would cause trouble if they were allowed to remain in the country.

Hugo was fed up with his native country and so *expatriated* to America. In doing so, Hugo became an *expatriate* (eks PAY tree ut).

To *repatriate* (ree PAY tree ayt) is to return to one's native citizen-ship; that is, to become a *repatriate* (ree PAY tree it).

EXPEDIENT (ik SPEE dee unt) *adj* providing an immediate advantage; serving one's immediate self-interest; practical

Since the basement had nearly filled with water, the plumber felt it would be *expedient* to clear out the drain.

The candidate's position in favor of higher pay for teachers was an *expedient* one adopted for the national teachers' convention and abandoned shortly afterward.

Expedient can also be used as a noun for something *expedient*. The car repairman did not have his tool kit handy, so he used chewing gum as an *expedient* to patch a hole.

The noun *expedience* or *expediency* is practicality, or being especially suited to a particular goal.

EXPEDITE (EK spi dyte) *v* to speed up or ease the progress of

The post office *expedited* mail delivery by hiring more letter carriers.

The lawyer *expedited* the progress of our case through the courts by bribing a few judges.

Our wait for a table was *expedited* by a waiter who mistook Angela for a movie star.

EXPLICIT (ik SPLIS it) *adj* clearly and directly expressed

The sexually *explicit* movie received an X rating.

The machine's instructions were *explicit*—they told us exactly what to do.

No one *explicitly* asked us to set the barn on fire, but we got the impression that that was what we were supposed to do.

Implicit means indirectly expressed or implied. Gerry's dissatisfaction with our work was *implicit* in his expression, although he never criticized us directly.

EXTOL (ik STOHL) *v* to praise highly; to laud

The millionaire *extolled* the citizen who returned his gold watch, and then rewarded him with a heartfelt handshake.

EXTRANEOUS (ik STRAY nee us) *adj* unnecessary; irrelevant; extra

To be *extraneous* is to be *extra*, but always with the sense of being unnecessary. Extra ice cream would never be *extraneous*, unless everyone had already eaten so much that no one wanted any more.

The book's feeble plot was buried in a lot of *extraneous* material about a talking dog.

The soup contained several *extraneous* ingredients, including hair, sand, and a single dead fly.

EXTRAPOLATE (ik STRAP uh layt) *v* to project or deduce from something known; to infer

George's estimates were *extrapolated* from last year's data; he simply took all the old numbers and doubled them.

Jacob came up with a probable recipe by *extrapolating* from the taste of the cookies he had eaten at the store.

By *extrapolating* from a handful of pottery fragments, the archaeologists formed a possible picture of the ancient civilization.

To *extrapolate,* a scientist uses the facts he has to project to facts outside; to *interpolate* (in TUR puh layt), he tries to fill the gaps within his data.

EXTRICATE (EK struh kayt) v to free from difficulty

It took two and a half days to *extricate* the little girl from the abandoned well into which she had fallen.

Sam had to pretend to be sick to *extricate* himself from the blind date with the mud wrestler.

Mary had no trouble driving her car into the ditch, but she needed a tow truck to *extricate* it.

Something that is permanently stuck is *inextricable* (in EKS tri kuh bul).

EXTROVERT (EKS truh vurt) n an open, outgoing person; a person whose attention is focused on others rather than on himself or herself

The little girl was quite an *extrovert;* she walked boldly into the roomful of strange adults and struck up a friendly conversation.

Hal was an *extrovert* in the sense that he was always more interested in other people's business than in his own.

An *introvert* (IN trah vurt) is a person whose attention is directed inward and who is concerned with little outside himself or herself. Bud was an *introvert;* he spent virtually all his time in his room, writing in his diary and talking to himself. An *introvert* is usually introspective.

EXULT (ig ZULT) v to rejoice; to celebrate

The women's team *exulted* in its victory over the men's team at the badminton finals. They were *exultant.*

Q•U•I•C•K • Q•U•I•Z #41

Match each word in the first column with its definition in the second column. Check your answers in the back of the book.

1. exigency
2. existential
3. exonerate
4. expatriate
5. expedient
6. expedite
7. explicit
8. implicit
9. extol
10. extraneous
11. extrapolate
12. extricate
13. extrovert
14. introvert
15. exult

a. free from blame
b. clearly expressed
c. indirectly expressed
d. having to do with existence
e. outgoing person
f. speed up
g. infer
h. free from difficulty
i. immediately advantageous
j. unnecessary
k. inwardly directed person
l. throw out of native land
m. emergency
n. rejoice
o. praise highly

F

FABRICATION (FAB ruh kay shun) *n* a lie; something made up

My story about being the Prince of Wales was a *fabrication*. I'm really the king of Denmark.

The suspected murderer's alibi turned out to be an elaborate *fabrication;* in other words, he was lying when he said that he hadn't killed the victim.

To create a *fabrication* is to *fabricate*.

FACETIOUS (fuh SEE shus) *adj* humorous; not serious; clumsily humorous

David was sent to the principal's office for making a *facetious* remark about the intelligence of the French teacher.

Our proposal about shipping our town's garbage to the moon was *facetious*, but the first selectman took it seriously.

FACILE (FAS il) *adj* fluent; skillful in a superficial way; easy

To say that a writer's style is *facile* is to say both that it is skillful and that it would be better if the writer exerted himself or herself more. The word *facile* almost always contains this sense of superficiality.

Joe's poems were *facile* rather than truly accomplished; if you read them closely, you soon realized they were filled with clichés.

The bank president was a *facile* speaker. He could speak engagingly on almost any topic with very little preparation. He spoke with great *facility*.

Note carefully the pronunciation of this word.

FACTION (FAK shun) *n* a group, usually a small part of a larger group, united around some cause; disagreement within an organization

At the Republican National Convention, the Ford *faction* spent much of its time shouting at the Reagan *faction*.

The faculty was relatively happy, but there was a *faction* that called for higher pay.

When the controversial topic of the fund drive came up, the committee descended into bitterness and *faction*. It was a *factious* topic.

FARCICAL (FARS i kul) *adj* absurd; ludicrous

Farcical means like a *farce*, which is a mockery or a ridiculous satire.

The serious play quickly turned *farcical* when the leading man's belt broke and his pants fell to his ankles.

The formerly secret documents detailed the CIA's *farcical* attempt to discredit Fidel Castro by sprinkling his shoes with a powder that was supposed to make his beard fall out.

FASTIDIOUS (fa STID ee us) *adj* meticulous; demanding; finicky

Mrs. Brown was a *fastidious* housekeeper; she cleaned up our crumbs almost before they hit the floor.

Jeb was so *fastidious* in his work habits that he needed neither a wastebasket nor an eraser.

The *fastidious* secretary was nearly driven mad by her boss, who used the floor as a file cabinet and his desk as a pantry.

FATALIST (FAYT uh list) *n* someone who believes that future events are already determined and that humans are powerless to change them

Fatalist is closely related to the word *fate*. A *fatalist* is someone who believes that *fate* determines everything.

The old man was a *fatalist* about his illness, believing there was no sense in worrying about something over which he had no control.

Bill was such a *fatalist* that he never wore a seat belt; he said that if he were meant to die in a car accident, there was nothing he could do to prevent it.

To be a *fatalist* is to be *fatalistic*.

FATUOUS (FACH oo us) *adj* foolish; silly; idiotic

Pauline is so pretty that her suitors are often driven to *fatuous* acts of devotion. They are *infatuated* with her.

FAUNA (FAW nuh) *n* animals

We saw little evidence of *fauna* on our walk through the woods. We did, however, see plenty of *flora*, or plants.

"Flora and *fauna"* means plants and animals. The terms are used particularly in describing what lives in a particular region or environment.

Arctic *fauna* are very different from tropical *fauna.*

In Jim's yard, the *flora* consists mostly of weeds.

It's easy to remember which of these words means what. Just remember *fawns* and *flowers.*

FECUND (FEE kund) *adj* fertile; productive

The *fecund* mother rabbit gave birth to hundreds and hundreds of little rabbits.

The philosopher's imagination was so *fecund* that ideas hopped out of him like so many baby rabbits.

Our compost heap became increasingly *fecund* as it decomposed.

The state of being *fecund* is *fecundity* (fi KUN di tee).

This word can also be pronounced "FEK und."

Q•U•I•C•K • Q•U•I•Z #42

Match each word in the first column with its definition in the second column. Check your answers in the back of the book.

1. fabrication	a. plants
2. facetious	b. fertile
3. facile	c. absurd
4. faction	d. one who believes in fate
5. farcical	e. humorous
6. fastidious	f. animals
7. fatalist	g. superficially skillful
8. fatuous	h. group with a cause
9. fauna	i. lie
10. flora	j. meticulous
11. fecund	k. foolish

FELICITY (fuh LIS uh tee) *n* happiness; skillfulness, especially at expressing things; adeptness

Love was not all *felicity* for Glen and Pam; they argued all the time. In fact their relationship was characterized by *infelicity.*

Shakespeare wrote with great *felicity.* His works are filled with *felicitous* expressions.

FERVOR (FUR vur) *n* great warmth or earnestness; ardor; zeal

Avid baseball fans frequently display their *fervor* for the game by throwing food at bad players.

FETTER (FET ur) *v* to restrain; to hamper

In his pursuit of the Nobel Prize for physics, Professor Jenkins was *fettered* by his near-total ignorance of the subject.

To be *unfettered* is to be unrestrained or free of hindrances. When his parents went to Europe for a few months, Jimmy invited all his friends for some *unfettered* partying in the empty house.

A *fetter* is literally a chain (attached to the foot) that is used to restrain a criminal or, for that matter, an innocent person. A figurative *fetter* can be anything that hampers or restrains someone. The housewife's young children were the *fetters* that prevented her from pursuing her love affair with the washing-machine repairman.

FIDELITY (fuh DEL uh tee) n faithfulness; loyalty

The motto of the United States Marine Corps is *semper fidelis,* which is Latin for always loyal.

A *high-fidelity* record player is one that is very faithful in reproducing the original sound of whatever was recorded.

The crusader's life was marked by *fidelity* to the cause of justice.

The soldiers couldn't shoot straight, but their *fidelity* to the cause of freedom was never in question.

Infidelity means faithlessness or disloyalty. Marital *infidelity* is another way of saying adultery. Early phonograph records were marked by *infidelity* to the original.

FIGURATIVE (FIG yur uh tiv) adj based on figures of speech; expressing something in terms usually used for something else; metaphorical

To say that the autumn hillside was a blaze of color is to use the word *blaze* in a *figurative* sense. The hillside wasn't really on fire, but the colors of the leaves made it appear (somewhat) as though it were.

When the mayor said that the housing market had sprouted wings, he was speaking *figuratively*. The housing market hadn't really sprouted wings; it had merely grown so rapidly that it had almost seemed to fly.

A *figurative* meaning of a word is one that is not *literal*. A *literal* statement is one in which every word means exactly what it says. If the housing market had *literally* sprouted wings, genuine wings would somehow have popped out of it.

People very, very often confuse these words, using one when they really mean the other. Andy could *literally* eat money if he chewed up and swallowed a dollar bill. Andy's car eats money only *figuratively*, in the sense that it is very expensive to operate.

FINESSE (fi NES) n skillful maneuvering; subtlety; craftiness

The doctor sewed up the wound with *finesse*, making stitches so small one could scarcely see them.

The boxer moved with such *finesse* that his opponent never knew what hit him.

FLAGRANT (FLAY grunt) adj glaringly bad; notorious; scandalous

A *flagrant* theft is stealing a car, for example, from the lot behind the police station. A *flagrant* spelling error is one that jumps right off the page. See the listing for *blatant*.

FLAUNT (flawnt) v to show off; to display ostentatiously

The brand-new millionaire annoyed all his friends by driving around his old neighborhood to *flaunt* his new Rolls-Royce.

Colleen *flaunted* her engagement ring, shoving it in the face of almost anyone who came near her.

This word is very often confused with *flout*.

FLOUT (flowt) v to disregard something out of disrespect

A driver *flouts* the traffic laws by driving through red lights and knocking down pedestrians.

To *flaunt* success is to make certain everyone knows that you are successful. To *flout* success is to be contemptuous of success or to act as though it means nothing at all.

FOIBLE (FOY bul) n a minor character flaw

Barbara's *foibles* included a tendency to prefer dogs to people.

The delegates to the state convention ignored the candidates' positions on the major issues and concentrated on their *foibles*.

FOMENT (foh MENT) v to stir up; to instigate

The bad news from abroad *fomented* pessimism among professional investors.

The radicals set off several bombs in an effort to *foment* rebellion among the peasants.

Q•U•I•C•K • Q•U•I•Z #43

Match each word in the first column with its definition in the second column. Check your answers in the back of the book.

1. felicity		a. loyalty
2. fervor		b. stir up
3. fetter		c. restrain
4. fidelity		d. meaning exactly what it says
5. figurative		e. minor character flaw
6. literal		f. show off
7. finesse		g. based on figures of speech
8. flagrant		h. to disregard contemptuously
9. flaunt		i. skillful maneuvering
10. flout		j. happiness
11. foible		k. glaringly bad
12. foment		l. zeal

FORBEAR (for BAYR) v to refrain from; to abstain

Stephen told me I could become a millionaire if I joined him in his business, but his company makes me nervous so I decided to *forbear*.

George *forbore* to punch me in the nose, even though I had told him that I thought he was a sniveling idiot.

The noun is *forbearance*.

A *forebear* (FOR bayr)—sometimes also spelled *forbear*—is an ancestor. William's *forebears* came to America on the *Mayflower*.

FORGO (for GOH) *v* to do without; to forbear

We had some of the chocolate cake, and some of the chocolate mousse, and some of the chocolate cream pie, but we were worried about our weight so we decided to *forgo* the chocolate-covered potato chips. That is, we *forwent* them.

FORSAKE (for SAYK) *v* to abandon; to renounce; to relinquish

We urged Buddy to *forsake* his life with the alien beings and return to his job at the drugstore.

All the guru's followers had *forsaken* him, so he became a real estate developer and turned his temple into an apartment building.

FORTUITOUS (for TOO uh tus) *adj* accidental; occurring by chance

The program's outcome was not the result of any plan but was entirely *fortuitous*.

The object was so perfectly formed that its creation could not have been *fortuitous*.

Fortuitous is often misused to mean lucky or serendipitous. Don't make that same mistake. It means merely accidental.

FOUNDER (FOWN dur) *v* to fail; to collapse; to sink

The candidate's campaign for the presidency *foundered* when it was revealed that he had once been married to an orangutan.

Zeke successfully struggled through the first part of the course but *foundered* when the final examination was given.

The ship *foundered* shortly after its hull fell off.

Be careful not to confuse this word with *flounder*, which means to move clumsily or in confusion. Our field hockey team *floundered* helplessly around the field while the opposing team scored point after point.

The witness began to *flounder* as the attorney fired question after question.

If you want to remember the difference between the two words, think that when a person *flounders*, he is flopping around like a flounder.

FRATERNAL (fruh TUR nul) *adj* like brothers

The *fraternal* feeling among the meeting's participants disappeared when one of them stood up at dinner and began firing a machine gun.

A *fraternity* is an organization of men who have bound themselves together in a relationship analogous to that of real brothers.

FRENETIC (fruh NET ik) *adj* frantic; frenzied

There was a lot of *frenetic* activity in the office, but nothing ever seemed to get accomplished.

The bird's *frenetic* attempt to free itself from the thorn bush finally exhausted it. Then the cat strolled over and ate it.

FRUGAL (FROO gul) *adj* economical; penny-pinching
Laura was so *frugal* that she even tried to bargain with the checkout girl at the supermarket.
We were as *frugal* as we could be, but we still ended up several thousand dollars in debt.
Hannah's *frugality* annoyed her husband, who loved nothing better than spending money.

FURTIVE (FUR tiv) *adj* secretive; sly
Cal wiggled his ears while the countess was talking to him in a *furtive* attempt to catch our attention.
The burglars were *furtive*, but not *furtive* enough; the alert policeman grabbed them as they carried the color TV through the Washingtons' back door.

Q•U•I•C•K • Q•U•I•Z #44

Match each word in the first column with its definition in the second column. Check your answers in the back of the book.

1. forbear	a. economical
2. forebear	b. ancestor
3. forgo	c. move in confusion
4. forsake	d. do without
5. fortuitous	e. refrain from
6. founder	f. sink
7. flounder	g. secretive
8. frenetic	h. accidental
9. frugal	i. abandon
10. furtive	j. frantic

FUTILE (FYOOT ul) *adj* useless; hopeless
A D+ average and no extracurricular interests to speak of meant that applying to Harvard was *futile*, but Lucinda hoped against hope.
Something *futile* is a *futility* (fyoo TIL uh tee). Lucinda doesn't know what a *futility* it is.

G

GARRULOUS (GAR uh lus) *adj* talkative; chatty
Gillette is gregarious and *garrulous;* he loves to hang out with the gang and gab.

GENRE (ZHAHN ruh) *n* a type or category, especially of art or writing
The novel is one *genre*. Poetry is another. Alan displayed a great talent for a particular *genre:* the bawdy limerick.

GENTEEL (jen TEEL) *adj* refined; polite; aristocratic; affecting refinement
The ladies at the ball were too *genteel* to accept our invitation to the wrestling match.
Jake had been born in a slum but now, in his mansion, his life was *genteel*.
A person who is *genteel* has *gentility*.

GESTICULATE (jes TIK yuh layt) *v* to make gestures, especially when speaking or in place of speaking
Harry *gesticulated* wildly on the other side of the theater in an attempt to get our attention.
The after-dinner speaker *gesticulated* in such a strange way that the audience paid more attention to his hands than to his words.
A person who *gesticulates* makes *gesticulations*.

GLUT (glut) *n* surplus; an overabundance
The international oil shortage turned into an international oil *glut* with surprising speed.
We had a *glut* of contributions but a *dearth,* or scarcity, of volunteers; it seemed that people would rather give their money than their time.

GRANDILOQUENT (gran DIL uh kwunt) *adj* pompous; using a lot of big, fancy words in an attempt to sound impressive
The president's speech was *grandiloquent* rather than eloquent; there were some six-dollar words and some impressive phrases, but he really had nothing to say.
The new minister's *grandiloquence* got him in trouble with deacons, who wanted him to be more restrained in his sermons.

GRANDIOSE (GRAN dee ohs) *adj* absurdly exaggerated
The scientist's *grandiose* plan was to build a huge shopping center on the surface of the moon.
Their house was genuinely impressive, although there were a few *grandiose* touches: a fireplace the size of a garage, a kitchen with four ovens, and a computerized media center in every room.
To be *grandiose* is to be characterized by *grandiosity* (gran dee AHS uh tee).

GRATUITOUS (gruh TOO uh tus) *adj* given freely (said of something bad); unjustified; unprovoked; uncalled for
The scathing review of the movie contained several *gratuitous* remarks about the sex life of the director.
Their attack against us was *gratuitous;* we had never done anything to offend them. *Gratuitous* is often misunderstood because it is confused with *gratuity*.
A *gratuity* is a tip, like the one you leave in a restaurant. A *gratuity* is a nice thing. *Gratuitous,* however, is not nice. Don't confuse these words.

GRAVITY (GRAV uh tee) *n* seriousness

Not the force that makes apples fall down instead of up, but a different sort of weightiness.

The anchorman's nervous giggling was entirely inappropriate, given the *gravity* of the situation.

No one realized the *gravity* of Myron's drug addiction until it was much too late to help him.

At the heart of the word *gravity* is the word *grave*, which means serious.

GREGARIOUS (gruh GAR ee us) *adj* sociable; enjoying the company of others

Dirk was too *gregarious* to enjoy the fifty years he spent in solitary confinement.

Anna wasn't very *gregarious;* she went to the party, but she spent most of her time hiding in the closet.

In biology, *gregarious* is used to describe animals that live in groups. Bees, which live together in large colonies, are said to be *gregarious* insects.

GUILE (gyle) *n* cunning; duplicity; artfulness

José used *guile,* not intelligence, to win the spelling bee; he cheated.

Stuart was shocked by the *guile* of the automobile mechanic, who had poked a hole in his radiator and then told him that it had sprung a leak.

To be *guileless* is to be innocent or naive. *Guileless* and *artless* are synonyms.

The word *beguile* also means to deceive, but in a charming and not always bad way. Clarence found Mary's beauty so *beguiling* that he did anything she asked of him.

Q•U•I•C•K • Q•U•I•Z #45

Match each word in the first column with its definition in the second column. Check your answers in the back of the book.

1. futile	a. chatty
2. garrulous	b. surplus
3. genre	c. cunning
4. genteel	d. unjustified
5. gesticulate	e. seriousness
6. glut	f. make gestures
7. grandiloquent	g. hopeless
8. grandiose	h. refined
9. gratuitous	i. sociable
10. gravity	j. pompous
11. gregarious	k. absurdly exaggerated
12. guile	l. type of art

H

HACKNEYED (HAK need) *adj* overused; trite; stale

"As cold as ice" is a *hackneyed* expression.

Michael's book was full of clichés and *hackneyed* phrases.

The creationism issue had been discussed so much as to become *hackneyed*.

HAPLESS (HAP lis) *adj* unlucky

Joe's *hapless* search for fun led him from one disappointment to another.

Alex led a *hapless* existence that made all his friends' lives seem fortunate by comparison.

HARBINGER (HAR bin jur) *n* a forerunner; a signal of

Warm weather is the *harbinger* of spring.

A cloud of bad breath and body odor, which preceded him by several yards everywhere he went, was Harold's *harbinger*.

Note carefully the pronunciation of this word.

HEDONISM (HEED uh niz um) *n* the pursuit of pleasure as a way of life

A *hedonist* practices *hedonism* twenty-four hours a day.

HEGEMONY (hi JEM uh nee) *n* leadership, especially of one nation over another

America once held an unchallenged nuclear *hegemony*.

Japan and Germany vie for *hegemony* in the foreign-car market.

Note carefully the pronunciation of this word.

HERESY (HER uh see) *n* any belief that is strongly opposed to established beliefs

Galileo was tried for the *heresy* of suggesting that the sun did not revolve around the earth. He was almost convicted of being a *heretic*, but he recanted his *heretical* (huh RET i kul) view.

HERMETIC (hur MET ik) *adj* impervious to external influence; airtight

The president led a *hermetic* existence in the White House, as his advisers attempted to seal him off from the outside world.

The old men felt vulnerable and unwanted outside the *hermetic* security of their club.

The poisonous substance was sealed *hermetically* inside a glass cylinder.

HEYDAY (HAY day) *n* golden age; prime

In his *heyday*, Vernon was a world-class athlete; today he's just Vernon.

The *heyday* of the British Navy ended a long, long time ago.

HIATUS (hye AY tus) *n* a break or interruption, often from work

Spencer looked forward to spring break as a welcome *hiatus* from the rigors of campus parties.

Note carefully the pronunciation of this word.

HIERARCHY (HYE uh rahr kee) *n* an organization based on rank or degree; pecking order

George was very low in the State Department *hierarchy*. In fact, his phone number wasn't even listed in the State Department directory.

There appeared to be no *hierarchy* in the newly discovered tribe; there was no leader and, for that matter, no followers.

The adjective is *hierarchical* (hye uh RAHRK i kul).

HISTRIONIC (his tree AHN ik) *adj* overly dramatic; theatrical

Adele's *histrionic* request for a raise embarrassed everyone in the office. She gesticulated wildly, jumped up and down, pulled out handfuls of hair, threw herself to the ground, and groaned in agony.

The chairman's *histrionic* presentation convinced no one.

Histrionic behavior is referred to as *histrionics*. The young actor's *histrionics* made everyone in the audience squirm.

HOMILY (HAHM uh lee) *n* a sermon

The football coach often began practice with a lengthy *homily* on the virtues of clean living.

HOMOGENEOUS (hoh muh JEE nee us) *adj* uniform; made entirely of one thing

Homogenized (huh MAHJ uh nyzed) milk is milk in which the cream, which usually floats on top, has been permanently mixed with the rest of the milk. (Skim milk is milk from which the layer of cream has been skimmed off.) When milk is *homogenized,* it becomes a *homogeneous* substance—that is, it's the same throughout, or uniform.

The kindergarten class was extremely *homogeneous:* all the children had blond hair, blue eyes, red shoes, and the same last name.

To be *heterogeneous* (het ur uh JEE nee us) is to be mixed or varied. On Halloween the children amassed a *heterogeneous* collection of candy, chewing gum, popcorn, cookies, and razor blades.

The nouns are *homogeneity* (hoh muh juh NEE uh tee) and *heterogeneity* (het uh roh juh NEE uh tee) respectively.

HUSBANDRY (HUZ bun dree) *n* thrifty management of resources; livestock farming

Husbandry is the practice of conserving money or resources. To *husband* is to economize. Everyone *husbanded* oil and electricity during the energy crisis of the seventies.

HYPERBOLE (hye PUR buh lee) *n* an exaggeration used as a figure of speech; exaggeration

When Joe said "I'm so hungry I could eat a horse," he was using *hyperbole* to convey the extent of his hunger.

WORD SMART

The candidate was guilty of *hyperbole;* all the facts in his speech were exaggerated.
Note carefully the pronunciation of this word.

HYPOTHETICAL (hye puh THET uh kul) *adj* uncertain; unproven
Ernie's skill as a baseball player was entirely *hypothetical,* since he had never played the game.
There were several *hypothetical* explanations for the strange phenomenon, but no one could say for certain what had caused it.
A *hypothetical* explanation is a *hypothesis* (hye PAHTH uh sis), the plural of which is *hypotheses* (hye PAHTH uh seez).

Q•U•I•C•K • Q•U•I•Z #46

Match each word in the first column with its definition in the second column. Check your answers in the back of the book.

1. hackneyed	a.	leadership
2. hapless	b.	uniform
3. harbinger	c.	airtight
4. hedonism	d.	forerunner
5. hegemony	e.	pecking order
6. heresy	f.	overused, trite
7. hermetic	g.	exaggeration
8. heyday	h.	golden age
9. hiatus	i.	varied
10. hierarchy	j.	obstruction
11. hindrance	k.	unlucky
12. histrionic	l.	uncertain; unproven
13. homily	m.	overly dramatic
14. homogeneous	n.	break
15. heterogeneous	o.	sermon
16. husbandry	p.	thrifty management of resources
17. hyperbole	q.	lifelong pursuit of pleasure
18. hypothetical	r.	strongly contrary belief

I

ICONOCLAST (eye KAHN uh klast) *n* one who attacks popular beliefs or institutions

Iconoclast comes from Greek words meaning image breaker. The original *iconoclasts* were opponents of the use of *icons*, or sacred images, in certain Christian churches. Today the word is used to refer to someone who attacks popular figures and ideas—a person to whom "nothing is sacred."

The popular columnist was an inveterate *iconoclast*, avidly attacking public figures no matter what their party affiliation.

To study and go to class is to be an *iconoclast* on that campus, which has a reputation for being the biggest party school in the country if not the world.

Herbert's *iconoclastic* (eye kahn uh KLAS tik) views were not popular with the older members of the board.

IDEOLOGY (eye dee AHL uh jee) *n* a system of social or political ideas

Conservatism and liberalism are competing *ideologies.*

The candidate never managed to communicate his *ideology* to the voters, so few people were able to grasp what he stood for.

The senator's tax proposal had more to do with *ideology* than with common sense; his plan, though consistent with his principles, was clearly impractical.

A dogmatic person attached to an *ideology* is an *ideologue* (EYE dee uh lawg). An *ideologue* is doctrinaire.

Ideology is sometimes pronounced "ID ee ahl uh jee."

IDIOSYNCRASY (id ee oh SINK ruh see) *n* a peculiarity; an eccentricity

Eating green beans drenched in ketchup for breakfast was one of Jordana's *idiosyncrasies.*

The doctor's interest was aroused by an *idiosyncrasy* in Bill's skull: there seemed to be a coin slot in the back of his head.

A person who has an *idiosyncrasy* is said to be *idiosyncratic* (id ee oh sin KRAT ik). Tara's driving was somewhat *idiosyncratic;* she sometimes seemed to prefer the sidewalk to the street.

IDYLLIC (eye DIL ik) *adj* charming in a rustic way; naturally peaceful

They built their house on an *idyllic* spot. There was a babbling brook in back and an unbroken view of wooded hills in front.

Our vacation in the country was *idyllic;* we went for long walks down winding dirt roads and didn't see a newspaper all week.

An *idyllic* vacation or other experience could also be called an *idyll.*

IGNOMINY (IG nuh min ee) *n* deep disgrace

After the big scandal, the formerly high-flying investment banker fell into a life of shame and *ignominy.*

The *ignominy* of losing the spelling bee was too much for Arnold, who decided to give up spelling altogether.

Something that is deeply disgraceful is *ignominious* (ig nuh MIN ee us). The massacre of the farm family was an *ignominious* act.

Note carefully the pronunciation of both parts of speech.

ILLICIT (i LIS it) *adj* illegal; not permitted

Criminals engage in *illicit* activities.

Don't confuse this word with *elicit*, listed previously. The police interviewed hundreds of witnesses, trying to *elicit* clues that might help them stop an *illicit* business.

IMMINENT (IM uh nunt) *adj* just about to happen

The pink glow in the east made it clear that sunrise was *imminent*.

George had a feeling that disaster was *imminent*, but he couldn't figure out why; then the jumbo jet crashed into his garage.

Don't confuse this word with *eminent*, listed previously.

IMMUTABLE (i MYOO tuh bul) *adj* unchangeable

Jerry's mother had only one *immutable* rule: no dancing on the dinner table.

The statue of the former principal looked down on the students with an *immutable* scowl.

Something that is changeable is said to be *mutable*. The *mutable* shoreline shifted continually as the tides moved sand first in one direction and then in another.

Helena's moods were *mutable*; one minute she was kind and gentle, the next minute she was screaming with anger.

Both *immutable* and *mutable* are based on a Latin root meaning change. So are *mutation* and *mutant*.

IMPARTIAL (im PAHR shul) *adj* fair; not favoring one side or the other; unbiased

Jurors are supposed to be *impartial* rather than *partial*; they aren't supposed to make up their minds until they've heard all the evidence.

Beverly tried to be an *impartial* judge at the beauty contest, but in the end she couldn't help selecting her own daughter to be the new Pork Queen.

The noun is *impartiality* (im pahr shee AL uh tee).

IMPECCABLE (im PEK uh bul) *adj* flawless; entirely without sin

The children's behavior was *impeccable*; they didn't set fire to the cat, and they didn't pour dye into the swimming pool.

Hal's clothes were always *impeccable*; even the wrinkles were perfectly creased.

By the way, *peccable* means liable to sin. And while we're at it, *peccadillo* is a minor sin.

IMPERIAL (im PEER ee ul) *adj* like an emperor or an empire

Imperial, emperor, and *empire* are all derived from the same root.

England's *imperial* days are over, now that the British Empire has crumbled away.

The palace was decorated with *imperial* splendor.

George's *imperial* manner was inappropriate, since he was nothing more exalted than the local dogcatcher.

A similar word is *imperious* (im PEER ee us), which means bossy and, usually, arrogant. The director's *imperious* style rubbed everyone the wrong way; he always seemed to be giving orders, and he never listened to what anyone said.

Q•U•I•C•K • Q•U•I•Z #47

Match each word in the first column with its definition in the second column. Check your answers in the back of the book.

1. iconoclast
2. ideology
3. idiosyncrasy
4. idyllic
5. ignominy
6. illicit
7. imminent
8. immutable
9. impartial
10. impeccable
11. imperial
12. imperious

a. peculiarity
b. naturally peaceful
c. like an emperor
d. flawless
e. attacker of popular beliefs
f. just about to happen
g. fair
h. system of social ideas
i. bossy
j. deep disgrace
k. unchangeable
l. illegal

IMPERVIOUS (im PUR vee us) *adj* not allowing anything to pass through; impenetrable

A raincoat, if it is any good, is *impervious* to water. It is made of an *impervious* material.

David was *impervious* to criticism—he did what he wanted to do no matter what anyone said.

IMPETUOUS (im PECH oo wus) *adj* impulsive; extremely impatient

Impetuous Dick always seemed to be running off to buy a new car, even if he had just bought one the day before.

Samantha was so *impetuous* that she never took more than a few seconds to make up her mind.

IMPLEMENT (IM pluh munt) *v* to carry out

Leo developed a plan for shortening the grass in his yard, but he was unable to *implement* it, because he didn't have a lawn mower.

The government was better at creating new laws than at *implementing* them.

IMPOTENT (IM puh tunt) *adj* powerless; helpless; unable to perform sexual intercourse

Impotent means not *potent*—not powerful.

Joe and Betty made a few *impotent* efforts to turn aside the steam-roller, but it squished their vegetable garden anyway.

We felt *impotent* in the face of their overpowering opposition to our plan.

Omnipotent (ahm NIP uh tunt) means all powerful. After winning a dozen games in a row, the football team began to feel *omnipotent*. *Note carefully the pronunciation of this word.*

IMPUGN (im PYOON) v to attack, especially to attack the truth or integrity of something

The critic *impugned* the originality of Jacob's novel, claiming that long stretches of it had been lifted from the work of someone else.

Fred said I was *impugning* his honesty when I called him a dirty liar, but I told him he had no honesty to *impugn*. This just seemed to make him angrier, for some reason.

INANE (i NAYN) adj silly; senseless

Their plan to make an indoor swimming pool by flooding their basement was *inane*.

Mel made a few *inane* comments about the importance of chewing only on the left side of one's mouth, and then he passed out beneath the table.

Something that is *inane* is an *inanity*.

INAUGURATE (in AW gyuh rayt) v to begin officially; to induct formally into office

The mayor *inaugurated* the new no-smoking policy and then celebrated by lighting up a big cigar.

The team's loss *inaugurated* an era of defeat that lasted for several years.

To *inaugurate* a president is to make him take the oath of office and then give him the keys to the White House.

Q•U•I•C•K • Q•U•I•Z #48

Match each word in the first column with its definition in the second column. Check your answers in the back of the book.

1. impervious	a.	begin officially
2. impetuous	b.	carry out
3. implement	c.	powerless
4. impotent	d.	impenetrable
5. impugn	e.	silly
6. inane	f.	attack the truth of
7. inaugurate	g.	impulsive

INCANDESCENT (in kun DES unt) *adj* brilliant; giving off heat or light

An *incandescent* light bulb is one containing a wire or filament that gives off light when it is heated. An *incandescent* person is one who gives off light or energy in a figurative sense.

Jan's ideas were so *incandescent* that simply being near her made you feel as though you understood the subject for the first time.

INCANTATION (in kan TAY shun) *n* a chant; the repetition of statements or phrases in a way reminiscent of a chant

Much to our delight, the wizard's *incantation* eventually caused the small stone to turn into a sleek black BMW.

The students quickly became deaf to the principal's *incantations* about the importance of school spirit.

INCENSE (in SENS) *v* to make very angry

Jeremy was *incensed* when I told him that even though he was stupid and loathsome, he would always be my best friend.

My comment about his lovely painting of a tree *incensed* the artist, who said it was actually a portrait of his mother.

INCESSANT (in SES unt) *adj* unceasing

I will go deaf and lose my mind if you children don't stop your *incessant* bickering.

The noise from the city street was *incessant;* there always seemed to be a fire engine or a police car screaming by.

A *cessation* is a ceasing.

INCIPIENT (in SIP ee unt) *adj* beginning; emerging

Sitting in class, Henrietta detected an *incipient* tingle of boredom that told her she would soon be asleep.

Support for the plan was *incipient,* and the planners hoped it would soon grow and spread.

The *inception* of something is its start or formal beginning.

INCISIVE (in SYE siv) *adj* cutting right to the heart of the matter

When a surgeon cuts into you, he or she makes an *incision.* To be *incisive* is to be as sharp as a scalpel in a figurative sense.

After hours of debate, Louis offered a few *incisive* comments that made it immediately clear to everyone how dumb the original idea had been.

Lloyd's essays were always *incisive;* he never wasted any words, and his reasoning was always sharp and persuasive.

INCONGRUOUS (in KAHN groo us) *adj* not harmonious; not consistent; not appropriate; not fitting in

The ultramodern kitchen seemed *incongruous* in the restored eighteenth-century farmhouse. It was an *incongruity* (in kun GROO uh tee).

Bill's membership in the motorcycle gang was *incongruous* with his mild personality and his career as a management consultant.

INCORRIGIBLE (in KOR uh juh bul) *adj* incapable of being reformed

The convict was an *incorrigible* criminal; as soon as he got out of prison, he said, he was going to rob another doughnut store.

Bill is *incorrigible*—he eats three bags of potato chips every day even though he knows that eating two would be better for him.

Ever-cheerful Annie is an *incorrigible* optimist.

Think of *incorrigible* as incorrectable. The word *corrigible* is rarely seen or used these days.

INCREMENT (IN cruh munt) *n* an increase; one in a series of increases

Bernard received a small *increment* in his salary each year, even though he did less and less work with every day that passed.

This year's fund-raising total represented an *increment* of 1 percent over last year's. This year's total represented an *incremental* change from last year's.

Orville built up his savings account *incrementally*, one dollar at a time.

INDIFFERENT (in DIF ur unt) *adj* not caring one way or the other; apathetic; mediocre

Red was *indifferent* about politics; he didn't care who was elected to office so long as no one passed a law against *Monday Night Football*.

Henry's *indifference* was extremely annoying to Melissa, who loved to argue but found it difficult to do so with people who had no opinions.

We planted a big garden but the results were *indifferent;* only about half of the flowers came up.

The painter did an *indifferent* job, but it was good enough for Susan, who was *indifferent* about painting.

Q•U•I•C•K • Q•U•I•Z #49

Match each word in the first column with its definition in the second column. Check your answers in the back of the book.

1. incandescent	a. increase
2. incantation	b. make very angry
3. incense	c. beginning
4. incessant	d. chant
5. incipient	e. not harmonious
6. incisive	f. incapable of being reformed
7. incongruous	g. not caring; mediocre
8. incorrigible	h. cutting right to the heart
9. increment	i. unceasing
10. indifferent	j. brilliant

INDIGENOUS (in DIJ uh nus) *adj* native; originating in that area
Fast-food restaurants are *indigenous* to America, where they were invented.
The grocer said the corn had been locally grown, but we didn't believe him because it didn't appear to be *indigenous.*
The botanist said that the small cactus was *indigenous* but that the large one had been introduced to the region by Spanish explorers.

INDIGENT (IN di junt) *adj* poor
The *indigent* family had little to eat, nothing to spend, and virtually nothing to wear.
Rusty had once been a lawyer but now was *indigent;* he spent most of his time sleeping on a bench in the park.
Don't confuse this word with *indigenous,* listed above.

INDIGNANT (in DIG nunt) *adj* angry, especially as a result of something unjust or unworthy; insulted
Bruno became *indignant* when the policewoman accused him of stealing the nuclear weapon.
Isabel was *indignant* when we told her all the nasty things that Blake had said about her over the public address system at the big party.

INDOLENT (IN duh lunt) *adj* lazy
The *indolent* teenagers slept late, moped around, and never looked for summer jobs.
Inheriting a lot of money enabled Rodney to do what he loved most: pursue a life of *indolence.*

INDULGENT (in DUL junt) lenient; yielding to desire
The nice mom was *indulgent* of her children, letting them have all the candy, cookies, and ice cream that they wanted, even for breakfast.
Our *indulgent* teacher never punished us for not turning in our homework. She was nice. She didn't want us to turn into ascetic grinds.
Someone who is *self-indulgent* yields to his or her every desire.

INEFFABLE (in EF uh bul) *adj* incapable of being expressed or described
The simple beauty of nature is often so *ineffable* that it brings tears to our eyes.
The word *effable*—expressible—is rarely used.

INEPT (in EPT) *adj* clumsy; incompetent; gauche
Joshua is an *inept* dancer; he is as likely to stomp on his partner's foot as he is to step on it.
Julia's *inept* attempt at humor drew only groans from the audience.
To be *inept* is to be characterized by *ineptitude,* which is the opposite of aptitude. The woodworking class's *ineptitude* was both broad and deep; there was little that they were able to do, and nothing that they were able to do well.

The opposite of *inept* is *adept* (uh DEPT). *Adept* and *adroit* are synonyms.

INERT (in URT) *adj* inactive; sluggish; not reacting chemically

The baseball team seemed strangely *inert;* it was as though they had lost the will not only to win but also even to play.

Having colds made the children *inert* and reluctant to get out of bed.

Helium is an *inert* gas: it doesn't burn, it doesn't explode, and it doesn't kill you if you inhale it.

To be *inert* is to be characterized by *inertia.* As it is most commonly used, *inertia* means lack of get-up-and-go, or an inability or unwillingness to move.

In physics, *inertia* refers to an object's tendency to continue doing what it's doing (either moving or staying still) unless it's acted on by something else.

INEXORABLE (in EK sur uh bul) *adj* relentless; inevitable; unavoidable

The *inexorable* waves pounded the shore, as they have always pounded it and as they always will pound it.

Eliot drove his father's car slowly but *inexorably* through the grocery store, wrecking aisle after aisle despite the manager's anguished pleading.

Inexorable death finds everyone sooner or later.

Note carefully the pronunciation of this word.

INFAMOUS (IN fuh mus) *adj* shamefully wicked; having an extremely bad reputation; disgraceful

Be careful with the pronunciation of this word.

To be *infamous* is to be *famous* for being evil or bad. An *infamous* cheater is one whose cheating is well known.

Deep within the prison was the *infamous* torture chamber, where hooded guards tickled their prisoners with feathers until they confessed.

Infamy is the state of being *infamous.* The former Nazi lived the rest of his life in *infamy* after the court convicted him of war crimes and atrocities.

President Roosevelt said that the date of the Japanese attack on Pearl Harbor would "live in *infamy.*"

INFATUATED (in FACH oo ay tid) *adj* foolish; foolishly passionate or attracted; made foolish; foolishly in love

To be *infatuated* is to be *fatuous* or foolish. I was so *infatuated* with Polly that I drooled and gurgled whenever she was near.

The *infatuated* candidate thought so highly of himself that he had the ceiling of his bedroom covered with his campaign posters.

My ride in Boris's racing car *infatuated* me; I knew immediately that I would have to have a racing car, too.

Q·U·I·C·K • Q·U·I·Z #50

Match each word in the first column with its definition in the second column. Check your answers in the back of the book.

1. indigenous	a. native
2. indigent	b. inactive
3. indignant	c. lazy
4. indolent	d. foolish
5. indulgent	e. shamefully wicked
6. ineffable	f. poor
7. inept	g. relentless
8. inert	h. angry
9. inexorable	i. clumsy
10. infamous	j. lenient
11. infatuated	k. inexpressible

INFER (in FUR) v to conclude; to deduce

Ruth said she loved the brownies, but I *inferred* from the size of the piece left on her plate that she had actually despised them.

She hadn't heard the score, but the silence in the locker room led her to *infer* that we had lost.

Infer is often confused with *imply*. To *imply* something is to hint at it, suggest it, or state it indirectly. To *infer* something is to figure out what it is without being told directly.

An *inference* is a deduction or conclusion.

INFINITESIMAL (in fin uh TES uh mul) *adj* very, very, very small; infinitely small

Infinitesimal does not mean huge, as some people incorrectly believe.

Dumb old Willy's brain, if he had one at all, was undoubtedly *infinitesimal*.

An *infinitesimal* bug of some kind crawled into Heather's ear and bit her in a place she couldn't scratch.

Our chances of winning were *infinitesimal*, but we played our hearts out anyway.

Note carefully the pronunciation of this word.

INGENUOUS (in JEN yoo us) *adj* frank; without deception; simple; artless; charmingly naive

A young child is *ingenuous*. He doesn't know much about the ways of the world, and certainly not enough to deceive anyone.

An *ingenue* (AHN ji noo) is a somewhat naive young woman, especially a young actress.

Disingenuous means crafty or artful. The movie producer was being *disingenuous* when he said, "I don't care if I make a cent on this movie. I just want every man, woman, and child in the country to see it."

INHERENT (in HAYR unt) *adj* part of the essential nature of something; intrinsic

Wetness is an *inherent* quality of water. (You could also say that wetness is *inherent* in water.)

There is an *inherent* strength in steel that is lacking from cardboard.

The man's *inherent* fatness, jolliness, and beardedness made it easy for him to play the part of Santa Claus.

Note carefully the pronunciation of this word.

INJUNCTION (in JUNGK shun) *n* a command or order, especially a court order

Wendy's neighbors got a court *injunction* prohibiting her from playing her radio loud.

Herbert, lighting up, disobeyed his doctor's *injunction* to stop smoking.

INNATE (i NAYT) *adj* existing since birth; inborn; inherent

Joseph's kindness was *innate*; it was part of his natural character.

Bill has an apparently *innate* ability to throw a football. You just can't teach someone to throw a ball as well as he can.

There's nothing *innate* about good manners; all children have to be taught to say "please" and "thank you."

INNOCUOUS (i NAHK yoo us) *adj* harmless; banal

Innocuous is closely related, in both origin and meaning, to *innocent.*

The supposedly obscene record sounded pretty *innocuous* to us; there weren't even any four-letter words in it.

The speaker's voice was loud but his words were *innocuous;* there was nothing to get excited about.

Meredith took offense at Bruce's *innocuous* comment about the saltiness of her soup.

INORDINATE (in OR duh nit) *adj* excessive; unreasonable

The young math teacher paid an *inordinate* amount of attention to the pretty blond senior.

The limousine was *inordinately* large, even for a limousine; there was room for more than a dozen passengers.

Romeo's love for Juliet was perhaps a bit *inordinate*, given the outcome of their relationship.

INSATIABLE (in SAY shuh bul) *adj* hard or impossible to satisfy; greedy; avaricious

Peter had an *insatiable* appetite for chocolate macadamia ice cream; he could never get enough. Not even a gallon of chocolate macadamia was enough to *sate* (sayt) or *satiate* (SAY shee ayt) his craving. Peter's addiction never reached *satiety* (suh TYE uh tee).

Note carefully the pronunciation of these words.

Q•U•I•C•K • Q•U•I•Z #51

Match each word in the first column with its definition in the second column. Check your answers in the back of the book.

1. infer	a. hard or impossible to satisfy
2. imply	b. intensify
3. infinitesimal	c. part of the nature of
4. inflame	d. hint at
5. ingenuous	e. artless
6. inherent	f. inborn
7. injunction	g. conclude
8. innate	h. excessive
9. innocuous	i. harmless
10. inordinate	j. infinitely small
11. insatiable	k. court order

INSIDIOUS (in SID ee us) *adj* treacherous; sneaky

The spy's *insidious* plan was to steal all the kryptonite in Metropolis.

Winter was *insidious;* it crept in under the doors and through cracks in the windows.

Cancer, which can spread rapidly from a small cluster of cells, is an *insidious* disease.

INSINUATE (in SIN yoo ayt) *v* to hint; to creep in

When I told her that I hadn't done any laundry in a month, Valerie *insinuated* that I was a slob.

He didn't ask us outright if we would leave; he merely *insinuated,* through his tone and his gestures, that it was time for us to go.

Jessica *insinuated* her way into the conversation by moving her chair closer and closer to where we were sitting.

Before we realized what was happening, the stray cat had *insinuated* itself into our household.

To *insinuate* is to make an *insinuation.*

INSIPID (in SIP id) *adj* dull; bland; banal

Barney's jokes were so *insipid* that no one in the room managed to force out so much as a chuckle.

We were bored to death at the party; it was full of *insipid* people making *insipid* conversation.

The thin soup was so *insipid* that all the spices in the world could not have made it interesting.

INSOLENT (IN suh lunt) *adj* arrogant; insulting

The ill-mannered four-year-old was so *insolent* that even adults were tempted to kick him in the rear end.

The *insolent* sales clerk said she was sorry but the store did not accept cash.

INSTIGATE (IN stuh gayt) *v* to provoke; to stir up
The strike was *instigated* by the ambitious union president, who wanted to get his name into the newspapers.
The CIA tried unsuccessfully to *instigate* rebellion in the tiny country by distributing pamphlets that, as it turned out, were printed in the wrong language.

INSULAR (IN suh lur) *adj* like an island; isolated
The Latin word for island is *insula*. From it we get the words *peninsula* ("almost an island"), *insulate* (*insulation* makes a house an island of heat), and *insular*, among others.
Lying flat on his back in bed for twenty-seven years, the 1,200-pound man led an *insular* existence.
The *insular* little community had very little contact with the world around it.
Something that is *insular* has *insularity*. The *insularity* of the little community was so complete that it was impossible to buy a big-city newspaper there.

INSURGENT (in SUR junt) *n* a rebel; someone who revolts against a government
The heavily armed *insurgents* rushed into the presidential palace, but they paused to taste the fresh blueberry pie on the dinner table and the president's bodyguards captured them.
This word can also be an adjective. A rebellion is an *insurgent* activity.
Insurgency is another word for rebellion; so is *insurrection*.

INTEGRAL (IN tuh grul) *adj* essential
A solid offense was an *integral* part of our football team; so was a strong defense.
Dave was *integral* to the organization; it could never have gotten along without him.

INTRACTABLE (in TRAK tuh bul) *adj* uncontrollable; stubborn; disobedient
The *intractable* child was a torment to his nursery school teacher.
Bill was *intractable* in his opposition to pay increases for the library employees; he swore he would never vote to give them a raise.
The disease was *intractable*. None of the dozens of medicines the doctor tried had the slightest effect on it.
The opposite of *intractable* is *tractable*.

INTRANSIGENT (in TRAN suh junt) *adj* uncompromising; stubborn
Roy was an *intransigent* hard-liner, and he didn't care how many people he offended with his views.
The jury was unanimous except for one *intransigent* member, who didn't believe that anyone should ever be forced to go to jail.
The noun is *intransigence*.

Q·U·I·C·K • Q·U·I·Z #52

*Match each word in the first column with its definition in the
second column. Check your answers in the back of the book.*

1. insidious	a. hint
2. insinuate	b. uncontrollable
3. insipid	c. treacherous
4. insolent	d. essential
5. instigate	e. provoke
6. insular	f. like an island
7. insurgent	g. rebel
8. integral	h. dull
9. intractable	i. uncompromising
10. intransigent	j. arrogant

INTRINSIC (in TRIN sik) *adj* part of the essential nature of something;
inherent

Larry's *intrinsic* boldness was always getting him into trouble.

There was an *intrinsic* problem with Owen's alibi: it was a lie.

The opposite of *intrinsic* is *extrinsic*.

INTROSPECTIVE (in truh SPEC tiv) *adj* tending to think about oneself;
examining one's feelings

The *introspective* six-year-old never had much to say to other
people but always seemed to be turning over something in her mind.

Randy's *introspective* examination of his motives led him to conclude that he must have been at fault in the breakup of his marriage.

See *extrovert*, listed previously.

INUNDATE (IN un dayt) *v* to flood; to cover completely with water; to
overwhelm

The tiny island kingdom was *inundated* by the tidal wave. Fortunately, no one died from the deluge.

The fifteen-year-old girl was *inundated* with telegrams and gifts
after she gave birth to octuplets.

INVECTIVE (in VEK tiv) *n* insulting or abusive speech

The critic's searing review was filled with bitterness and *invective*.

Herman wasn't much of an orator, but he was brilliant at *invective*.

INVETERATE (in VET ur it) *adj* habitual; firm in habit; deeply rooted

Eric was such an *inveterate* liar on the golf course that when he
finally made a hole-in-one, he marked it on his score card as a zero.

Larry's practice of spitting into the fireplace became *inveterate*
despite his wife's protestations.

IRASCIBLE (i RAS uh bul) *adj* easily angered or provoked; irritable

A grouch is *irascible*. The CEO was so *irascible*, his employees were afraid to talk to him, for fear he might hurl paperweights at them.

IRONIC (eye RAHN ik) *adj* meaning the opposite of what you seem to say; using words to mean something other than what they seem to mean

Don't use the alternate form, *ironical*.

Eddie was being *ironic* when he said he loved Peter like a brother; in truth, he hated him.

Blake's discussion of Reagan's brilliance was, of course, *ironic;* he really thinks that Reagan is idiotic. Blake is a writer known for his *irony*.

Credulous George never realized that the speaker was being *ironic* as he discussed what he called his plan to put a nuclear-missile silo in every backyard in America.

IRREVOCABLE (i REV uh kuh bul) *adj* irreversible

To *revoke* (ri VOHK) is to take back. Something *irrevocable* cannot be taken back. My decision not to wear a Tarzan costume and ride on a float in the Macy's Thanksgiving Day Parade is *irrevocable;* there is absolutely nothing you could do or say to make me change my mind.

Shortly after his car began to plunge toward the sea, Tom decided not to drive off the cliff after all, but by that point his decision to do so was *irrevocable*.

Something that can be reversed is *revocable* (REV uh kuh bul). *Note carefully the pronunciation of both words.*

ITINERANT (eye TIN ur unt) *adj* moving from place to place

The life of a traveling salesman is an *itinerant* one.

The *itinerant* junk dealer passes through our neighborhood every month or so, pulling his wagon of odds and ends.

The international banker's *itinerant* lifestyle began to seem less glamorous to him after his first child was born.

A closely related word is *itinerary*, which is the planned route or schedule of a trip. The traveling salesman taped his *itinerary* to the refrigerator before every trip so that his wife would know how to reach him on the telephone.

Q•U•I•C•K • Q•U•I•Z #53

Match each word in the first column with its definition in the second column. Check your answers in the back of the book.

1.	intrinsic	a.	irreversible
2.	introspective	b.	insulting speech
3.	inundate	c.	planned trip route
4.	invective	d.	flood
5.	inveterate	e.	inherent
6.	irascible	f.	examining one's feelings
7.	ironic	g.	meaning other than what's said
8.	irrevocable	h.	moving from place to place
9.	itinerant	i.	irritable
10.	itinerary	j.	habitual

J

JUDICIOUS (joo DISH us) *adj* exercising sound judgment

The judge was far from *judicious;* he told the jury that he thought the defendant looked guilty and said that anyone who would wear a red bow tie into a courtroom deserved to be sent to jail.

The firefighters made *judicious* use of flame-retardant foam as the burning airplane skidded along the runway.

The mother of twin boys *judiciously* used an electron microscope and a laser to divide the ice cream into equal parts.

The word *judicial* is obviously closely related, but there is a critically important difference in meaning between it and *judicious*. A judge is *judicial* simply by virtue of being a judge; *judicial* means having to do with judges, judgment, or justice. But a judge is *judicious* only if he or she exercises sound judgment.

JUXTAPOSE (JUK stuh pohz) *v* to place side by side

Comedy and tragedy were *juxtaposed* in the play, which was alternately funny and sad.

Juxtaposing the genuine painting and the counterfeit made it much easier to tell which was which.

The final examination requires students to *juxtapose* two unrelated works of fiction.

The noun is *juxtaposition* (juk stuh puh ZISH un).

K

KINETIC (ki NET ik) *adj* having to do with motion; lively; active
Kinetic energy is energy associated with motion. A speeding bullet has a lot of *kinetic* energy.
Kinetic art is art with things in it that move. A mobile is an example of *kinetic* art.
A *kinetic* personality is a lively, active, moving personality.

L

LABYRINTH (LAB uh rinth) *n* a maze; something like a maze
Each of the fifty floors in the office building was a *labyrinth* of dark corridors and narrow passageways.
The bill took many months to pass through the *labyrinth* of congressional approval.
A *labyrinth* is *labyrinthine,* or mazelike. Before beginning construction on the new house, the contractor had to weave his way through the *labyrinthine* (lab uh RINTH in) bureaucracy in order to obtain a building permit.

LACONIC (luh KAHN ik) *adj* using few words, especially to the point of seeming rude
The manager's *laconic* dismissal letter left the fired employees feeling angry and hurt.
When she went backstage, June discovered why the popular rock musician was so *laconic* in public: his voice was high and squeaky.

LAMENT (luh MENT) *v* to mourn
From the balcony of the bullet-pocked hotel, the foreign correspondents could hear hundreds of women and children *lamenting* the fallen soldiers.
As the snowstorm gained in intensity, Stan *lamented* his decision that morning to dress in shorts and a T-shirt.
Lamentable (LAM en tuh bul) or (luh MEN tuh bul) means regrettable.
Note carefully the pronunciation of both parts of speech.

LAMPOON (lam POON) *v* to satirize; to mock; to parody
The irreverent students mercilessly *lampooned* their Latin teacher's lisp in a skit at the school talent show.
The Harvard Lampoon, the nation's oldest humor magazine, has *lampooned* just about everything there is to *lampoon* in its 112-year history.

LANGUISH (LANG gwish) *v* to become weak, listless, or depressed

The formerly eager and vigorous accountant *languished* in his tedious job at the international conglomerate.

The longer Jill remained unemployed, the more she *languished* and the less likely it became that she would find another job.

To *languish* is to be *languid*. The child seemed so *languid* that his father thought he was sick and called the doctor. It turned out that the little boy had simply had an overdose of television.

LARGESS (lahr JES) *n* generous giving of gifts (or the gifts themselves); generosity; philanthropy

Sam was marginally literate at best. Only the *largess* of his uncle got Sam into Princeton.

Largess can also be spelled *largesse*.

Note carefully the pronunciation of this word.

LATENT (LAYT unt) *adj* present but not visible or apparent; potential

A photographic image is *latent* in a piece of exposed film; it's there, but you can't see it until the film is developed.

LAUD (lawd) *v* to praise; to applaud; to extol; to celebrate

The bank manager *lauded* the hero who trapped the escaping robber. The local newspaper published a laudatory editorial on this intrepid individual. *Laudatory* means praising.

Giving several million dollars to charity is a *laudable* act of philanthropy. *Laudable* means praiseworthy.

LEGACY (LEG uh see) *n* something handed down from the past; a bequest

The *legacy* of the corrupt administration was chaos, bankruptcy, and despair.

A shoebox full of baseball cards was the dead man's only *legacy*.

To be a *legacy* at a college sorority is to be the daughter of a former sorority member.

LETHARGY (LETH ur jee) *n* sluggishness; laziness; drowsiness; indifference

The couch potato had fallen into a state of such total *lethargy* that he never moved except to change channels or get another bag of Doritos from the kitchen.

The *lethargy* of the library staff caused what should have been a quick errand to expand into a full day's work.

To be filled with *lethargy* is to be *lethargic*. The *lethargic* (luh THAR jik) teenagers took all summer to paint the Hendersons' garage.

LEVITY (LEV uh tee) *n* lightness; frivolity; unseriousness

To *levitate* something is to make it so light that it floats up into the air. *Levity* comes from the same root and has to do with a different kind of lightness.

The speaker's *levity* was not appreciated by the convention of funeral directors, who felt that a convention of funeral directors was no place to tell jokes.

The judge's attempt to inject some *levity* into the dreary court proceedings (by setting off a few firecrackers in the jury box) was entirely successful.

Q•U•I•C•K • Q•U•I•Z #54

Match each word in the first column with its definition in the second column. Check your answers in the back of the book.

1. judicious	a. sluggishness
2. juxtapose	b. lightness
3. kinetic	c. using few words
4. labyrinth	d. maze
5. laconic	e. place side by side
6. lament	f. present but not visible
7. lampoon	g. bequest
8. languish	h. active
9. latent	i. become weak
10. laud	j. satirize
11. legacy	k. mourn
12. lethargy	l. praise
13. levity	m. exercising sound judgment

LIBEL (LYE bul) *n* a written or published falsehood that injures the reputation of, or defames, someone

The executive said that the newspaper had committed *libel* when it called him a stinking, no-good, corrupt, incompetent, overpaid, lying, worthless moron. He claimed that the newspaper had *libeled* him, and that its description of him had been *libelous*. At the trial, the jury disagreed, saying that the newspaper's description of the executive had been substantially accurate.

Don't confuse this word with *liable,* which has an entirely different meaning.

Slander is just like *libel* except that it is spoken instead of written. To *slander* someone is to say something untrue that injures that person's reputation.

LITIGATE (LIT uh gayt) *v* to try in court; to engage in legal proceedings

His lawyer thought a lawsuit would be fruitless, but the client wanted to *litigate.* He was feeling *litigious* (li TIJ us); that is, he was feeling in a mood to go to court.

When the company was unable to recover its money outside of court, its only option was to *litigate.*

To *litigate* is to engage in *litigation;* a court hearing is an example of *litigation.*

Note carefully the pronunciation of litigious.

LOQUACIOUS (loh KWAY shus) *adj* talking a lot or too much

The child was surprisingly *loquacious* for one so small.

Mary is so *loquacious* that Belinda can sometimes put down the telephone receiver and run a load of laundry while Mary is talking.

A *loquacious* person is one who is characterized by *loquaciousness* or *loquacity* (loh KWAS uh tee).

The English teacher's *loquacity* in class left little time for any of the students to speak, which was fine with most of the students.

LUCID (LOO sid) *adj* clear; easy to understand

The professor's explanation of the theory of relativity was so astonishingly *lucid* that even I could understand it.

Hubert's remarks were few but *lucid:* he explained the complicated issue with just a handful of well-chosen words.

The extremely old man was *lucid* right up until the moment he died; his body had given out but his mind was still going strong.

To *elucidate* something is to make it clear, to explain it. The poem was an enigma until a second grader in Encino, California, *elucidated* it for his admiring elders.

LUGUBRIOUS (loo GOO bree us) *adj* exaggeratedly mournful

To be mournful is to be sad and sorrowful. To be *lugubrious* is to make a big show of being sad and sorrowful.

Harry's *lugubrious* eulogy at the funeral of his dog eventually made everyone start giggling.

The valedictorian suddenly turned *lugubrious* and began sobbing and tearing her hair at the thought of graduating from high school.

Note carefully the pronunciation of this word.

LUMINOUS (LOO muh nus) *adj* giving off light; glowing; bright

The moon was a *luminous* disk in the cloudy nighttime sky.

The snow on the ground appeared eerily *luminous* at night—it seemed to glow.

The dial on my watch is *luminous;* it casts a green glow in the dark.

Q•U•I•C•K • Q•U•I•Z #55

Match each word in the first column with its definition in the second column. Check your answers in the back of the book.

1. libel	a. giving off light
2. slander	b. try in court
3. litigate	c. exaggeratedly mournful
4. loquacious	d. easy to understand
5. lucid	e. written injurious falsehood
6. lugubrious	f. spoken injurious falsehood
7. luminous	g. talking a lot

M

MACHINATION (mak uh NAY shun) *n* scheming activity for an evil purpose

This word is almost always used in the plural—*machinations*—in which form it means the same thing.

The ruthless *machinations* of the mobsters left a trail of blood and bodies.

The *machinations* of the conspirators were aimed at nothing less than the overthrow of the government.

This word is often used imprecisely to mean something like "machinelike activity." It should not be used in this way.

Note carefully the pronunciation of this word.

MAGNANIMOUS (mag NAN uh mus) *adj* forgiving; unresentful; noble in spirit; generous

The boxer was *magnanimous* in defeat, telling the sports reporters that his opponent had simply been too talented for him to beat.

Mrs. Jones *magnanimously* offered the little boy a cookie when he came over to confess that he had broken her window while attempting to shoot her cat with his pellet gun.

To be *magnanimous* is to have *magnanimity* (mag nuh NIM uh tee). The *magnanimity* of the conquering general was much appreciated by the defeated soldiers.

MAGNATE (MAG nayt) *n* a rich, powerful, or very successful businessperson

John D. Rockefeller was a *magnate* who was never too busy to give a shoeshine boy a dime for his troubles.

MALAISE (ma LAYZ) *n* a feeling of depression, uneasiness, or queasiness

Malaise descended on the calculus class when the teacher announced a quiz.

MALFEASANCE (mal FEE zuns) *n* an illegal act, especially by a public official

President Ford officially pardoned former president Nixon before the latter could be convicted of any *malfeasance*.

MALINGER (muh LING ger) *v* to pretend to be sick to avoid doing work

Indolent Leon always *malingered* when it was his turn to clean up the house. Arthur is artful and he always manages to *malinger* before a big exam.

MALLEABLE (MAL ee uh bul) *adj* easy to shape or bend

Modeling clay is very *malleable*.

So is Stuart. We can make him do whatever we want him to do.

MANDATE (MAN dayt) *n* a command or authorization to do something; the will of the voters as expressed by the results of an election

Our *mandate* from the executive committee was to find the answer to the problem as quickly as possible.

The newly elected president felt that the landslide vote had given him a *mandate* to do whatever he wanted to do.

Mandate can also be a verb. To *mandate* something is to command or require it.

A closely related word is *mandatory,* which means required or obligatory.

MANIFEST (MAN uh fest) *adj* visible; evident

Daryl's anger at us was *manifest:* you could see it in his expression and hear it in his voice.

There is *manifest* danger in riding a pogo stick along the edge of a cliff.

Manifest can also be a verb, in which case it means to show, to make visible, or to make evident. Rusty has been sick for a very long time, but it was only recently that he began to *manifest* symptoms.

Rebecca *manifested* alarm when we told her that the end of her ponytail was on fire, but she didn't do anything to put it out.

A visible sign of something is called a *manifestation* of it. A lack of comfort and luxury is the most obvious *manifestation* of poverty.

MANIFESTO (man uh FES toh) *n* a public declaration of beliefs or principles, usually political ones

The *Communist Manifesto* was a document that spelled out Karl Marx's vision of a Communist world.

Jim's article about the election was less a piece of reporting than a *manifesto* of his political views.

MARSHAL (MAHR shul) *v* to arrange in order; to gather together for the purpose of doing something

The statistician *marshaled* his facts before making his presentation.

The general *marshaled* his troops in anticipation of making an attack on the enemy fortress.

We *marshaled* half a dozen local groups in opposition to the city council's plan to bulldoze our neighborhood.

MARTIAL (MAHR shul) *adj* warlike; having to do with combat

Martial is often confused with *marital* (MAR uh tul), which means having to do with marriage. Marriages are sometimes *martial,* but don't confuse these words.

Karate and judo are often referred to as *martial* arts.

The parade of soldiers was *martial* in tone; the soldiers carried rifles and were followed by a formation of tanks.

The school principal declared *martial* law when food riots erupted in the cafeteria.

MARTYR (MAHR tur) *n* someone who gives up his or her life in pursuit of a cause, especially a religious one; one who suffers for a cause; one who makes a show of suffering in order to arouse sympathy

Many of the saints were also *martyrs;* they were executed, often gruesomely, for refusing to renounce their religious beliefs.

Jacob is a *martyr* to his job; he would stay at his desk twenty-four hours a day if his wife and the janitor would let him.

Eloise played the *martyr* during hay fever season, trudging wearily from room to room with a jumbo box of Kleenex in each hand.

MATRICULATE (muh TRIK yuh layt) *v* to enroll, especially at a college

Benny told everyone he was going to Harvard, but when he actually *matriculated* it was at the local junior college.

Q•U•I•C•K • Q•U•I•Z #56

Match each word in the first column with its definition in the second column. Check your answers in the back of the book.

1. machination	a. forgiving
2. macroeconomic	b. easy to shape
3. magnanimous	c. depression
4. magnate	d. command to do something
5. malaise	e. scheming evil activity
6. malfeasance	f. public declaration
7. malinger	g. pretend to be sick
8. malleable	h. visible
9. mandate	i. one who dies for a cause
10. manifest	j. arrange in order
11. manifesto	k. illegal act
12. marshal	l. enroll
13. martial	m. warlike
14. martyr	n. rich businessperson
15. matriculate	o. dealing with the economy at large

MAUDLIN (MAWD lin) *adj* silly and overly sentimental

The high school reunion grew more and more *maudlin* as the participants had more and more to drink.

The old lady had a *maudlin* concern for the worms in her yard; she would bang a gong before walking in the grass in order to give them a chance to get out of her way.

MAVERICK (MAV ur ik) *n* a nonconformist; a rebel

The word *maverick* originated in the Old West. It is derived from the name of Samuel A. Maverick, a Texas banker who once accepted a herd of cattle in payment of a debt. Maverick was a banker, not a rancher. He failed to confine or brand his calves, which habitually wandered into his neighbors' pastures. Local ranchers got in the habit of referring to any unbranded calf as a *maverick*. The word is now used for anyone who has refused to be "branded"—who has refused to conform.

The political scientist was an intellectual *maverick;* most of his theories had no followers except himself.

Maverick can also be an adjective. The *maverick* police officer got in trouble with the department for using illegal means to track down criminals.

MAXIM (MAK sim) *n* a fundamental principle; an old saying

We always tried to live our lives according to the *maxim* that it is better to give than to receive.

No one in the entire world is entirely certain of the differences in meaning among the words *maxim, adage, proverb,* and *aphorism.*

MEDIATE (MEE dee ayt) *v* to help settle differences

The United Nations representative tried to *mediate* between the warring countries, but the soldiers just kept shooting at one another.

Joe carried messages back and forth between the divorcing husband and wife in the hope of *mediating* their differences.

To *mediate* is to engage in *mediation*. When two opposing groups, such as a trade union and the management of a company, try to settle their differences through *mediation,* they call in a *mediator* to listen to their cases and make an equitable decision.

MELLIFLUOUS (muh LIF loo us) *adj* sweetly flowing

Mellifluous comes from Greek words meaning, roughly, "honey flowing." We use the word almost exclusively to describe voices, music, or sounds that flow sweetly, like honey.

Melanie's clarinet playing was *mellifluous;* the notes flowed smoothly and beautifully.

The choir's *mellifluous* singing made us feel as though we were being covered with a sticky yellow liquid.

MENDACIOUS (men DAY shus) *adj* lying; dishonest

Children are naturally *mendacious*. If you ask them what they are doing, they will automatically answer, "Nothing."

The jury saw through the *mendacious* witness and convicted the defendant.

To be *mendacious* is to engage in *mendacity,* or lying. I have no flaws, except occasional *mendacity*. Don't confuse this word with *mendicant,* listed below.

MENDICANT (MEN di kunt) *n* a beggar

The presence of thousands of *mendicants* in every urban area is a sad commentary on our national priorities.

MENTOR (MEN tur) *n* a teacher, tutor, counselor, or coach; especially in business, an experienced person who shows an inexperienced person the ropes

Mentor is too big a word to apply to just an ordinary teacher. A student might have many teachers but only one *mentor*—the person who taught him what was really important.

Chris's *mentor* in the pole vault was a former track star who used to hang out by the gym and give the students pointers.

Young men and women in business often talk about the importance of having a *mentor*—usually an older person at the same company who takes an interest in them and helps them get ahead by showing them the ropes.

Mentor is often used as a verb, but you shouldn't do it.

MERCENARY (MUR suh ner ee) *n* a hired soldier; someone who will do anything for money

If an army can't find enough volunteers or draftees, it will sometimes hire *mercenaries.* The magazine *Soldier of Fortune* is aimed at *mercenaries* and would-be *mercenaries;* it even runs classified advertisements by soldiers looking for someone to fight.

You don't have to be a soldier to be a *mercenary.* Someone who does something strictly for the money is often called a *mercenary.*

Our business contains a few dedicated workers and many, many *mercenaries,* who want to make a quick buck and then get out.

Mercenary can also be used as an adjective.

Larry's motives in writing the screenplay for the trashy movie were strictly *mercenary*—he needed the money.

MERCURIAL (mur KYOOR ee ul) *adj* emotionally unpredictable; rapidly changing in mood

A person with a *mercurial* personality is one who changes rapidly and unpredictably between one mood and another.

Mercurial Helen was crying one minute, laughing the next.

METAMORPHOSIS (met uh MOR fuh sis) *n* a magical change in form; a striking or sudden change

When the magician passed his wand over Eileen's head, she underwent a bizarre *metamorphosis:* she turned into a hamster.

Damon's *metamorphosis* from college student to Hollywood superstar was so sudden that it seemed a bit unreal.

To undergo a *metamorphosis* is to *metamorphose.* No matter how hard he tried, the accountant was unable to *metamorphose* the losses into gains.

THE WORDS

Q•U•I•C•K • Q•U•I•Z #57

Match each word in the first column with its definition in the second column. Check your answers in the back of the book.

1. maudlin
2. maverick
3. maxim
4. mediate
5. mellifluous
6. mendacious
7. mendicant
8. mentor
9. mercenary
10. mercurial
11. metamorphosis

a. teacher
b. fundamental principle
c. lying
d. help settle differences
e. sweetly flowing
f. nonconformist
g. emotionally unpredictable
h. magical change in form
i. overly sentimental
j. hired soldier
k. beggar

MICROCOSM (MYE kruh kahz um) *n* the world in miniature

The *cosmos* is the heavens, *cosmopolitan* means worldly, and a *microcosm* is a miniature version of the world. All three words are related.

The opposite of *microcosm* is a *macrocosm* (MAK ruh kahz um). A *macrocosm* is a large-scale representation of something, or the universe at large.

MILIEU (mil YOO) *n* environment; surroundings

A caring and involved community is the proper *milieu* for raising a family.

The farmer on vacation in the big city felt out of his *milieu.*

MINUSCULE (MIN uh skyool) *adj* very tiny

Be careful with the spelling of this word. People tend to spell it "miniscule." Think of *minus.*

Bob's *minuscule* brain was just enough to get him out of junior high school and into a job at the gas station.

Hank's salary was *minuscule,* but the benefits were pretty good: he got to sit next to the refrigerator and eat all day long.

Minute (mye NOOT) is a synonym for *minuscule.* The small details of something are the *minutiae* (mi NOO shi ee).

MISANTHROPIC (mis un THRAHP ik) *adj* hating mankind

A *misogynist* (mis AH juh nist) hates women. A *misanthropic* person doesn't make distinctions; he or she hates everyone. The opposite of a *misanthrope* (MIS un throhp) is a *philanthropist* (fuh LAN thruh pist). Curiously, there is no word for someone who hates men only.

MITIGATE (MIT uh gayt) v to moderate the effect of something

The sense of imminent disaster was *mitigated* by the guide's calm behavior and easy smile.

The effects of the disease were *mitigated* by the experimental drug treatment.

Nothing Joel said could *mitigate* the enormity of forgetting his mother-in-law's birthday.

Unmitigated means absolute, unmoderated, not made less intense or severe.

MOLLIFY (MAHL uh fye) v to soften; to soothe; to pacify

Lucy *mollified* the angry police officer by kissing him on the tip of his nose.

My father was not *mollified* by my promise never to crash his car into a brick wall again.

The baby-sitter was unable to *mollify* the cranky child, so she put him in the clothes dryer and spun him around for a little while.

MONOLITHIC (mah nuh LITH ik) adj massive, solid, uniform, and un-yielding

A *monolith* is a huge stone shaft or column. Many other things can be said to be *monolithic*.

A huge corporation is often said to be *monolithic*, especially if it is enormous and powerful and all its parts are dedicated to the same purpose.

If the opposition to a plan were said to be *monolithic*, it would probably consist of a very large group of people who all felt the same way.

MORIBUND (MOR uh bund) adj dying

The steel industry in this country was *moribund* a few years ago, but now it seems to be reviving somewhat.

The senator's political ideas were *moribund;* no one thinks that way anymore.

A dying creature could be said to be *moribund*, too, although this word is usually used in connection with things that die only figuratively.

MOROSE (muh ROHS) adj gloomy; sullen

Louise was always so *morose* about everything that she was never any fun to be with.

New Yorkers always seemed *morose* to the writer who lived in the country; they seemed beaten down by the vast, unfriendly city in which they lived.

MORTIFY (MOR tuh fye) adj to humiliate

I was *mortified* when my father asked my girlfriend whether she thought I was a dumb, pathetic wimp.

We had a *mortifying* experience at the opera; when Stanley sneezed, the entire orchestra stopped playing and stared at him for several minutes.

MUNDANE (mun DAYN) *adj* ordinary; pretty boring; not heavenly and eternal

My day was filled with *mundane* chores: I mowed the lawn, did the laundry, fed the dog, and fed the dog to the gorilla.

Dee's job was so *mundane* she sometimes had trouble remembering whether she was at work or asleep.

The monk's thoughts were far removed from *mundane* concerns; he was contemplating all the fun he was going to have in heaven.

MUNIFICENT (myoo NIF uh sunt) *adj* very generous; lavish

The *munificent* millionaire gave lots of money to any charity that came to him with a request.

Mrs. Bigelow was a *munificent* hostess; there was so much wonderful food and wine at her dinner parties that the guests had to rest between courses. She was known for her *munificence.*

MYOPIA (mye OH pee uh) *adj* nearsightedness; lack of foresight

Myopia is the fancy medical name for the inability to see clearly at a distance. It's also a word used in connection with people who lack other kinds of visual acuity.

The president suffered from economic *myopia;* he was unable to see the consequences of his fiscal policies.

The workers' dissatisfaction was inflamed by management's *myopia* on the subject of wages.

To suffer myopia is to be *myopic* (mye AHP ik). Some people who wear glasses are *myopic.* So are the people who can't see the consequences of their actions.

MYRIAD (MIR ee ud) *n* a huge number

A country sky on a clear night is filled with a *myriad* of stars.

There are *myriad* reasons why I don't like school.

This word can also be used as an adjective. *Myriad* stars is a lot of stars. The teenager was weighted down by the *myriad* anxieties of adolescence.

Note carefully the pronunciation of this word.

Q•U•I•C•K • Q•U•I•Z #58

Match each word in the first column with its definition in the second column. Check your answers in the back of the book.

1. microcosm
2. milieu
3. minuscule
4. misanthropic
5. mitigate
6. mollify
7. monolithic
8. moribund
9. morose
10. mortify
11. mundane
12. munificent
13. myopia
14. myriad

a. a huge number
b. moderate the effect of
c. massive and unyielding
d. humiliate
e. ordinary
f. soften
g. nearsightedness
h. very tiny
i. gloomy
j. environment
k. very generous
l. dying
m. world in miniature
n. hating mankind

N

NARCISSISM (NAHR si siz um) *n* excessive love of one's body or oneself

In Greek mythology, Narcissus was a boy who fell in love with his own reflection and, after lying around for a long time staring at it, turned into a flower. To engage in *narcissism* is to be like Narcissus.

Throwing a kiss to your reflection in the mirror is an act of *narcissism*. So is filling your living room with all your bowling trophies or telling everyone how smart and good-looking you are. You are a *narcissist* (NAHR suh sist).

Someone who suffers from *narcissism* is said to be *narcissistic* (nahr si SIS tik). The selfish students were bound up in *narcissistic* concerns and gave no thought to other people.

NEBULOUS (NEB yuh lus) *adj* vague; hazy; indistinct

Oscar's views are so *nebulous* that no one can figure out what he thinks about anything.

The community's boundaries are somewhat *nebulous;* where they are depends on whom you ask.

Molly's expensive new hairdo was a sort of *nebulous* mass of wisps, waves, and hair spray.

A *nebula* (NEB yuh luh) is an interstellar cloud, the plural of which is *nebulae* (NEB yuh lee).

NEFARIOUS (ni FAR ee us) *adj* evil; flagrantly wicked

The radicals' *nefarious* plot was to destroy New York by filling the reservoir with strawberry Jell-O.

The convicted murderer had committed a myriad of *nefarious* acts.

NEOLOGISM (nee OL uh jiz um) *n* a new word or phrase; a new usage of a word

Pedants don't like *neologisms*. They like the words we already have. But at one time every word was a *neologism*. Someone somewhere had to be the first to use it.

NEPOTISM (NEP uh tiz um) *n* showing favoritism to friends or family in business or politics

Clarence had no business acumen, so he was counting on *nepotism* when he married the boss's daughter.

NIHILISM (NYE uh liz um) *n* the belief that there are no values or morals in the universe

A *nihilist* does not believe in any objective standards of right or wrong.

Note carefully the pronunciation of this word.

NOMINAL (NOM uh nul) *adj* in name only; insignificant; A-OK (during rocket launches)

Bert was the *nominal* chairman of the committee, but Sue was really the one who ran things.

The cost was *nominal* in comparison with the enormous value of what you received.

"All systems are *nominal*," said the NASA engineer as the space shuttle successfully headed into orbit.

NOSTALGIA (nahs TAL juh) *n* sentimental longing for the past; homesickness

A wave of *nostalgia* overcame me when the old Temptations song came on the radio; hearing it took me right back to 1967.

Some people who don't remember what the decade was really like feel a misplaced *nostalgia* for the 1950s.

To be filled with *nostalgia* is to be *nostalgic*. As we talked about the fun we'd had together in junior high school, we all began to feel a little *nostalgic*.

NOTORIOUS (noh TOR ee us) *adj* famous for something bad

A well-known actor is famous; a well-known criminal is *notorious*.

No one wanted to play poker with Jeremy, because he was a *notorious* cheater.

Luther's practical jokes were *notorious;* people always kept their distance when he came into the room.

To be *notorious* is to have *notoriety* (noh tuh RYE uh tee). Jesse's *notoriety* as a bank robber made it difficult for him to find a job in banking.

NOVEL (NAHV ul) *adj* new; original

Ray had a *novel* approach to homework: he didn't do it. Ray failed geometry as a result of this *novelty*.

There was nothing *novel* about the author's latest novel; the characters were old and the plot was borrowed.

NOXIOUS (NAHK shus) *adj* harmful; offensive

Smoking is a *noxious* habit in every sense.

Poison ivy is a *noxious* weed.

Carbon monoxide is a *noxious* gas.

The mothers' committee believed that rock 'n' roll music exerted a *noxious* influence on their children.

NUANCE (NOO ahns) *n* a subtle difference or distinction

The artist's best work explored the *nuance* between darkness and deep shadow.

Harry was incapable of *nuance;* everything for him was either black or white.

In that Chinese dialect, the difference between one word and its opposite is sometimes nothing more than a *nuance* of inflection.

Q•U•I•C•K • Q•U•I•Z #59

Match each word in the first column with its definition in the second column. Check your answers in the back of the book.

1. narcissism	a. excessive love of self
2. nebulous	b. in name only
3. nefarious	c. harmful
4. neologism	d. original
5. nepotism	e. evil
6. nihilism	f. subtle difference
7. nominal	g. famous for something bad
8. nostalgia	h. vague
9. notorious	i. longing for the past
10. novel	j. favoritism
11. noxious	k. belief in the absence of all
12. nuance	values and morals
	l. new word

O

OBDURATE (AHB dyoo rit) *adj* stubborn and insensitive

Obdurate contains one of the same roots as *durable* and *endurance;* each word conveys a different sense of hardness.

The committee's *obdurate* refusal to listen to our plan was heartbreaking to us, since we had spent ten years coming up with it.

The child begged and begged to have a bubble-gum machine installed in his bedroom, but his parents were *obdurate* in their insistence that he have a soft-drink machine instead.

Note carefully the pronunciation of this word.

OBFUSCATE (AHB fuh skayt) *v* to darken; to confuse; to make confusing

The spokesman's attempt to explain what the president had meant merely *obfuscated* the issue further. People had hoped the spokesman would elucidate the issue.

Too much gin had *obfuscated* the old man's senses.

The professor's inept lecture gradually *obfuscated* a subject that had been crystal clear to us before.

To *obfuscate* something is to engage in *obfuscation.* Lester called himself a used-car salesman, but his real job was *obfuscation:* he sold cars by confusing his customers.

OBLIQUE (oh BLEEK) *adj* indirect; at an angle

In geometry, lines are said to be *oblique* if they are neither parallel nor perpendicular to one another. The word has a related meaning outside of mathematics. An *oblique* statement is one that does not directly address the topic at hand, that approaches it as if from an angle.

An allusion could be said to be an *oblique* reference.

An *oblique* argument is one that does not directly confront its true subject.

To insult someone *obliquely* is to do so indirectly.

Harry sprinkled his student council speech with *oblique* references to the principal's new toupee; the principal is so dense that he never figured out what was going on, but the rest of us were rolling on the floor.

OBLIVION (uh BLIV ee un) *n* total forgetfulness; the state of being forgotten

A few of the young actors would find fame, but most were headed for *oblivion.*

After tossing and turning with anxiety for most of the night, Richie finally found the *oblivion* of sleep.

To be *oblivious* is to be forgetful or unaware. Old age had made the retired professor *oblivious* of all his old theories.

The workmen stomped in and out of the room, but the happy child, playing on the floor, was *oblivious* of all distraction.

OBSCURE (ub SKYOOR) *adj* unknown; hard to understand; dark

The comedy nightclub was filled with *obscure* comedians who stole one another's jokes and seldom got any laughs.

The artist was so *obscure* that even his parents had trouble remembering his name.

The noted scholar's dissertation was terribly *obscure;* it had to be translated from English into English before anyone could make head or tail of it.

Some contemporary poets apparently believe that the only way to be great is to be *obscure.*

The features of the forest grew *obscure* as night fell.

The state of being *obscure* in any of its senses is called *obscurity.*

OBSEQUIOUS (ub SEE kwee us) *adj* fawning; subservient; sucking up to

Ann's assistant was so *obsequious* that she could never tell what he really thought about anything.

My *obsequious* friend seemed to live only to make me happy and never wanted to do anything if I said I didn't want to do it.

OBTUSE (ahb TOOS) *adj* insensitive; blockheaded

Mabel was so *obtuse* that she didn't realize for several days that Carl had asked her to marry him.

The *obtuse* student couldn't seem to grasp the difference between addition and subtraction.

OFFICIOUS (uh FISH us) *adj* annoyingly eager to help or advise

The *officious* officer could never resist sticking his nose into other people's business.

The *officious* salesperson refused to leave us alone, so we finally left without buying anything.

Note carefully the pronunciation of this word.

ONEROUS (AHN ur us) *adj* burdensome; oppressive

We were given the *onerous* task of cleaning up the fairgrounds after the carnival.

The job had long hours but the work wasn't *onerous;* Bill spent most of his time sitting with his feet on the desk.

This word can be pronounced (OH nur us).

OPAQUE (oh PAYK) *adj* impossible to see through; impossible to understand

The windows in the movie star's house were made not of glass but of some *opaque* material that was intended to keep his fans from spying on him.

We tried to figure out what Horace was thinking, but his expression was *opaque:* it revealed nothing.

Marvin's mind, assuming he had one, was *opaque.*

The statement was *opaque;* no one could make anything of it.

The noun form of *opaque* is *opacity* (oh PAS uh tee).

OPULENT (AHP yuh lunt) *adj* luxurious

Everything in the *opulent* palace was made of gold—except the toilet-paper holder, which was made of platinum.

The investment banker had grown so accustomed to an *opulent* lifestyle that he had trouble adjusting to the federal penitentiary.

Opulence is often ostentatious.

ORTHODOX (OR thuh dahks) *adj* conventional; adhering to established principles or doctrines, especially in religion; by the book

The doctor's treatment for Lou's cold was entirely *orthodox:* plenty of liquids and aspirin, and lots of rest.

Austin's views were *orthodox;* there was nothing shocking about any of them.

The body of what is *orthodox* is called *orthodoxy.* The teacher's lectures were characterized by strict adherence to *orthodoxy.*

To be unconventional is to be *unorthodox.* "Green cheese" is an *unorthodox* explanation for the composition of the moon.

OSTENSIBLE (ah STEN suh bul) *adj* apparent (but misleading); professed

Blake's *ostensible* mission was to repair a broken telephone, but his real goal was to plant a bomb that would blow up the building.

Trevor's *ostensible* kindness to squirrels belied his deep hatred of them.

OSTENTATIOUS (ahs ten TAY shus) *adj* excessively conspicuous; showing off

The designer's use of expensive materials was *ostentatious;* every piece of furniture was covered with silk or velvet, and every piece of hardware was made of silver or gold.

The donor was *ostentatious* in making his gift to the hospital. He held a big press conference to announce it and then walked through the wards to give patients an opportunity to thank him personally.

The young lawyer had *ostentatiously* hung his Harvard diploma on the door to his office.

To be *ostentatious* is to engage in *ostentation.* Jerry wore solid-gold shoes to the party; I was shocked by his *ostentation.*

P

PACIFY (PAS uh fye) *v* to calm someone down; to placate

A parent gives a baby a *pacifier* to *pacify* him or her. A *pacifist* is someone who does not believe in war.

Q•U•I•C•K • Q•U•I•Z #60

Match each word in the first column with its definition in the second column. Check your answers in the back of the book.

1. obdurate		a.	forgetfulness
2. obfuscate		b.	hard to understand
3. oblique		c.	stubborn
4. oblivion		d.	insensitive
5. obscure		e.	burdensome
6. obsequious		f.	luxurious
7. obtuse		g.	indirect
8. officious		h.	misleadingly apparent
9. onerous		i.	showing off
10. opaque		j.	impossible to see through
11. opulent		k.	calm someone down
12. orthodox		l.	confuse
13. ostensible		m.	fawning
14. ostentatious		n.	conventional
15. pacify		o.	annoyingly helpful

PAINSTAKING (PAYN stay king) *adj* extremely careful; taking pains
   Painstaking = pains-taking = taking pains.
   The jeweler was *painstaking* in his effort not to ruin the $50 million diamond.
   We made a *painstaking* effort to move the piano without harming it; first we wrapped it in Kleenex, then we covered it with balloons, then we put it on roller skates and pushed it down the ramp.

PALLIATE (PAL ee ayt) *v* to relieve or alleviate something without getting rid of the problem; to assuage; to mitigate
   You take aspirin in the hope that it will *palliate* your headache. Aspirin is a *palliative* (PAL yuh tiv).

PALPABLE (PAL puh bul) *adj* capable of being touched; obvious; tangible
   The tumor was *palpable;* the doctor could feel it with his finger.
   Harry's disappointment at being rejected by every college in America was *palpable;* it was so obvious that you could almost reach out and touch it.
   There was *palpable* danger in flying the kite in a thunderstorm.
   The opposite of *palpable* is *impalpable*.

PALTRY (PAWL tree) *adj* insignificant; worthless
   The lawyer's efforts in our behalf were *paltry;* they didn't add up to anything.
   The *paltry* fee he paid us was scarcely large enough to cover our expenses.

PANACEA (pan uh SEE uh) *n* something that cures everything

The administration seemed to believe that a tax cut would be a *panacea* for the country's economic ills.

Granny believed that her "rheumatiz medicine" was a *panacea*. No matter what you were sick with, that was what she prescribed.

Note carefully the pronunciation of this word.

PARADIGM (PAR uh dime) *n* a model or example

Mr. King is the best teacher in the whole world; his classroom should be the *paradigm* for all classrooms.

In selecting her wardrobe, messy Gertrude apparently used a scarecrow as her *paradigm*.

A *paradigm* is *paradigmatic* (par uh dig MAT ik). Virtually all the cars the company produced were based on a single, *paradigmatic* design.

Note carefully the pronunciation of this word.

PARADOX (PAR uh dahks) *n* a true statement or phenomenon that nonetheless seems to contradict itself; an untrue statement or phenomenon that nonetheless seems logical

Mr. Cooper is a political *paradox;* he's a staunch Republican who votes only for Democrats.

One of Xeno's *paradoxes* seems to prove the impossibility of an arrow's ever reaching its target: if the arrow first moves half the distance to the target, then half the remaining distance, then half the remaining distance, and so on, it can never arrive.

A *paradox* is *paradoxical*. Hubert's dislike of ice cream was *paradoxical*, considering that he worked as an ice-cream taster.

PAROCHIAL (puh ROH kee ul) *adj* narrow or confined in point of view; provincial

The townspeople's concerns were entirely *parochial;* they worried only about what happened in their town and not about the larger world around it.

The journalist's *parochial* point of view prevented him from becoming a nationally known figure.

A lot of people think a *parochial* school is a religious school. Actually, a *parochial* school is the school of the parish or neighborhood. In other contexts, though, *parochial* has negative connotations.

PARODY (PAR uh dee) *n* a satirical imitation

On the cover of *The Harvard Lampoon*'s parody of *People* magazine was a photograph of Brooke Shields holding a great big fish.

At the talent show the girls sang a terrible *parody* of a Beatles song called "I Want to Hold Your Foot."

Some *parodies* are unintentional and not very funny. The unhappy student accused Mr. Benson of being not a teacher but a *parody* of one.

Parody can also be a verb. To *parody* something is to make a *parody* of it. A *parody* is *parodic*.

PARSIMONIOUS (pahr suh MOH nee us) *adj* stingy

The old widow was so *parsimonious* that she hung used teabags out to dry on her clothesline so that she would be able to use them again. We tried to be *parsimonious,* but without success. After just a couple of days at the resort we realized that we had spent all the money we had set aside for our entire month-long vacation.

To be *parsimonious* is to practice *parsimony.*

PARTISAN (PAHR tuh zun) *n* one who supports a particular person, cause, or idea

Henry's plan to give himself the award had no *partisan* except himself.

I am the *partisan* of any candidate who promises not to make promises.

The mountain village was attacked by *partisans* of the rebel chieftain.

Partisan can also be used as an adjective meaning biased, as in *partisan* politics. An issue that everyone agrees on regardless of the party he or she belongs to is a *nonpartisan* issue. *Bipartisan* means supported by two (bi) parties.

Both the Republican and Democratic senators voted to give themselves a raise. The motion had *bipartisan* support.

Q•U•I•C•K • Q•U•I•Z #61

Match each word in the first column with its definition in the second column. Check your answers in the back of the book.

1. painstaking	a. obvious
2. palliate	b. model
3. palpable	c. supporter of a cause
4. paltry	d. narrow in point of view
5. panacea	e. contradictory truth
6. paradigm	f. stingy
7. paradox	g. cure for everything
8. parochial	h. insignificant
9. parody	i. extremely careful
10. parsimonious	j. satirical imitation
11. partisan	k. alleviate

PATENT (PAYT unt) *adj* obvious

To say that the earth is flat is a *patent* absurdity, since the world is obviously spherical.

It was *patently* foolish of Lee to think that he could sail across the Pacific Ocean in a washtub.

PATERNAL (puh TUR nul) *adj* fatherly; fatherlike
Fred is *paternal* toward his niece. *Maternal* (muh TUR nul) means motherly or momlike.

PATHOLOGY (puh THAHL uh jee) *n* the science of diseases
Pathology is the science or study of diseases, but not necessarily in the medical sense. *Pathological* means relating to *pathology*, but it also means arising from a disease. So if we say Brad is an inveterate, incorrigible, *pathological* (path uh LAHJ uh kul) liar, we are saying that Brad's lying is a sickness.

PATRIARCH (PAY tree ahrk) *n* the male head of a family or tribe
A *patriarch* is generally a strong male head of a family or tribe.

PATRICIAN (puh TRISH un) *n* a person of noble birth; an aristocrat
Mr. Anderson was a *patrician*, and he was never truly happy unless his place at the dinner table was set with at least half a dozen forks.
Patrician can also be an adjective. Polo is a *patrician* sport. The noisy crowd on the luxury ocean liner was *patrician* in dress but not in behavior; they were wearing tuxedos but throwing deck chairs into the ocean.

PATRONIZE (PAY truh nyze) *v* to treat as an inferior; to condescend to
Our guide at the art gallery was extremely *patronizing*, treating us as though we wouldn't be able to distinguish a painting from a piece of sidewalk without her help.
We felt *patronized* by the waiter at the fancy French restaurant; he ignored all our efforts to attract his attention and then pretended not to understand our accents.
Patronize also means to frequent or be a regular customer of. To *patronize* a restaurant is to eat there often, not to treat it as an inferior.

PAUCITY (PAW suh tee) *n* scarcity
There was a *paucity* of fresh vegetables at the supermarket, so we had to buy frozen.
The plan was defeated by a *paucity* of support.
There is no *paucity* of water in the ocean.

PECCADILLO (pek uh DIL oh) *n* a minor offense
The smiling defendant acted as though first-degree murder were a mere *peccadillo* rather than a hideous crime.
The reporters sometimes seemed more interested in the candidates' sexual *peccadillos* than in their inane programs and proposals.

PEDANTIC (puh DAN tik) *adj* boringly scholarly or academic
The discussion quickly turned *pedantic* as each participant tried to sound more learned than all the others.
Percival's feelings about love were mostly *pedantic;* he'd read about love in books but had never really encountered it in his life.
The professor's interpretation of the poem was *pedantic* and empty of genuine feeling.

A *pedantic* person is called a *pedant* (PED unt). A *pedant* is fond of *pedantry* (PED un tree).

PEDESTRIAN (puh DES tree un) *adj* unimaginative; banal
This is one of the favorite words of the people who write the SAT. A *pedestrian* is someone walking, but to be *pedestrian* is to be something else altogether.

Mary Anne said the young artist's work was brilliant, but I found it to be *pedestrian;* I've seen better paintings in kindergarten classrooms.

The menu was *pedestrian;* I had encountered each of the dishes dozens of times before.

PEJORATIVE (pi JOR uh tiv) *adj* negative; disparaging
"Hi, stupid" is a *pejorative* greeting.

"Loudmouth" is a nickname with a *pejorative* connotation.

Abe's description of the college as "a pretty good school" was unintentionally *pejorative*.

PENCHANT (PEN chunt) *n* a strong taste or liking for something; a predilection
Dogs have a *penchant* for chasing cats and mailmen.

PENITENT (PEN uh tunt) *adj* sorry; repentant; contrite
Julie was *penitent* when Hank explained how much pain she had caused him.

The two boys tried to sound *penitent* at the police station, but they weren't really sorry that they had herded the sheep into Mr. Ingersoll's house. They were *impenitent*.

PENSIVE (PEN siv) *adj* thoughtful and sad
Norton became suddenly *pensive* when Jack mentioned his dead father.

The gloomy weather made everyone feel *pensive,* so we cheered them up by shooting off a few firecrackers in the living room.

Q•U•I•C•K • Q•U•I•Z #62

Match each word in the first column with its definition in the second column. Check your answers in the back of the book.

1. patent	a. male head of a family
2. paternal	b. minor offense
3. pathology	c. unimaginative
4. patriarch	d. thoughtful and sad
5. patrician	e. boringly scholarly
6. patronize	f. science of diseases
7. paucity	g. treat as an inferior
8. peccadillo	h. negative
9. pedantic	i. obvious
10. pedestrian	j. aristocrat
11. pejorative	k. scarcity
12. penchant	l. fatherly
13. penitent	m. sorry
14. pensive	n. strong liking

PEREMPTORY (puh REMP tuh ree) *adj* final; categorical; dictatorial

Someone who is *peremptory* says or does something without giving anyone a chance to dispute it. Frank's father *peremptorily* banished him to his room.

Note carefully the pronunciation of this word.

PERENNIAL (puh REN ee ul) *adj* continual; happening again and again or year after year

Mr. Phillips is a *perennial* favorite of students at the high school because he always gives everyone an A.

Milton was a *perennial* candidate for governor; every four years he printed up another batch of his BINGO AND HORSE RACING bumper stickers.

Flowers called *perennials* are flowers that bloom year after year without being replanted.

Biennial (bye EN ee ul) and *centennial* (sen TEN ee ul) are related words. *Biennial* means happening once every two years (biannual means happening twice a year). *Centennial* means happening once every century.

PERFIDY (PUR fuh dee) *n* treachery

It was the criminals' natural *perfidy* that finally did them in, as each one became an informant on the other.

I was appalled at Al's *perfidy*. He had sworn to me that he was my best friend, but then he asked my girlfriend to the prom.

To engage in *perfidy* is to be *perfidious* (pur FID ee us).

PERFUNCTORY (pur FUNGK tuh ree) *adj* unenthusiastic; careless

Larry made a couple of *perfunctory* attempts at answering the questions on the test, but then he put down his pencil and his head and slept until the end of the period.

Sandra's lawn mowing was *perfunctory* at best: she skipped all the difficult parts and didn't rake up any of the clippings.

PERIPATETIC (per uh peh TET ik) *adj* wandering; traveling continually; itinerant

Groupies are a *peripatetic* bunch, traveling from concert to concert to follow their favorite rock stars.

PERIPHERY (puh RIF uh ree) *n* the outside edge of something

José never got involved in any of our activities; he was always at the *periphery*.

The professional finger painter enjoyed his position at the *periphery* of the art world.

To be at the *periphery* is to be *peripheral* (puh RIF uh rul). A *peripheral* interest is a secondary or side interest.

Your *peripheral* vision is your ability to see to the right and left while looking straight ahead.

PERJURY (PUR jur ee) *n* lying under oath

The defendant was acquitted of bribery but convicted of *perjury*, because he had lied on the witness stand during his trial.

To commit *perjury* is to *perjure* oneself. The former cabinet official *perjured* himself when he said that he had not committed *perjury* during his trial for bribery.

PERMEATE (PUR mee ayt) *v* to spread or seep through; to penetrate

A stinky smell quickly *permeated* the room after Jock lit a cigarette.

Corruption had *permeated* the company; every single one of its executives belonged in jail.

Something that can be *permeated* is said to be *permeable*. A *permeable* raincoat is one that lets water seep through.

PERNICIOUS (pur NISH us) *adj* deadly; extremely evil

The drug dealers conducted their *pernicious* business on every street corner in the city.

Lung cancer is a *pernicious* disease.

PERQUISITE (PUR kwuh zit) *n* a privilege that goes along with a job; a "perk"

Free access to a photocopier is a *perquisite* of most office jobs.

The big corporate lawyer's *perquisites* included a chauffeured limousine, a luxurious apartment in the city, and all the chocolate ice cream he could eat.

A *perquisite* should not be confused with a *prerequisite* (pree REK wuh zit), which is a necessity. Health and happiness are two *prerequisites* of a good life.

A college degree is a *prerequisite* for many high-paying jobs.

PERTINENT (PUR tuh nunt) *adj* relevant; dealing with the matter at hand

The suspect said that he was just borrowing the jewelry for a costume ball. The cop said he did not think that was *pertinent*.

By the way, *impertinent* means disrespectful.

PERTURB (pur TURB) *v* to disturb greatly

Rudolph's mother was *perturbed* by his aberrant behavior at the dinner table. Rudolph's father was not bothered. Nothing bothered Rudolph Sr. He was *imperturbable*.

PERUSE (puh ROOZ) *v* to read carefully

This word is misused more often than it is used correctly. To *peruse* something is not to skim it or read it quickly. To *peruse* something is to study it or read it with great care.

The lawyer *perused* the contract for many hours, looking for a loophole that would enable his client to back out of the deal.

To *peruse* something is to engage in *perusal*. My *perusal* of the ancient texts brought me no closer to my goal of discovering the meaning of life.

Q•U•I•C•K • Q•U•I•Z #63

Match each word in the first column with its definition in the second column. Check your answers in the back of the book.

1. peremptory
2. perennial
3. perfidy
4. perfunctory
5. peripatetic
6. periphery
7. perjury
8. permeate
9. pernicious
10. perquisite
11. prerequisite
12. pertinent
13. perturb
14. peruse

a. outside edge of something
b. unenthusiastic
c. penetrate
d. lying under oath
e. job-related privilege
f. continual
g. disturb greatly
h. necessity
i. read carefully
j. treachery
k. final
l. wandering
m. relevant
n. deadly

PERVADE (pur VAYD) *v* to spread throughout

A terrible smell *pervaded* the apartment building after the sewer main exploded.

On examination day, the classroom was *pervaded* by a sense of imminent doom.

Something that *pervades* is *pervasive*. There was a *pervasive* feeling of despair on Wall Street on the day the Dow-Jones industrial average fell more than 500 points.

There was a *pervasive* odor of fuel oil in the house, and we soon discovered why: the basement was filled with the stuff.

PETULANT (PECH uh lunt) *adj* rude; cranky; ill-tempered

Gloria became *petulant* when we suggested that she leave her pet cheetah at home when she came to spend the weekend; she said that we had insulted her cheetah and that an insult to her cheetah was an insult to her.

The *petulant* waiter slammed down our water glasses and spilled a tureen of soup onto Roger's toupee.

To be *petulant* is to engage in *petulance*, or rudeness.

PHILANTHROPY (fi LAN thruh pee) *n* love of mankind, especially by doing good deeds

A charity is a *philanthropic* institution. An altruist is someone who cares about other people. A *philanthropist* is actively doing things to help, usually by giving time or money.

PHILISTINE (FIL i steen) *n* a smugly ignorant person with no appreciation of intellectual or artistic matters

The novelist dismissed his critics as *philistines*, saying they wouldn't recognize a good book if it crawled up and bit them on the nose; the critics, in reply, dismissed the novelist as a *philistine* who wouldn't recognize a good book if it crawled up and rolled itself into his typewriter.

Philistine can also be an adjective. To be *philistine* is to act like a *philistine*.

PIOUS (PYE us) *adj* reverent or devout; outwardly (and sometimes falsely) reverent or devout; hypocritical

This is a sometimes confusing word with meanings that are very nearly opposite each other.

A *pious* Presbyterian is one who goes to church every Sunday and says his prayers every night before bed. *Pious* in this sense means something like religiously dutiful.

Pious can also be used to describe behavior or feelings that aren't religious at all but are quite hypocritical. The adulterous minister's sermon on marital fidelity was filled with *pious* disregard for his own sins.

The state of being *pious* is *piety* (PYE uh tee). The opposite of *pious* is *impious* (IM pee us).

Note carefully the pronunciation of this word.

PIVOTAL (PIV uh tul) *adj* crucial

Pivotal is the adjective form of the verb to *pivot*. To *pivot* is to turn on a single point or shaft. A basketball player *pivots* when he turns while leaving one foot planted in the same place on the floor.

A *pivotal* comment is a comment that turns a discussion. It is a very important comment.

A *pivotal* member of a committee is a crucial or extremely important member of a committee.

Harry's contribution was *pivotal;* without it, we would have failed.

PLACATE (PLAY kayt) *v* to pacify; to appease; to soothe

The tribe *placated* the angry volcano by tossing a few teenagers
into the raging crater.

The beleaguered general tried to *placate* his fierce attacker by
sending him a pleasant flower arrangement. His duplicitous enemy
decided to attack anyway. He was *implacable.*

PLAINTIVE (PLAYN tiv) *adj* expressing sadness or sorrow

The lead singer's *plaintive* love song expressed his sorrow at being
abandoned by his girlfriend for the lead guitarist.

The chilly autumn weather made the little bird's song seem *plaintive.*

You could also say that there was *plaintiveness* in that bird's song.

Don't confuse *plaintive* with *plaintiff.* A *plaintiff* is a person who
takes someone to court—who makes a legal complaint.

PLATITUDE (PLAT uh tood) *n* a dull or trite remark; a cliché

The principal thinks he is a great orator, but his loud, boring speech
was full of *platitudes.*

Instead of giving us any real insight into the situation, the lecturer
threw *platitudes* at us for the entire period. It was a *platitudinous*
speech.

PLEBEIAN (pluh BEE un) *adj* common; vulgar; low class; bourgeois

Plebeian is the opposite of *aristocratic.*

Sarah refused to eat frozen dinners, saying they were too *plebeian*
for her discriminating palate.

Note carefully the pronunciation of this word.

PLETHORA (PLETH ur uh) *n* an excess

We ate a *plethora* of candy on Halloween and a *plethora* of turkey
on Thanksgiving.

Letting the air force use our backyard as a bombing range created a
plethora of problems.

Note carefully the pronunciation of this word.

POIGNANT (POYN yunt) *adj* painfully emotional; extremely moving;
sharp or astute

The words *poignant* and *pointed* are very closely related, and they
share much of the same range of meaning.

A *poignant* scene is one that is so emotional or moving that it is
almost painful to watch.

All the reporters stopped taking notes as they watched the old
woman's *poignant* reunion with her daughter, whom she hadn't seen in
eighty-five years.

Poignant can also mean pointed in the sense of sharp or astute. A
poignant comment might be one that shows great insight.

To be *poignant* is to have *poignancy.*

Q•U•I•C•K • Q•U•I•Z #64

Match each word in the first column with its definition in the second column. Check your answers in the back of the book.

1. pervade	a. painfully emotional
2. petulant	b. spread throughout
3. philanthropy	c. pacify
4. philistine	d. smugly ignorant person
5. pious	e. excess
6. pivotal	f. expressing sadness
7. placate	g. reverent
8. plaintive	h. trite remark
9. platitude	i. rude
10. plebeian	j. crucial
11. plethora	k. love for mankind
12. poignant	l. low class

POLARIZE (POH luh ryze) *v* to break up into opposing factions or groupings

The issue of what kind of sand to put in the sandbox *polarized* the nursery school class; some students would accept nothing but wet, while some wanted only dry.

The increasingly acrimonious debate between the two candidates *polarized* the political party.

POLEMIC (puh LEM ik) *n* a powerful argument often made to attack or refute a controversial issue

The book was a convincing *polemic* that revealed the fraud at the heart of the large corporation.

Instead of the traditional Groundhog Day address, the state senator delivered a *polemic* against the sales tax.

A *polemic* is *polemical.*

PONDEROUS (PAHN dur us) *adj* so large as to be clumsy; massive; dull

The wedding cake was a *ponderous* blob of icing and jelly beans.

The fat man was unable to type, because his *ponderous* belly prevented him from pushing his chair up to his desk.

The chairman, as usual, gave a *ponderous* speech that left half his listeners snoring in their plates.

PORTENT (POR tent) *n* an omen; a sign of something coming in the future

The distant rumbling we heard this morning was a *portent* of the thunderstorm that hit our area this afternoon.

Stock market investors looked for *portents* in their complicated charts and graphs; they hoped that the market's past behavior would give them a clue as to what would happen in the future.

Portentous ((por TENT uhs) is the adjective form of *portent,* meaning ominous or filled with *portent.* But it is very often used to mean pompous, or self-consciously serious or ominous sounding. It can also mean amazing or prodigious.

A *portentous* speech is not one that you would enjoy listening to.

A *portentous* announcement might be one that tried to create an inappropriate sense of alarm in those listening to it.

Portentous can also mean amazing or astonishing. A *portentous* sunset might be a remarkably glorious one rather than an ominous or menacing one.

POSTULATE (PAHS chuh lut) *n* something accepted as true without proof; an axiom

A *postulate* is taken to be true because it is convenient to do so. We might be able to prove a *postulate* if we had the time, but not now. A theorem is something that is proven using *postulates.*

Postulate (PAHS chuh layt) can be used as a verb, too. Sherlock Holmes rarely *postulated* things, waiting for evidence before he made up his mind.

PRAGMATIC (prag MAT ik) *adj* practical; down to earth; based on experience rather than theory

A *pragmatic* person is one who deals with things as they are rather than as they might be or should be.

Erecting a gigantic dome of gold over our house would have been the ideal solution to the leak in our roof, but the small size of our bank account forced us to be *pragmatic;* we patched the hole with a dab of tar instead.

Pragmatism (PRAG muh tiz um) is the belief or philosophy that the value or truth of something can be measured by its practical consequences.

PRECEDENT (PRES uh dunt) *n* an earlier example or model of something

Precedent is a noun form of the verb to *precede,* or go before. To set a *precedent* is to do something that sets an example for what may follow.

Last year's million-dollar prom set a *precedent* that the current student council hopes will not be followed in the future. That is, the student council hopes that future proms won't cost a million dollars.

To be *unprecedented* is to have no *precedent,* to be something entirely new. George's consumption of 10,677 hot dogs was *unprecedented;* no one had ever eaten so many hot dogs before.

PRECEPT (PREE sept) *n* a rule to live by; a principle establishing a certain kind of action or behavior; a maxim

"Love thy neighbor" is a *precept* we have sometimes found difficult to follow; our neighbor is a noisy oaf who painted his house electric blue and who throws his empty beer cans into our yard.

PRECIPITATE (pri SIP uh tayt) v to cause to happen abruptly

A panic among investors *precipitated* last Monday's crisis in the stock market.

The police were afraid that distributing machine guns to the angry protestors might *precipitate* a riot.

Precipitate (pri SIP uh tit) can also be an adjective, meaning unwisely hasty or rash. A *precipitate* decision is one made without enough thought beforehand.

The guidance counselor, we thought, was *precipitate* when he had the tenth grader committed to a mental hospital for saying that homework was boring.

PRECIPITOUS (pri SIP uh tus) *adj* steep

Precipitous means like a precipice, or cliff. It and *precipitate* are very closely related, as you probably guessed. But they don't mean the same thing, even though *precipitous* is often used loosely to mean the same thing as *precipitate*.

A mountain can be *precipitous*, meaning either that it is steep or that it comprises lots of steep cliffs.

Precipitous can also be used to signify things that are only figuratively steep. For example, you could say that someone had stumbled down a *precipitous* slope into drug addiction.

Q•U•I•C•K • Q•U•I•Z #65

Match each word in the first column with its definition in the second column. Check your answers in the back of the book.

1. polarize	a. massive and clumsy
2. polemic	b. rule to live by
3. ponderous	c. practical
4. portent	d. powerful refutation
5. portentous	e. steep
6. postulate	f. cause to happen abruptly
7. pragmatic	g. cause opposing positions
8. precedent	h. ominous
9. precept	i. earlier example
10. precipitate	j. omen
11. precipitous	k. axiom

PRECLUDE (pri KLOOD) v to prevent something from ever happening

Ann feared that her abysmal academic career might *preclude* her becoming a brain surgeon.

PRECURSOR (pri KUR sur) n forerunner; something that goes before and anticipates or paves the way for whatever it is that follows

The arrival of a million-dollar check in the mail might very well be the *precursor* of a brand-new car.

A sore throat is often the *precursor* of a cold.

Hard work on the practice field might be the *precursor* of success on the playing field.

PREDILECTION (pred uh LEK shun) *n* a natural preference for something

The impatient judge had a *predilection* for well-prepared lawyers who said what they meant and didn't waste his time.

Joe's *predilection* for saturated fats has added roughly a foot to his waistline in the past twenty years.

PREEMINENT (pree EM uh nunt) *adj* better than anyone else; outstanding; supreme

The nation's *preeminent* harpsichordist would be the best harpsichordist in the nation.

The Nobel Prize–winning physicist was *preeminent* in his field but he was still a lousy teacher.

See our listing for *eminent*.

PREEMPT (pree EMPT) *v* to seize something by prior right

When television show A *preempts* television show B, television show A is shown at the time usually reserved for television show B. The word *preempt* implies that television show A is more important than television show B and thus has a greater right to the time slot.

A *preemptive* action is one that is undertaken in order to prevent some other action from being undertaken. When the air force launched a *preemptive* strike against the missile base, the air force was attacking the missiles in order to prevent the missiles from attacking the air force.

PREMISE (PREM is) *n* an assumption; the basis for a conclusion

In deciding to eat all the ice cream in the freezer, my *premise* was that if I didn't do it, you would.

Based on the *premise* that two wrongs don't make a right, I hit him three times.

PREPOSSESS (pree puh ZES) *v* to preoccupy; to influence beforehand or prejudice; to make a good impression on beforehand

This word has several common meanings. Be careful.

When a person is *prepossessed* by an idea, he or she can't get it out of his or her mind. My dream of producing energy from old chewing-gum wrappers *prepossessed* me, and I lost my job, my home, my wife, and my children.

Experience had *prepossessed* Larry's mother not to believe him when he said that someone else had broken the window; Larry had broken it every other time, so she assumed that he had broken it this time.

The new girl in the class was extremely *prepossessing*. The minute she walked into the room, all the boys rushed over to introduce themselves. *Unprepossessing* means unimpressive, but the word is only mildly negative. The quaint farmhouse had an unprepossessing exterior, but a beautiful interior. Who would have imagined?

PREROGATIVE (pri RAHG uh tiv) *n* a right or privilege connected exclusively with a position, a person, a class, a nation, or some other group or classification

Giving traffic tickets to people he didn't like was one of the *prerogatives* of Junior's job as a policeman.

Sentencing people to death is a *prerogative* of kings and queens.

Big mansions and fancy cars are among the *prerogatives* of wealth.

PREVAIL (pri VAYL) *v* to triumph; to overcome rivals; (with *on, upon,* or *with*) to persuade

When justice *prevails*, it means that good defeats evil.

The prosecutor *prevailed* in the murder trial; the defendant was found guilty.

My mother *prevailed* on me to make my bed. She told me she would belt me if I didn't, so I did.

The adjective *prevailing* means most frequent or predominant. The *prevailing* opinion on a topic is the one that most people hold. If the *prevailing* winds are out of the north, then the wind is out of the north most of the time. A *prevailing* theory is the one most widely held at the time. It is *prevalent* (PREV uh lunt).

PRISTINE (PRIS teen) *adj* original; unspoiled; pure

An antique in *pristine* condition is one that hasn't been tampered with over the years. It's still in its original condition.

A *pristine* mountain stream is a stream that hasn't been polluted.

PRODIGAL (PRAHD uh gul) *adj* wastefully extravagant

The chef was *prodigal* with his employer's money, spending thousands of dollars on ingredients for what was supposed to be a simple meal.

The young artist was *prodigal* with his talents: he wasted time and energy on greeting cards that might have been devoted to serious paintings.

The *prodigal* gambler soon found that he couldn't afford even a two-dollar bet.

To be *prodigal* is to be characterized by *prodigality*.

Q•U•I•C•K • Q•U•I•Z #66

Match each word in the first column with its definition in the second column. Check your answers in the back of the book.

1. preclude
2. precursor
3. predilection
4. preeminent
5. preempt
6. premise
7. prepossess
8. prerogative
9. prevail
10. pristine
11. prodigal

a. outstanding
b. triumph
c. seize by prior right
d. wastefully extravagant
e. unspoiled
f. natural preference
g. preoccupy
h. right or privilege
i. assumption
j. forerunner
k. prevent

PRODIGIOUS (pruh DIJ us) *adj* extraordinary; enormous

To fill the Grand Canyon with Ping-Pong balls would be a *prodigious* undertaking; it would be both extraordinary and enormous.

The little boy caught a *prodigious* fish—it was ten times his size and might more easily have caught him had their situations been reversed.

See also *prodigy.*

PRODIGY (PRAHD uh jee) *n* an extremely talented child; an extraordinary accomplishment or occurrence

The three-year-old *prodigy* could play all of Beethoven and most of Brahms on his harmonica.

Larry was a mathematical *prodigy;* he had calculated *pi* to 100 decimal places almost before he could walk.

Josephine's tower of dominoes and Popsicle sticks was a *prodigy* of engineering.

PROFANE (proh FAYN) *adj* not having to do with religion; irreverent; blasphemous

Profane is the opposite of sacred. Worshiping the almighty dollar is *profane. Profane* can also mean disrespectful of religion. Sticking out your tongue in church would be a *profane* gesture.

Profane can also be a verb. You *profaned* the church by sticking out your tongue in it. Nick *profaned* his priceless Egyptian statue by using it as a doorstop.

The noun form of *profane* is *profanity* (proh FAN uh tee). Throwing a gallon of red paint at the front door of the church was an act of *profanity.*

PROFESS (pruh FES) *v* to declare; to declare falsely or pretend

Jason *professed* to teach himself calculus; he declared that he was going to do it.

No one in our town was fooled by the candidate's *professed* love for llama farmers; everyone knew he was just trying to win votes from the pro-llama faction.

PROFICIENT (pruh FISH unt) *adj* thoroughly competent; skillful; very good (at something)

Jerry was a *proficient* cabinetmaker. He could make a cabinet that would make you sit back and say, "Now, there's a cabinet."

I fiddled around at the piano for many years but never became *proficient* at playing.

Lucy was merely competent but Molly was *proficient* at plucking canaries.

Proficiency is the state of being *proficient*.

PROFLIGATE (PRAHF luh git) *adj* extravagantly wasteful and, usually, wildly immoral

The fraternity members were a *profligate* bunch; they held all-night orgies on weeknights and nearly burned down their fraternity house with their parties every weekend.

The young heir was *profligate* with his fortune, spending millions on champagne and racehorses.

PROFOUND (pruh FOUND) *adj* deep (in several senses)

Profound understanding is deep understanding.

To say something *profound* is to say something deeply intelligent or discerning.

Profound respect is deep respect. *Profound* horror is deep horror.

The noun of *profound* is *profundity* (pruh FUN duh tee).

PROFUSE (pruh FYOOS) *adj* flowing; extravagant

When we gave Marian our house, our car, and all our clothes, her gratitude was *profuse*.

My teacher said I had done a good job, but his praise was far from *profuse*. I got the feeling he hadn't really liked my epic poems about two dinosaurs who fall in love just before they go extinct.

The grieving widow's tears were *profuse*. She had tears in *profusion*.

PROLETARIAT (proh luh TER ee ut) *n* the industrial working class

The *proletariat* is the laboring class—blue-collar workers or people who roll up their shirtsleeves to do an honest day's work.

PROLIFERATE (proh LIF uh rayt) *v* to spread or grow rapidly

Honey bees *proliferated* when we filled our yard with flowering plants.

Coughs and colds *proliferate* when groups of children are cooped up together during the winter.

The police didn't know what to make of the *proliferation* of counterfeit money in the north end of town.

PROLIFIC (proh LIF ik) *adj* abundantly productive; fruitful or fertile

A *prolific* writer is a writer who writes a lot of books. A *prolific* artist is an artist who paints a lot of pictures.

The old man had been extraordinarily *prolific;* he had thirty children and more than one hundred grandchildren.

Q•U•I•C•K • Q•U•I•Z #67

Match each word in the first column with its definition in the second column. Check your answers in the back of the book.

1. prodigious	a. declare
2. prodigy	b. irreverent
3. profane	c. abundantly productive
4. profess	d. flowing
5. proficient	e. extremely talented child
6. profligate	f. extraordinary
7. profound	g. spread rapidly
8. profuse	h. deep
9. proletariat	i. thoroughly competent
10. proliferate	j. extravagantly wasteful
11. prolific	k. industrial working class

PROMULGATE (PRAHM ul gayt) *v* to proclaim; to publicly or formally declare something

The principal *promulgated* a new dress code over the loudspeaker system: red, green, yellow, and blue were the only permissible artificial hair colors.

PROPENSITY (pruh PEN suh tee) *n* a natural inclination or tendency; a predilection

Jessie has a *propensity* for saying stupid things: every time she opens her mouth, something stupid comes out.

Bill's *propensity* to sit around all day doing nothing came into conflict with his mother's *propensity* to kick him out of the house.

PROPITIOUS (pruh PISH us) *adj* marked by favorable signs or conditions

Rush hour is not a *propitious* time to drive into the city.

The early negotiations between the union and the company had been so *propitious* that no one was surprised when a new contract was announced well before the strike deadline.

PROPONENT (pruh POH nunt) *n* an advocate; a supporter of a position

Proponent and *opponent* are antonyms. The *proponents* of a tax increase will probably not be reelected next fall.

PROPRIETARY (pruh PRYE uh ter ee) *adj* characteristic of an owner of property; constituting property

To take a *proprietary* interest in something is to act as though you own it. George felt very *proprietary* about the chocolate-cookie recipe; he had invented it himself.

The company's design for musical toilet paper is *proprietary;* the company owns it, and outsiders can't look at it for nothing.

A *proprietor* (pruh PRYE uh tur) is an owner.

PROPRIETY (pruh PRYE uh tee) *n* properness; good manners

The old lady viewed the little girl's failure to curtsy as a flagrant breach of *propriety.* She did not approve of or countenance such *improprieties.*

Propriety prevented the young man from trashing the town in celebration of his unexpected acceptance by the college of his choice.

Propriety derives from *proper,* not *property.*

PROSAIC (proh ZAY ik) *adj* dull; unimaginative; like prose (as opposed to poetry)

His description of the battle was so *prosaic* that it was hard for his listeners to believe that any of the soldiers had even been wounded, much less blown to smithereens.

The little boy's ambitions were all *prosaic:* he said he wanted to be an accountant, an auditor, or a claims adjuster.

PROSCRIBE (proh SKRYBE) *v* to outlaw; to prohibit

Spitting on the sidewalk and shooting at road signs were both *proscribed* activities under the new administration.

The young doctor *proscribed* smoking in the waiting room of his office.

The act of *proscribing* is *proscription;* an individual act of *proscribing* is also a *proscription.*

PROSELYTIZE (PRAHS uh luh tyze) *v* to convert (someone) from one religion or doctrine to another; to recruit converts to a religion or doctrine

The former Methodist had been *proselytized* by a Lutheran deacon.

The airport terminal was filled with *proselytizers* from a dozen different sects, cults, and religions. They were attempting to *proselytize* the passengers walking through the terminal.

PROTAGONIST (proh TAG uh nist) *n* the leading character in a novel, play, or other work; a leader or champion

Martin Luther King, Jr., was a *protagonist* in the long and continuing struggle for racial equality.

The *protagonist* of the movie was an eleven-year-old boy who saved his hometown from destruction by eating all the doughnuts that the mad scientist had been using to fuel his nuclear reactor. The mad scientist was the boy's chief *antagonist.* An *antagonist* is an opponent or adversary.

PROTRACT (proh TRAKT) *v* to prolong

The trial was so *protracted* that one of the jurors died of old age and another gave birth.

The commencement speaker promised not to *protract* his remarks, but then he spoke for two solid hours. It was a *protracted* speech.

PROVIDENT (PRAHV uh dunt) *adj* preparing for the future; providing for the future; frugal

We were *provident* with our limited food supplies, knowing that the winter ahead would be long and cold.

The *provident* father had long ago set aside money for the college educations of each of his children.

To be *improvident* is to fail to provide for the future. It was *improvident* of the grasshopper not to store any food for the winter, unlike his acquaintance the *provident* ant.

Q•U•I•C•K • Q•U•I•Z #68

Match each word in the first column with its definition in the second column. Check your answers in the back of the book.

1. promulgate	a. natural inclination
2. propensity	b. good manners
3. propitious	c. advocate
4. proponent	d. prohibit
5. proprietary	e. prolong
6. propriety	f. leading character
7. prosaic	g. constituting property
8. proscribe	h. frugal
9. proselytize	i. dull
10. protagonist	j. marked by favorable signs
11. protract	k. convert
12. provident	l. proclaim

PROVINCIAL (pruh VIN shul) *adj* limited in outlook to one's own small corner of the world; narrow

The farmers were very *provincial*; they had no opinions about anything but the price of corn and no interest in anything except growing more of it.

New Yorkers have reputations for being very sophisticated and cosmopolitan, but most of them are actually very *provincial*; they act as though nothing of interest had ever happened on the other side of the Hudson River.

PROVISIONAL (pruh VIZH uh nul) *adj* conditional; temporary; tentative

Louis had been accepted as a *provisional* member of the club. He wouldn't become a permanent member until the other members had had a chance to see what he was really like.

The old man's offer to donate $10,000 to the charity was *provisional;* he said that he would give the money only if the charity could manage to raise a matching sum.

PROXIMITY (prok SIM uh tee) *n* nearness

I can't stand being in the *proximity* of a nuclear explosion. The radiation leaves my hair a mess.

In a big city, one is almost always in the *proximity* of a restaurant.

PRUDENT (PROOD unt) *adj* careful; having foresight

Joe is a *prudent* money manager. He doesn't invest heavily in racehorses, and he puts only a small part of his savings in the office football pool. Joe is the epitome of *prudence.*

The opposite of *prudent* is *imprudent.* It was *imprudent* of us to pour gasoline all over the floor of our living room and then light a fire in the fireplace.

PURPORTED (pur PORT id) *adj* rumored; claimed

The heiress is *purported* to have been kidnapped by adventurers and buried in a concrete vault beneath the busiest intersection in Times Square. No one believes this story except the psychic who was consulted by the police.

To *purport* something is to claim or allege it.

PUTATIVE (PYOO tuh tiv) *adj* commonly accepted; supposed; reputed

The *putative* reason for placing the monument downtown is that nobody had wanted it uptown. When you use the word *putative,* you emphasize that the reason is only supposed, not proven.

Q•U•I•C•K • Q•U•I•Z #69

Match each word in the first column with its definition in the second column. Check your answers in the back of the book.

1. provincial   a. commonly accepted
2. provisional   b. nearness
3. proximity   c. narrow in outlook
4. prudent   d. rumored
5. purported   e. careful
6. putative   f. conditional

Q

QUALIFY (KWAHL uh fye) *v* to modify or restrict

You already know the primary meaning of *qualify*. Here's another meaning.

Susan *qualified* her praise of Judith by saying that her kind words applied only to Judith's skillful cooking and not to her abhorrent personality. Judith was upset by Susan's *qualification*.

The library trustees rated their fund-raiser a *qualified* success; many more people than expected had come, but virtually no money had been raised.

An *unqualified* success is a complete, unrestricted success.

QUALITATIVE (KWAHL uh tay tiv) *adj* having to do with the *quality* or *qualities* of something (as opposed to the *quantity*)

If a school achieves a *qualitative* improvement in attendance, it means the school is being attended by better students. If the school achieves a *quantitative* improvement, it means the school is being attended by more students.

The difference between the two restaurants was *quantitative* rather than *qualitative*. Both served the same dreadful food, but the second restaurant served more of it.

QUERULOUS (KWER uh lus) *adj* complaining; grumbling; whining

Although a *query* is a question, *querulous* does not mean questioning.

The exasperated mother finally managed to hush her *querulous* child.

The *querulous* voices of the students, who believed that their quiz had been graded too harshly, could be heard all the way at the other end of the school building.

QUIXOTIC (kwik SAHT ik) *adj* romantic or idealistic to a foolish or impractical degree

The word *quixotic* is derived from the name of Don Quixote, the protagonist of Miguel de Cervantes's classic seventeenth-century novel. Don Quixote had read so many romances about the golden age of chivalry that he set out to become a knight himself and have chivalrous adventures. Instead, his romantic idealism almost invariably got him into trouble. To be *quixotic* is to be as foolish or impractical as Don Quixote in pursuing an ideal.

For many years Mr. Morris had led a *quixotic* effort to repeal the federal income tax.

The political organization had once been a powerful force in Washington, but its membership had dwindled and its causes had become increasingly *quixotic*.

Q•U•I•C•K • Q•U•I•Z #70

Match each word in the first column with its definition in the second column. Check your answers in the back of the book.

1. qualify
2. qualitative
3. quantitative
4. querulous
5. quixotic

a. having to do with quantity
b. foolishly romantic
c. complaining
d. modify or restrict
e. having to do with quality

R

RAMIFICATION (ram uh fuh KAY shun) *n* a consequence; a branching out

A tree could be said to *ramify,* or branch out, as it grows. A *ramification* is a consequence that grows out of something in the same way that a tree branch grows out of a tree trunk.

The professor found a solution to the problem, but there are many *ramifications;* some experts are afraid that he has created more problems than he has solved.

RANCOR (RANG kur) *n* bitter, long-lasting ill will or resentment

The mutual *rancor* felt by the two nations eventually led to war.

Jeremy's success produced such feelings of *rancor* in Jessica, his rival, that she was never able to tolerate being in the same room with him again.

To feel *rancor* is to be *rancorous.* The *rancorous* public exchanges between the two competing boxers are strictly for show; outside the ring, they are the best of friends.

RAPACIOUS (ruh PAY shus) *adj* greedy; plundering; avaricious

Wall Street investment bankers are often accused of being *rapacious,* but they claim they are performing a valuable economic function.

The noun form is *rapacity* (ruh PAS uh tee).

REBUKE (ri BYOOK) *v* to criticize sharply

The judge *rebuked* the convicted murderer for chopping up so many people and burying them in the woods.

We trembled as Mr. Solomon *rebuked* us for flipping over his car and taking off the tires.

A piece of sharp criticism is called a *rebuke.* When the students pushed their French teacher out the window, the principal delivered a *rebuke* that made their ears twirl.

REBUT (ri BUT) *v* to contradict; to argue in opposition to; to prove to be false

They all thought I was crazy, but none of them could *rebut* my argument.

The defense attorney attempted to *rebut* the prosecutor's claim that the defendant's fingerprints, hair, clothing, signature, wallet, wristwatch, credit cards, and car had been found at the scene of the crime.

An act or instance of *rebutting* is called a *rebuttal*. *Rebut* and *refute* are synonyms.

RECALCITRANT (ri KAL suh trunt) *adj* stubbornly defiant of authority or control; disobedient

The *recalcitrant* cancer continued to spread through the patient's body despite every therapy and treatment the doctors tried.

The country was in turmoil, but the *recalcitrant* dictator refused even to listen to the pleas of the international representatives.

RECANT (ri KANT) *v* to publicly take back and deny (something previously said or believed); to openly confess error

The chagrined scientist *recanted* his theory that mice originated on the moon; it turned out that he had simply mixed up the results of two separate experiments.

The secret police tortured the intellectual for a week, by tickling his feet with a feather duster, until he finally *recanted*.

An act of *recanting* is called a *recantation*.

RECIPROCAL (ri SIP ruh kul) *adj* mutual; shared; interchangeable

The Rochester Club had a *reciprocal* arrangement with the Duluth Club. Members of either club had full privileges of membership at the other.

Their hatred was *reciprocal;* they hated each other.

To *reciprocate* is to return in kind, to interchange, or to repay.

Our new neighbors had had us over for dinner several times, but we were unable to *reciprocate* immediately because our dining room was being remodeled.

Peter hit Paul over the head with a stick. Paul *reciprocated* by punching Peter in the nose.

A *reciprocity* (res uh PRAHS uh tee) is a *reciprocal* relation between two parties, often whereby both parties gain.

RECLUSIVE (ri KLOOS iv) *adj* hermitlike; withdrawn from society

The crazy millionaire led a *reclusive* existence, shutting himself up in his labyrinthine mansion and never setting foot in the outside world.

Our new neighbors were so *reclusive* that we didn't even meet them until a full year after they had moved in.

A *reclusive* person is a *recluse*. After his wife's death, the grieving old man turned into a *recluse* and seldom ventured out of his house.

RECONDITE (REK un dyte) *adj* hard to understand; over one's head

The philosopher's thesis was so *recondite* that I couldn't get past the first two sentences.

Every now and then the professor would lift his head from his desk and deliver some *recondite* pronouncement that left us scratching our heads and trying to figure out what he meant.

The scholarly journal was so *recondite* as to be utterly incomprehensible.

Note carefully the pronunciation of this word.

Q•U•I•C•K • Q•U•I•Z #71

Match each word in the first column with its definition in the second column. Check your answers in the back of the book.

1. ramification	a. hard to understand
2. rancor	b. criticize sharply
3. rapacious	c. consequence
4. rebuke	d. mutual
5. rebut	e. hermitlike
6. recalcitrant	f. bitter resentment
7. recant	g. stubbornly defiant
8. reciprocal	h. publicly deny
9. reclusive	i. contradict
10. recondite	j. greedy

RECRIMINATION (ri krim uh NAY shun) *n* a bitter counteraccusation, or the act of making a bitter counteraccusation

Mary was full of *recrimination*. When I accused her of stealing my pen, she angrily accused me of being careless, evil, and stupid.

The word is often used in the plural. The courtroom echoed with the *recriminations* of the convicted defendant as he was taken off to the penitentiary.

To make a *recrimination* is to *recriminate*. The adjective is *recriminatory* (ruh KRIM uh nuh tor ee).

REDOLENT (RED uh lunt) *adj* fragrant

The air in autumn is *redolent* of wood smoke and fallen leaves.

The flower arrangements on the tables were both beautiful and *redolent*.

Something that is *redolent* has *redolence*.

Redolent also means suggestive. The new play was *redolent* of one I had seen many years ago.

REDUNDANT (ri DUN dunt) *adj* unnecessarily repetitive; excessive; excessively wordy

Bill had already bought paper plates, so our purchase of paper plates was *redundant*.

Harry's article was *redundant*—he kept saying the same thing over and over again.

An act of being *redundant* is a *redundancy*. The title "Department of Redundancy Department" is *redundant*.

REFUTE (ri FYOOT) *v* to prove to be false; to disprove

His expensive suit and imported shoes clearly *refuted* his claim that he was poor.

I *refuted* Larry's mathematical proof by showing him that it depended on two and two adding up to five.

An act of *refuting* is called a *refutation*. The audience enjoyed the panelist's humorous *refutation* of the main speaker's theory about the possibility of building an antigravity airplane.

Something that is indubitable, something that cannot be disproven, is *irrefutable*. Carrie's experiments with jelly beans and pencil erasers offered *irrefutable* proof that jelly beans taste better than pencil erasers.

REITERATE (ree IT uh rayt) *v* to say again; to repeat

The candidate had *reiterated* his position so many times on the campaign trail that he sometimes even muttered it in his sleep.

To *reiterate,* let me say once again that I am very happy to have been invited to the birthday celebration of your adorable Pekingese.

An act of *reiterating* is called a *reiteration*. Bobby's *reiteration* of his demands was entirely unnecessary, since we already knew what they were.

RELEGATE (REL uh gayt) *v* to banish; to send away

The most junior of the junior executives was *relegated* to a tiny, windowless office that had once been a broom closet.

The new father's large collection of jazz records was *relegated* to the cellar to make room for the new baby's larger collection of stuffed animals. The father objected to the *relegation* of his record collection to the cellar, but his objection did no good.

RELENTLESS (ri LENT lis) *adj* continuous; unstoppable

To *relent* is to stop or give up. *Relentless,* or *unrelenting,* means not stopping. The insatiable rabbit was *relentless;* it ate and ate until nothing was left in the botanical garden. The torrential rains were *relentless,* eventually creating a deluge.

RELINQUISH (ri LING kwish) *v* to release or let go of; to surrender; to stop doing

The hungry dog refused to *relinquish* the enormous beef bone that he had stolen from the butcher's shop.

The retiring president *relinquished* control of the company only with the greatest reluctance.

Sandra was forty-five years old before she finally *relinquished* her view of herself as a glamorous teenaged beauty.

REMONSTRATE (ri MAHN strayt) *v* to argue against; to protest; to raise objections

My boss *remonstrated* with me for telling all the secretaries they could take the rest of the week off.

The manager *remonstrated,* but the umpire continued to insist that the base runner had been out at third. When the manager continued to *remonstrate,* the umpire threw him out of the game.

An act of *remonstrating* is a *remonstration.*

RENAISSANCE (REN uh sahns) *n* a rebirth or revival

The capital R *Renaissance* was a great blossoming of art, literature, science, and culture in general that transformed Europe between the fourteenth and seventeenth centuries. The word is also used in connection with lesser rebirths.

The declining neighborhood underwent a *renaissance* when a group of investors bought several crumbling tenements and turned them into attractive apartment buildings.

The small college's football team had endured many losing seasons but underwent a dramatic renaissance when the new coach recruited half a dozen 400-pound freshmen.

Renaissance can also be spelled *renascence* (ri NAY suns).

RENOUNCE (ri NOWNCE) *v* to give up formally or resign; to disown; to have nothing to do with anymore

Despite the pleadings and protestations of her parents, Deborah refused to *renounce* her love for the leader of the motorcycle gang.

The presidential candidate *renounced* his manager after it was revealed that the zealous manager had tried to murder the candidate's opponent in the primary.

To *renounce* is to make a *renunciation* (ri nun see AY shun).

Q•U•I•C•K • Q•U•I•Z #72

Match each word in the first column with its definition in the second column. Check your answers in the back of the book.

1. recrimination	a. surrender
2. redolent	b. disown
3. redundant	c. rebirth
4. refute	d. argue against
5. reiterate	e. fragrant
6. relegate	f. banish
7. relinquish	g. say again
8. remonstrate	h. bitter counteraccusation
9. renaissance	i. unnecessarily repetitive
10. renounce	j. prove to be false

REPARATION (rep uh RAY shun) *n* paying back; making amends; compensation

To make a *reparation* is to *repair* some damage that has occurred. This word is often used in the plural. The defeated country demanded *reparations* for the destruction it had suffered at the hands of the victorious army.

After the accident we sought *reparation* in court, but our lawyer was not competent and we didn't win a cent.

Something that cannot be *repaired* is *irreparable* (i REP uh ruh bul).

Note carefully the pronunciation of these words.

REPERCUSSION (ree pur KUSH un) *n* a consequence; an indirect effect

One *repercussion* of the new tax law was that accountants found themselves with a lot of new business.

The declaration of war had many *repercussions,* including a big increase in production at the bomb factory.

REPLENISH (ri PLEN ish) *v* to fill again; to resupply; to restore

The manager of the hardware store needed to *replenish* his stock; quite a few of the shelves were empty.

The commanding general *replenished* his army with a trainload of food and other supplies.

After the big Thanksgiving meal, everyone felt *replenished.*

An act of *replenishing* is a *replenishment.*

The *replenishment* of our firewood supply was our first thought after the big snowstorm.

REPLETE (ri PLEET) *adj* completely filled; abounding

The once polluted stream was now *replete* with fish of every description.

The bride wore a magnificent sombrero *replete* with fuzzy dice and campaign buttons.

Tim ate all nine courses at the wedding banquet. He was filled to the point of *repletion.*

REPREHENSIBLE (rep ri HEN suh bul) *adj* worthy of blame or censure

He put the cat in the laundry chute, tied the dog to the chimney, and committed several other *reprehensible* acts.

Malcolm's manners were *reprehensible:* he ate his soup by drinking it from his empty wineglass and flipped his peas into his mouth with the back of his salad fork.

REPRISAL (ri PRYE zul) *n* a military action undertaken in revenge for another; an act of taking "an eye for an eye"

The raid on the Iranian oil-drilling platform was a *reprisal* for the Iranians' earlier attack on the American tanker.

Fearing *reprisals* from the terrorists, the CIA beefed up its security after capturing the terrorist leader.

REPROACH (ri PROHCH) v to scold, usually in disappointment; to blame; to disgrace

My doctor *reproached* me for gaining twenty pounds after he had advised me to lose fifteen.

The police officer *reproached* me for leaving my car parked overnight in a no-standing zone.

Reproach can also be a noun. To look at someone with *reproach* is to look at that person critically or accusingly. To be filled with *self-reproach* can mean to be ashamed.

Impeccable behavior is beyond fault, it is *irreproachable*. Even though Jerome did split Aunt Mabel's skull with an ax, his motive was *irreproachable:* he had merely been trying to kill a fly perched on her hairnet.

REPROVE (ri PROOV) v to criticize mildly

Aunt May *reproved* us for eating too much, but we could tell she was actually thrilled that we had enjoyed the meal.

My wife *reproved* me for leaving my dirty dish in the sink.

An act of *reproving* is called a *reproof.* The judge's decision was less a sentence than a gentle *reproof;* he put Jerry on probation and told him never to get in trouble again.

REPUDIATE (ri PYOO dee ayt) v to reject; to renounce; to disown; to have nothing to do with

Hoping to receive a lighter sentence, the convicted gangster *repudiated* his former connection with the mob.

REQUISITE (REK wuh zit) adj required; necessary

Howard bought a hunting rifle and the *requisite* ammunition.

As the *requisite* number of members was not in attendance, the chairman adjourned the meeting just after it had begun.

Requisite can also be a noun, meaning a requirement or a necessity. A hammer and a saw are among the *requisites* of the carpenter's trade.

A *prerequisite* is something required before you can get started. A high school diploma is usually a *prerequisite* to entering college.

RESOLUTE (REZ uh loot) adj determined; firm; unwavering

Uncle Ted was *resolute* in his decision not to have a good time at our Christmas party; he stood alone in the corner and muttered to himself all night long.

The other team was strong, but our players were *resolute*. They kept pushing and shoving until, in the final moments, they won the roller-derby tournament.

Someone who sticks to his New Year's *resolution* is *resolute. Resolute* and *resolved* are synonyms.

To be *irresolute* is to be wavering or indecisive. Our *irresolute* leader led us first one way and then the other way in the process of getting us thoroughly and completely lost.

Q•U•I•C•K • Q•U•I•Z #73

Match each word in the first column with its definition in the second column. Check your answers in the back of the book.

1. reparation	a. act of revenge
2. repercussion	b. determined
3. replenish	c. worthy of blame
4. replete	d. consequence
5. reprehensible	e. scold
6. reprisal	f. completely filled
7. reproach	g. paying back
8. reprove	h. necessary
9. repudiate	i. criticize mildly
10. requisite	j. fill again
11. resolute	k. reject

RESPITE (RES pit) *n* a period of rest or relief

We worked without *respite* from five in the morning until five in the afternoon.

The new mother fell asleep when her baby stopped crying, but the *respite* was brief; the baby started up again almost immediately.

Note carefully the pronunciation of this word.

RETICENT (RET uh sunt) *adj* quiet; restrained; reluctant to speak, especially about oneself

Luther's natural *reticence* made him an ideal speaker: his speeches never lasted more than a few minutes.

Jeffrey was *reticent* on the subject of his accomplishments; he didn't like to talk about himself.

To be *reticent* is to be characterized by *reticence*.

REVERE (ri VEER) *v* to respect highly; to honor

Einstein was a preeminent scientist who was *revered* by everyone, even his rivals. Einstein enjoyed nearly universal *reverence* (REV uh rins). To be *irreverent* is to be mildly disrespectful. Peter made jokes about his younger sister's painting. She was perturbed at his *irreverence* and began to cry.

RHETORIC (RET ur ik) *n* the art of formal speaking or writing; inflated discourse

A talented public speaker might be said to be skilled in *rhetoric*.

The word is often used in a pejorative sense to describe speaking or writing that is skillfully executed but insincere or devoid of meaning. A political candidate's speech that was long on drama and promises but short on genuine substance might be dismissed as "mere *rhetoric*."

To use *rhetoric* is to be *rhetorical* (ruh TOR ik uhl). A *rhetorical* question is one the speaker intends to answer himself or herself—that is, a question asked only for *rhetorical* effect.

RIGOROUS (RIG ur us) *adj* strict; harsh; severe
To be *rigorous* is to act with *rigor*.
Our exercise program was *rigorous* but effective; after just a few months, our eighteen hours of daily exercise had begun to pay off.
The professor was popular largely because he wasn't very *rigorous;* there were no tests in his course and only one paper, which was optional.

ROBUST (roh BUST) *adj* strong and healthy; vigorous
The hundred-year-old man was still *robust.* Every morning he ran several miles down to the ocean and jumped in.
The tree we planted last year isn't looking very *robust.* Most of the leaves have fallen off, and the bark has begun to peel.

ROGUE (rohg) *n* a criminally dishonest person; a scoundrel
A *rogue* is someone who can't be trusted. This word is often used, however, to characterize a playfully mischievous person.

RUDIMENTARY (roo duh MEN tuh ree) *adj* basic; crude; unformed or undeveloped
The primitive tribe's tools were very *rudimentary.* In fact, they looked more like rocks than like tools.
The boy who had lived with wolves for fifteen years lacked even the most *rudimentary* social skills.
The strange creature had small bumps on its torso that appeared to be *rudimentary* limbs.

RUMINATE (ROO muh nayt) *v* to contemplate; to ponder; to mull over
Ruminate comes from a Latin word meaning to chew cud. Cows, sheep, and other cud-chewing animals are called *ruminants.* To *ruminate* is to quietly chew on or ponder your own thoughts.
The teacher's comment about the causes of weather set me to *ruminating* about what a nice day it was and to wishing that I were outside.
The very old man spent his last days *ruminating* about death and eating box after box of vanilla wafers.
An act of *ruminating* is called a *rumination.* Serge was a very private man; he kept his *ruminations* to himself.

RUSTIC (RUS tik) *adj* rural; lacking urban comforts or sophistication; primitive
Life in the log cabin was too *rustic* for Leah; she missed hot showers, cold beer, and electricity.
Rustic can be used as a noun. A *rustic* is an unsophisticated person from the country. We enjoyed the *rustic* scenery as we traveled through the countryside. To *rusticate* is to spend time in the country.

Q•U•I•C•K • Q•U•I•Z #74

Match each word in the first column with its definition in the second column. Check your answers in the back of the book.

1. respite	a. basic
2. reticent	b. contemplate
3. retract	c. vigorous
4. reverberate	d. withdraw
5. revere	e. formal writing or speaking
6. rhetoric	f. restrained
7. rigorous	g. rural
8. robust	h. period of rest
9. rogue	i. echo
10. rudimentary	j. strict
11. ruminate	k. honor
12. rustic	l. scoundrel

S

SACCHARINE (SAK uh rin) *adj* sweet; excessively or disgustingly sweet

Saccharin is a calorie-free sweetener; *saccharine* means sweet. Except for the spelling, this is one of the easiest-to-remember words there is. Don't screw up.

Saccharine can be applied to things that are literally sweet, such as sugar, *saccharin*, fruit, and so on. It can also be applied to things that are sweet in a figurative sense, such as children, personalities, and sentiments—especially things that are *too* sweet, or sweet in a sickening way.

We wanted to find a nice card for Uncle Moe, but the cards in the display at the drugstore all had such *saccharine* messages that we would have been too embarrassed to send any of them.

The love story was so *saccharine* that I ended up loathing the heroine and wishing the hero would belch or pick his nose just to break the gooey monotony.

SACRILEGE (SAK ruh lij) *n* a violation of something sacred; blasphemy

The minister committed the *sacrilege* of delivering his sermon while wearing his golf shoes; he didn't want to be late for his tee-off time, which was just a few minutes after the scheduled end of the service.

The members of the fundamentalist sect believed that dancing, going to movies, and watching television were *sacrileges*.

To commit a *sacrilege* is to be *sacrilegious*. Be careful with the spelling of these words.

SACROSANCT (SAK roh sangkt) *adj* sacred; held to be inviolable

A church is *sacrosanct.* So, for Christians, is belief in the divinity of Jesus Christ.

Sacrosanct is also used loosely, and often ironically, outside of religion. Mr. Peters's lunchtime trip to his neighborhood bar was *sacrosanct;* he would no sooner skip it than he would skip his mother's funeral.

SAGACIOUS (suh GAY shus) *adj* discerning; shrewd; keen in judgment; wise

Edgar's decision to move the chickens into the barn turned out to be *sagacious;* about an hour later, the hailstorm hit.

The announcer's *sagacious* commentary made the baseball game seem vastly more interesting than we had expected it to be.

To be *sagacious* is to have *sagacity* (suh GAS uh tee). A similar word is *sage,* which means wise, possessing wisdom derived from experience or learning.

When we were contemplating starting our own popcorn business, we received some *sage* advice from a man who had lost all his money selling candied apples.

The professor's critique, which consisted of just a few *sage* comments, sent me back to my room feeling pretty stupid.

Sage can also be a noun. A wise person, especially a wise old person, is often called a *sage.*

SALIENT (SAYL yunt) *adj* sticking out; conspicuous; leaping

A *salient* characteristic is one that leaps right out at you.

Ursula had a number of *salient* features including, primarily, her nose, which stuck out so far that she was constantly in danger of slamming it in doors and windows.

Note carefully the pronunciation of this word.

SALUTARY (SAL yuh ter ee) *adj* healthful; remedial; curative

Lowered blood pressure is among the *salutary* effects of exercise.

The long sea voyage was *salutary;* when Elizabeth landed she looked ten years younger than she had when she set sail.

SANCTIMONIOUS (sangk tuh MOH nee us) *adj* pretending to be devout; affecting religious feeling

The *sanctimonious* old bore pretended to be deeply offended when Lucius whispered a mild swearword after dropping the anvil on his bare foot.

Simon is an egoist who speaks about almost nothing but caring for one's fellow man. His altruism is *sanctimonious.*

SANGUINE (SANG gwin) *adj* cheerful; optimistic; hopeful

Peter was *sanguine* about his chances of winning the Nobel Peace Prize, even though, as an eighth grader, he hadn't really done anything to deserve it.

The ebullient checkers champion remained *sanguine* in defeat; he was so sure of himself that he viewed even catastrophe as merely a temporary setback.

Don't confuse *sanguine* (a nice word) with *sanguinary* (not a nice word). *Sanguinary* means bloodthirsty.

SARDONIC (sahr DAHN ik) *adj* mocking; scornful

Robert's weak attempts at humor were met by nothing but a few scattered pockets of *sardonic* laughter.

Even George's friends found him excessively *sardonic;* he couldn't discuss anything without mocking it, and there was almost nothing about which he could bring himself to say two nice words in a row.

Q•U•I•C•K • Q•U•I•Z #75

Match each word in the first column with its definition in the second column. Check your answers in the back of the book.

1. saccharine	a. blasphemy
2. sacrilege	b. wise
3. sacrosanct	c. sweet
4. sagacious	d. pretending to be devout
5. sage	e. healthful
6. salient	f. mocking
7. salutary	g. cheerful
8. sanctimonious	h. sacred
9. sanguine	i. sticking out
10. sardonic	j. discerning

SCINTILLATE (SIN tuh layt) *v* to sparkle, either literally or figuratively

Stars and diamonds *scintillate.* So do witty comments, charming personalities, and anything else that can be said to sparkle.

Warner was a quiet drudge at home, but at a party he could be absolutely *scintillating,* tossing off witty remarks and charming everyone in the room.

Benny's grades last term weren't *scintillating,* to put it mildly; he had four Ds and an F.

The act of *scintillating* is called *scintillation.*

SCRUPULOUS (SKROO pyuh lus) *adj* strict; careful; hesitant for ethical reasons

Doug was *scrupulous* in keeping his accounts; he knew where every penny came from and where every penny went.

We tried to be *scrupulous* about not dripping paint, but by the time the day was over there was nearly as much paint on the floor as there was on the walls.

Philip was too *scrupulous* to make a good armed robber; every time he started to point his gun at someone, he was overcome by ethical doubts.

A *scruple* is a qualm or moral doubt. To have no *scruples*—to be *unscrupulous*—is to have no conscience.

SCRUTINIZE (SKROOT uh nyze) *v* to examine very carefully

I *scrutinized* the card catalog at the library but couldn't find a single book on the topic I had chosen for my term paper.

The rocket scientists *scrutinized* thousands of pages of computer printouts, looking for a clue to why the rocket had exploded.

My mother *scrutinized* my clothes and my appearance before I left for the evening, but even after several minutes of careful analysis she was unable to find anything to complain about.

To *scrutinize* something is to subject it to *scrutiny*. The clever forgery fooled the museum curator but did not withstand the *scrutiny* of the experts; after studying for several weeks, the experts pronounced the painting to be a fake.

Something that cannot be examined is *inscrutable*. *Inscrutable* means mysterious, impossible to understand. We had no idea what Bill was thinking since his smile was *inscrutable*. Poker players try to be *inscrutable* to their opponents.

SECULAR (SEK yuh lur) *adj* having nothing to do with religion or spiritual concerns

The halfway house had several nuns on its staff, but it was an entirely *secular* operation; it was run by the city, not the church.

The priest's *secular* interests include German food and playing the trombone.

SEDITION (si DISH un) *n* treason; the incitement of public disorder or rebellion

Revolutions usually begin as a small band of *seditious* individuals plot to change the established order.

SENSORY (SEN suh ree) *adj* having to do with the senses or sensation

Babies enjoy bright colors, moving objects, pleasant sounds, and other forms of *sensory* stimulation.

Your ears, eyes, and tongue are all *sensory* organs. It is through them that your *senses* operate.

Extrasensory perception is the supposed ability of some people to perceive things without using the standard senses of sight, hearing, smell, touch, or taste.

Two similar-sounding and often confusing words are *sensual* and *sensuous*. To be *sensual* is to be devoted to gratifying one's senses through physical pleasure, especially sexual pleasure; to be *sensuous* is to delight the senses. A *sensual* person is one who eagerly indulges his or her physical desires. A *sensuous* person is one who stimulates the senses of others (sometimes, though by no means invariably, inspiring in them thoughts of *sensual* gratification).

SENTIENT (SEN shunt) *adj* able to perceive by the senses; conscious

Human beings are *sentient*. Rocks are not.

Note carefully the pronunciation of this word.

SEQUESTER (si KWES tur) *v* to set or keep apart

Since much of the rest of the city had become a battle zone, the visiting entertainers were *sequestered* in the international hotel.

The struggling writer *sequestered* himself in his study for several months, trying to produce the Great American Novel.

Juries are sometimes *sequestered* during trials to prevent them from talking to people or reading newspapers.

Q•U•I•C•K • Q•U•I•Z #76

Match each word in the first column with its definition in the second column. Check your answers in the back of the book.

1. scintillate
2. scrupulous
3. scrutinize
4. secular
5. sedition
6. sensory
7. sensual
8. sensuous
9. sentient
10. sequester

a. sparkle
b. having nothing to do with religion
c. treason
d. having to do with the senses
e. set apart
f. strict
g. delighting the senses
h. examine very carefully
i. devoted to pleasure
j. conscious

SERENDIPITY (ser un DIP uh tee) *n* accidental good fortune; discovering good things without looking for them

It was *serendipity* rather than genius that led the archaeologist to his breathtaking discovery of the ancient civilization. While walking his dog in the desert, he tripped over the top of a buried tomb.

Something that occurs through *serendipity* is *serendipitous*. Our arrival at the airport *serendipitously* coincided with that of the queen, and she offered us a ride to our hotel in her carriage.

SERVILE (SUR vyle) *adj* submissive and subservient; like a servant

Cat lovers sometimes say that dogs are too *servile;* they follow their owners everywhere and slobber all over them at every opportunity.

The horrible boss demanded *servility* from his employees; when he said "Jump!" he expected them to ask "How high?"

A very similar word is *slavish* (SLAY vish), which means even more subservient than *servile. Slavish* devotion to a cause is devotion in spite of everything. An artist's *slavish* imitator would be an imitator who imitated everything about the artist.

SINGULAR (SING gyuh lur) *adj* unique; superior; exceptional; strange

Dale had the *singular* ability to stand on one big toe for several hours at a stretch.

The man on the train had a *singular* deformity: both of his ears were on the same side of his head.

A *singularity* is a unique occurrence. *Singularity* is also the quality of being unique.

SLANDER (SLAN dur) *v* to speak badly about someone publicly; to defame; to spread malicious rumor

Jonathan *slandered* Mr. Perriwinkle by telling everyone in school that the principal wore a toupee; Mr. Perriwinkle resented this *slander*. Since he was the principal, he expelled the *slanderous* student.

SLOTH (slawth) *n* laziness; sluggishness

You may have seen a picture of an animal called a *sloth*. It hangs upside down from tree limbs and is never in a hurry to do anything. To fall into *sloth* is to act like a *sloth*.

Ivan's weekends were devoted to *sloth*. He never arose before noon, and he seldom left the house before Monday morning.

To be lazy and sluggish is to be *slothful*. Ophelia's *slothful* husband virtually lived on the couch in the living room, and the television remote-control device was in danger of becoming grafted to his hand.

SOBRIETY (suh BRYE uh tee) *n* the state of being sober; seriousness

A *sober* person is a person who isn't drunk. A *sober* person can also be a person who is serious, solemn, or not ostentatious. *Sobriety* means both "undrunkness" and seriousness or solemnity.

Sobriety was such an unfamiliar condition that the reforming alcoholic didn't recognize it at first.

Sobriety of dress is one characteristic of the hardworking Amish.

Note carefully the pronunciation of this word.

SOLICITOUS (suh LIS uh tus) *adj* eager and attentive, often to the point of hovering; anxiously caring or attentive

Every time we turned around, we seemed to step on the foot of the *solicitous* salesman, who appeared to feel that if he left us alone for more than a few seconds, we would decide to leave the store.

When the sick movie star sneezed, half a dozen *solicitous* nurses came rushing into his hospital room.

The noun is *solicitude*.

SOLVENT (SAHL vunt) *adj* not broke or bankrupt; able to pay one's bills

Jerry didn't hope to become a millionaire; all he wanted to do was remain *solvent*.

The struggling company was battered but still *solvent* after it paid its billion-dollar fine for selling exploding Christmas ornaments.

To be broke is to be *insolvent*. An *insolvent* company is one that can't cover its debts.

The state of being *solvent* is called *solvency;* the state of being *insolvent* is called *insolvency*.

SOPORIFIC (sahp uh RIF ik) *adj* sleep inducing; extremely boring; very sleepy

The doctor calmed his hysterical patient by injecting him with some sort of *soporific* medication.

Sam's *soporific* address was acknowledged not by applause but by a chorus of snores.

The *soporific* creature from the bottom of the sea lay in a gigantic blob on the beach for several days, and then roused itself enough to consume the panic-stricken city.

Q•U•I•C•K • Q•U•I•Z #77

Match each word in the first column with its definition in the second column. Check your answers in the back of the book.

1. serendipity	a. accidental good fortune
2. servile	b. sleep inducing
3. singular	c. eager and attentive
4. slavish	d. not bankrupt
5. sloth	e. submissive
6. sobriety	f. broke
7. solicitous	g. laziness
8. solvent	h. state of being sober
9. insolvent	i. extremely subservient
10. soporific	j. unique

SORDID (SOR did) *adj* vile; filthy; squalid

The college roommates led a *sordid* existence whose principal ingredients were dirty laundry, rotting garbage, and body odor.

The conspirators plotted their *sordid* schemes at a series of secret meetings in an abandoned warehouse.

The drug dealers had turned a once-pretty neighborhood into a *sordid* outpost of despair and crime.

SPAWN (spawn) *v* to bring forth; to produce a large number

A bestselling book or blockbuster movie will *spawn* dozens of imitators.

SPECIOUS (SPEE shus) *adj* deceptively plausible or attractive

The charlatan's *specious* theories about curing baldness with used tea bags charmed the television studio audience but did not convince the experts, who believed that fresh tea bags were more effective.

The river's beauty turned out to be *specious;* what had looked like churning rapids from a distance was, on closer inspection, some sort of foamy industrial waste.

To be *specious* is to be characterized by *speciousness.*

SPORADIC (spuh RAD ik) *adj* stopping and starting; scattered; occurring in bursts every once in a while

The bathers were made jittery by *sporadic* gunfire that peppered the beach.

Kyle's attention to his schoolwork was *sporadic* at best; he tended to lose his concentration after a few minutes of effort.

SPURIOUS (SPYOOR ee us) *adj* false; fake

An apocryphal story is one whose truth is uncertain. A *spurious* story, however, is out-and-out false, no doubt about it. The political candidate attributed his loss to numerous *spurious* rumors that hounded him throughout his campaign.

SQUALOR (SKWAHL ur) *n* filth; wretched, degraded, or repulsive living conditions

If people live in *squalor* for too long, the ruling elite can count on an insurgency.

SQUANDER (SKWAHN dur) *v* to waste

Jerry failed to husband his inheritance; instead, he *squandered* it on stuffed toys.

STAGNATION (stag NAY shun) *n* motionlessness; inactivity

The company grew quickly for several years, then fell into *stagnation*.

Many years of carelessly dumping pollutants led to the gradual *stagnation* of the river.

To fall into *stagnation* is to *stagnate*. To be in a state of *stagnation* is to be *stagnant*.

STATIC (STAT ik) *adj* stationary; not changing or moving

Sales of the new book soared for a few weeks, then became *static*.

The movie was supposed to be a thriller, but we found it to be tediously *static;* nothing seemed to happen from one scene to the next.

STAUNCH (stawnch) *adj* firmly committed; firmly in favor of; steadfast

A *staunch* Republican is someone who always votes for Republican candidates. A *staunch* supporter of tax reform would be someone who firmly believes in tax reform. To be *staunch* in your support of something is to be unshakable.

STEADFAST (STED fast) *adj* loyal; faithful

Steadfast love is love that never wavers. To be *steadfast* in a relationship is to be faithfully committed. To be *steadfast* is to be like a rock: unchanging, unwavering, unmoving.

STIGMATIZE (STIG muh tyze) *v* to brand with disgrace; to set a mark of disgrace upon

Steve's jeans were Lee's instead of Levi's, and this mistake *stigmatized* him for the rest of his high school career.

A *stigma* is a mark of disgrace.

STIPULATE (STIP yuh layt) *v* to require something as part of an agreement

You are well advised to *stipulate* the maximum amount you will pay in any car-repair contract.

Guarantees often *stipulate* certain conditions that must be met if the guarantee is to be valid.

STOIC (STOH ik) *adj* indifferent (at least outwardly) to pleasure or pain, to joy or grief, to fortune or misfortune

Nina was *stoic* about the death of her canary; she went about her business as though nothing sad had happened.

We tried to be *stoic* about our defeat, but as soon as we got into the locker room, we all began to cry and bang our foreheads on the floor.

STRATUM (STRAT um) *n* a layer; a level

The middle class is one *stratum* of society.

The plural of *stratum* is *strata*. A hierarchy is composed of *strata*.

To *stratify* is to make into layers.

This word can also be pronounced "STRAY tum."

STRICTURE (STRIK chur) *n* a restriction; a limitation; a negative criticism

Despite the *strictures* of apartment living, we enjoyed the eight years we spent in New York City.

The unfavorable lease placed many *strictures* on how the building could be used.

The poorly prepared violinist went home trembling after his concert to await the inevitable *strictures* of the reviewers.

Q•U•I•C•K • Q•U•I•Z #78

Match each word in the first column with its definition in the second column. Check your answers in the back of the book.

1. sordid	a. disgrace
2. spawn	b. stopping and starting
3. specious	c. restriction
4. sporadic	d. inactivity
5. spurious	e. require
6. squander	f. indifferent to pain, pleasure
7. stagnation	g. bring forth
8. static	h. vile
9. staunch	i. firmly committed (2)
10. steadfast	j. layer
11. stigmatize	k. stationary
12. stipulate	l. deceptively plausible
13. stoic	m. false
14. stratum	n. waste
15. stricture	

STRIFE (stryfe) *n* bitter conflict; discord; a struggle or clash
Marital *strife* often leads to divorce.

STRINGENT (STRIN junt) *adj* strict; restrictive
The restaurant's *stringent* dress code required diners to wear paper hats, army boots, and battery-operated twirling bow ties.

The IRS accountant was quite *stringent* in his interpretation of the tax code; he disallowed virtually all of Leslie's deductions.

STYMIE (STYE mee) *v* to thwart; to get in the way of; to hinder
Stymie is a golfing term. A golfer is *stymied* when another player's ball lies on the direct path between his or her own ball and the cup.

Off the golf course, one might be *stymied* by one's boss. In my effort to make a name for myself in the company, I was *stymied* by my boss, who always managed to take credit for all the good things I did and to blame me for his mistakes.

SUBJUGATE (SUB juh gayt) *v* to subdue and dominate; to enslave
I bought the fancy riding lawn mower because I thought it would make my life easier, but it quickly *subjugated* me; all summer long, it seems, I did nothing but change its oil, sharpen its blades, and drive it back and forth between my house and the repair shop.

The tyrant *subjugated* all the peasants living in the kingdom; once free, they were now forced to do his bidding.

SUBLIME (suh BLYME) *adj* awesome; extremely exalted; lofty; majestic
After winning $70 million in the lottery and quitting our jobs as sewer workers, our happiness was *sublime.*

Theodore was a *sublime* thinker; after pondering even a difficult problem for just a few minutes, he would invariably arrive at a concise and elegant solution.

The soup at the restaurant was *sublime.* I've never tasted anything so good.

The noun form of *sublime* is *sublimity* (suh BLIM i tee). Don't confuse *sublime* with *subliminal* (suh BLIM uh nuhl), which means subconscious, or *sublimate*, which means to suppress one's subconscious mind.

SUBORDINATE (suh BOR duh nit) *adj* lower in importance, position, or rank; secondary
My desire to sit on the couch and watch television all night long was *subordinate* to my desire to stand in the kitchen eating junk food all night long, so I did the latter instead of the former.

A vice president is *subordinate* to a president.

Subordinate (suh BOR duh nayt) can also be a verb. To *subordinate* something in relation to something else is to make it secondary or less important.

To be *insubordinate* (in suh BOR duh nit) is not to acknowledge the authority of a superior. An army private who says "Bug off!" when ordered to do something by a general is guilty of being *insubordinate* or of committing an act of *insubordination.*

SUBSTANTIVE (SUB stan tiv) *adj* having substance; real; essential; solid; substantial

The differences between the two theories were not *substantive;* in fact, the two theories said the same thing with different words.

The gossip columnist's wild accusations were not based on anything *substantive;* her source was a convicted criminal, and she had made up all the quotations.

SUBTLE (SUT ul) *adj* not obvious; able to make fine distinctions; ingenious; crafty

The alien beings had created a very shrewd replica of Mr. Jenson, but his wife did notice a few *subtle* differences, including the fact that the new Mr. Jenson had no pulse or internal organs.

Joe's *subtle* mind enables him to see past problems that confuse the rest of us.

The burglar was very *subtle;* he had come up with a plan that would enable him to steal all the money in the world without arousing the suspicions of the authorities.

Something *subtle* is a *subtlety.*

SUBVERSIVE (sub VUR siv) *adj* corrupting; overthrowing; undermining; insurgent

The political group planted bombs in the White House, destroyed the Pentagon's computer files, hijacked *Air Force One,* and engaged in various other *subversive* activities.

Madeline's efforts to teach her first-grade students to read were thwarted by that most *subversive* of inventions, the television set.

SUCCINCT (suk SINGKT) *adj* brief and to the point; concise

Harry's *succinct* explanation of why the moon doesn't fall out of the sky and crash into the earth quickly satisfied even the dullest of the anxious investment bankers.

We were given so little room in which to write on the examination that we had no choice but to keep our essays *succinct.*

Note carefully the pronunciation of this word.

Q•U•I•C•K • Q•U•I•Z #79

Match each word in the first column with its definition in the second column. Check your answers in the back of the book.

1. strife	a. not obvious
2. stringent	b. awesome
3. stymie	c. brief and to the point
4. subjugate	d. thwart
5. sublime	e. subdue
6. subordinate	f. corrupting
7. insubordinate	g. not respectful of authority
8. substantive	h. strict
9. subtle	i. lower in importance
10. subversive	j. having substance
11. succinct	k. bitter conflict

SUCCUMB (suh KUM) v to yield or submit; to die

I had said I wasn't going to eat anything at the party, but when Ann held the tray of imported chocolates under my nose, I quickly *succumbed* and ate all of them.

The Martians in *The War of the Worlds* survived every military weapon known to man but *succumbed* to the common cold.

When Willard reached the age of 110, his family began to think that he would live forever, but he *succumbed* not long afterward.

SUPERCILIOUS (soo pur SIL ee us) *adj* haughty; patronizing

The *supercilious* Rolls-Royce salesman treated us like peasants until we opened our suitcase full of one-hundred-dollar bills.

The newly famous author was so *supercilious* that he pretended not to recognize members of his own family, whom he now believed to be beneath him.

SUPERFICIAL (soo pur FISH ul) *adj* on the surface only; shallow; not thorough

Tom had indeed been shot, but the wound was *superficial;* the bullet had merely creased the tip of his nose.

The mechanic, who was in a hurry, gave my car what appeared to be a very *superficial* tune-up. In fact, if he checked the oil, he did it without opening the hood.

A person who is *superficial* can be accused of *superficiality*. The *superficiality* of the editor's comments made us think that he hadn't really read the manuscript.

SUPERFLUOUS (soo PUR floo us) *adj* extra; unnecessary; redundant

Andrew's attempt to repair the light bulb was *superfluous*, since the light bulb had already been repaired.

Roughly 999 of the 1,000-page book's pages were *superfluous*.
The noun is *superfluity* (soo pur FLOO uh tee).
Note carefully the pronunciation of this word.

SURFEIT (SUR fit) *n* excess; an excessive amount; excess or overindulgence in eating or drinking

   Thanksgiving meals are usually a *surfeit* for everyone involved.
Note carefully the pronunciation of this word.

SURREPTITIOUS (sur up TISH us) *adj* sneaky; secret

   The dinner guest *surreptitiously* slipped a few silver spoons into his jacket as he was leaving the dining room.
   The baby-sitter mixed herself a *surreptitious* cocktail as soon as Mr. and Mrs. Robinson had driven away.

SURROGATE (SUR uh git) *adj* substitute

   A *surrogate* mother is a woman who bears a child for someone else.
   This word is often a noun. A *surrogate* is a substitute. The nice father offered to go to prison as a *surrogate* for his son, who had been convicted of extortion.

SYCOPHANT (SIK uh funt) *n* one who sucks up to others

   The French class seemed to be full of *sycophants;* the students were always bringing apples to the teacher and telling her how nice she looked.
   A *sycophant* is *sycophantic* (sik uh FAN tik). The exasperated boss finally fired his *sycophantic* secretary because he couldn't stand being around someone who never had anything nasty to say.
Note carefully the pronunciation of this word.

SYNTHESIS (SIN thuh sis) *n* the combining of parts to form a whole

   It seemed as though the meeting might end in acrimony and confusion until Raymond offered his brilliant *synthesis* of the two diverging points of view.
   A hot fudge sundae is the perfect *synthesis* of hot fudge and vanilla ice cream.

Q•U•I•C•K • Q•U•I•Z #80

Match each word in the first column with its definition in the second column. Check your answers in the back of the book.

1. succumb		a. haughty
2. supercilious		b. yield
3. superficial		c. flatterer
4. superfluous		d. substitute
5. surfeit		e. unnecessary
6. surreptitious		f. on the surface only
7. surrogate		g. sneaky
8. sycophant		h. excess
9. synthesis		i. combining of parts

T

TACIT (TAS it) *adj* implied; not spoken

Mrs. Rodgers never formally asked us to murder her husband, but we truly believed that we were acting with her *tacit* consent.

There was *tacit* agreement among the men that women had no business at their weekly poker game.

Tacit is related to *taciturn*.

TACITURN (TAS i turn) *adj* untalkative by nature

The chairman was so *taciturn* that we often discovered that we had absolutely no idea what he was thinking.

The *taciturn* physicist was sometimes thought to be brilliant simply because no one had ever heard him say anything stupid. Everyone misconstrued his *taciturnity*; he was actually quite stupid. *Taciturn* is related to *tacit*.

TANGENTIAL (tan JEN schul) *adj* only superficially related to the matter at hand; not especially relevant; peripheral

The mayor's speech bore only a *tangential* relationship to the topic that had been announced.

Stuart's connection with our organization is *tangential*; he once made a phone call from the lobby of our building, but he never worked here.

When a writer or speaker "goes off on a *tangent*," he or she is making a digression or straying from the original topic.

Note carefully the pronunciation of this word.

TANGIBLE (TAN juh bul) *adj* touchable; palpable

A mountain of cigarette butts was the only *tangible* evidence that Luther had been in our house.

There was no *tangible* reason I could point to, but I did have a sneaking suspicion that Ernest was an ax murderer.

The opposite of *tangible* is *intangible*.

TANTAMOUNT (TAN tuh mownt) *adj* equivalent to

Waving a banner for the visiting team at that football game would be *tantamount* to committing suicide; the home-team fans would tear you apart in a minute.

Yvonne's method of soliciting donations from her employees was *tantamount* to extortion; she clearly implied that she would fire them if they didn't pitch in.

TAUTOLOGICAL (tawt uh LAH juh kul) *adj* redundant; circular

"When everyone has a camera, cameras will be universal" is a *tautological* statement, because "everyone having a camera" and "cameras being universal" mean the same thing.

The testing company's definition of intelligence—"that which is measured by intelligence tests"—is *tautological*.

A *tautology* (taw TAHL uh jee) is a needless repetition of words, or saying the same thing using different words. For example: The trouble with bachelors is that they aren't married.

TEMERITY (tuh MER uh tee) *n* boldness; recklessness; audacity
Our waiter at the restaurant had the *temerity* to tell me he thought my table manners were atrocious.

The mountain climber had more *temerity* than skill or sense. He tried to climb a mountain that was much too difficult and ended up in a heap at the bottom.

TEMPERATE (TEM pur it) *adj* mild; moderate; restrained
Our climate is *temperate* during the spring and fall, but very nearly unbearable during the summer and winter.

The teacher's *temperate* personality lent a feeling of calm and control to the kindergarten class.

The opposite of *temperate* is *intemperate*, which means not moderate. Bucky's *intemperate* use of oregano ruined the chili.

To *temper* something is to make it milder. Wilma laughed and shrieked so loudly at every joke that even the comedian wished she would *temper* her appreciation.

Temperance is moderation, especially with regard to alcoholic drinks.

TENABLE (TEN uh bul) *adj* defensible, as in one's position in an argument; capable of being argued successfully; valid
Members of the Flat Earth Society continue to argue that the earth is flat, although even children dismiss their arguments as not *tenable*.

Untenable means unable to be defended.

TENACIOUS (tuh NAY shus) *adj* persistent; stubborn; not letting go
The foreign student's *tenacious* effort to learn English won him the admiration of all the teachers at our school.

Louise's grasp of geometry was not *tenacious*. She could handle the simpler problems most of the time, but she fell apart on quizzes and tests.

The ivy growing on the side of our house was so *tenacious* that we had to tear the house down to get rid of it.

To be *tenacious* is to have *tenacity* (tuh NAS us tee).

Q•U•I•C•K • Q•U•I•Z #81

Match each word in the first column with its definition in the second column. Check your answers in the back of the book.

1. tacit	a. persistent
2. taciturn	b. naturally untalkative
3. tangential	c. boldness
4. tangible	d. equivalent to
5. tantamount	e. not deeply relevant
6. tautological	f. redundant
7. temerity	g. mild
8. temperate	h. defensible
9. tenable	i. implied
10. tenacious	j. touchable

TENET (TEN it) *n* a shared principle or belief

One of the most important *tenets* of our form of government is that people can be trusted to govern themselves.

The *tenets* of his religion prevented him from dancing and going to movies.

TENTATIVE (TEN tuh tiv) *adj* experimental; temporary; uncertain

George made a *tentative* effort to paint his house by himself; he slapped some paint on the front door and his clothes, tipped over the bucket, and called a professional.

Our plans for the party are *tentative* at this point, but we are considering hiring a troupe of accordionists to play polkas while our guests are eating dessert.

Hugo believed himself to be a great wit, but his big joke was rewarded by nothing more than a very *tentative* chuckle from his audience.

TENUOUS (TEN yoo us) *adj* flimsy; extremely thin

The organization's financial situation has always been *tenuous;* the balance of the checking account is usually close to zero.

The hostess's *tenuous* gown, which had been made from a sheet of clear plastic, certainly made her popular with her male guests.

To *attenuate* is to make thin. *Extenuating* circumstances are those that lessen the magnitude of something, especially a crime. Percy admitted that he stole the Cracker Jacks but claimed that there were *extenuating* circumstances: he had no money to buy food for his pet armadillo.

TERSE (turs) *adj* using no unnecessary words; succinct

The new recording secretary's minutes were so *terse* that they were occasionally cryptic.

Terseness is not one of Rex's virtues; he would talk until the crack of dawn if someone didn't stop him.

THEOLOGY (thee AHL uh jee) *n* the study of God or religion
Ralph was a paradox: he was an atheist yet he passionately studied *theology*.

TIRADE (TYE rayd) *n* prolonged, bitter speech
Percival launched into a *tirade* against imitation cheese on the school lunch menu.

TORPOR (TOR pur) *n* sluggishness; inactivity; apathy
After consuming the guinea pig, the boa constrictor fell into a state of contented *torpor* that lasted several days.

The math teacher tried to reduce the *torpor* of his students by setting off a few firecrackers on his desk, but the students scarcely blinked.

To be in a state of *torpor* is to be *torpid*.

TOUCHSTONE (TUCH stohn) *n* a standard; a test of authenticity or quality
In its original usage, a *touchstone* was a dark stone against which gold and other precious metals were rubbed in order to test their purity. Now the word is used more loosely to describe a broad range of standards and tests.

The size of a student's vocabulary is a useful *touchstone* for judging the quality of his or her education.

A candidate's pronouncements about the economy provided a *touchstone* by which his or her fitness for office could be judged.

TOUT (tout) *v* to praise highly; to brag publicly about
Advertisements *touted* the chocolate-flavored toothpaste as getting rid of your sweet tooth while saving your teeth.

TRANSCEND (tran SEND) *v* to go beyond or above; to surpass
The man who claimed to have invented a perpetual motion machine believed that he had *transcended* the laws of physics.

The basketball player was so skillful that he seemed to have *transcended* the sport altogether; he was so much better than his teammates that he seemed to be playing an entirely different game.

To be *transcendent* is to be surpassing or preeminent. Something *transcendent* is *transcendental* (tran sen DEN tul).

TRANSGRESS (trans GRES) *v* to violate (a law); to sin
The other side had *transgressed* so many provisions of the treaty that we had no choice but to go to war.

We tried as hard as we could not to *transgress* their elaborate rules, but they had so many prohibitions that we couldn't keep track of all of them.

An act of *transgressing* is a *transgression*. The bully's innumerable *transgressions* included breaking all the windows in the new gymnasium and pushing several first graders off the jungle gym.

TRANSIENT (TRAN shunt) *adj* not staying for a long time; temporary
The *transient* breeze provided some relief from the summer heat, but we were soon perspiring again.

The child's smile was *transient;* it disappeared as soon as the candy bar was gone.

A hotel's inhabitants are *transient;* they come and go and the population changes every night.

Transient can also be a noun. A *transient* person is sometimes called a *transient.* Hoboes, mendicants, and other homeless people are often called *transients.*

A very similar word is *transitory,* which means not lasting very long. A *transient* breeze might provide *transitory* relief from the heat. The breeze didn't stay very long; the relief didn't last very long.

Note carefully the pronunciation of this word.

TREPIDATION (trep uh DAY shun) *n* fear; apprehension; nervous trembling

The nursery school students were filled with *trepidation* when they saw the other children in their class dressed in their Halloween costumes.

The *trepidation* of the swimming team was readily apparent: their knees were knocking as they lined up along the edge of the pool.

To be fearless is to be *intrepid.* The *intrepid* captain sailed his ship around the world with only a handkerchief for a sail.

TURPITUDE (TUR puh tood) *n* shameful wickedness; depravity

Larry was sacked by his boss because of a flagrant act of *turpitude:* he slept with the boss's wife.

Q·U·I·C·K • Q·U·I·Z #82

Match each word in the first column with its definition in the second column. Check your answers in the back of the book.

1. tenet		a. without unnecessary words
2. tentative		b. go beyond
3. tenuous		c. brag publicly about
4. terse		d. fearless
5. torpor		e. experimental
6. theology		f. not lasting long (2)
7. tirade		g. bitter speech
8. touchstone		h. shared principle
9. tout		i. wickedness
10. transcend		j. sluggishness
11. transgress		k. flimsy
12. transient		l. fear
13. transitory		m. study of religion
14. trepidation		n. standard
15. intrepid		o. violate
16. turpitude		

U

UBIQUITOUS (yoo BIK wuh tus) *adj* being everywhere at the same time

The new beer commercial was *ubiquitous*—it seemed to be on every television channel at once.

Personal computers, once a rarity, have become *ubiquitous.*

To be *ubiquitous* is to be characterized by *ubiquity* (yoo BIK wuh tee). The *ubiquity* of fast-food restaurants is one of the more depressing features of American culture.

Note carefully the pronunciation of both parts of speech.

UNCONSCIONABLE (un KAHN shuh nuh bul) *adj* not controlled by conscience; unscrupulous

Leaving a small child unattended all day long is an *unconscionable* act.

Murdering every citizen of that town was *unconscionable.* Bert should be ashamed of himself for doing it.

Don't confuse this word with *unconscious.*

UNCTUOUS (UNGK choo us) *adj* oily, both literally and figuratively; insincere

Salad oil is literally *unctuous.* A used-car salesman might be figuratively *unctuous*—that is, oily in the sense of being slick, sleazy, and insincere.

UNIFORM (YOO nuh form) *adj* consistent; unchanging; the same for everyone

Traffic laws are similar from one state to the next, but they aren't *uniform;* each state has its own variations.

The school did not have a *uniform* grading policy; each teacher was free to mark students according to any system that he or she thought appropriate.

Something that is *uniform* has *uniformity* (yoo nuh FOR muh tee).

Uniforms are suits of clothing that are *uniform* in appearance from one person to the next.

UNREMITTING (un ri MIT ing) *adj* unceasing; unabated; relentless

Superman waged an *unremitting* battle against evildoers everywhere.

UNWITTING (un WIT ing) *adj* unintentional; ignorant; not aware

When Leo agreed to hold open the door of the bank, he became an *unwitting* accomplice to the bank robbery.

My theft was *unwitting;* I hadn't meant to steal the car, but had unintentionally driven it away from the automobile dealership and parked it in my garage.

On the camping trip, Josephine *unwittingly* stepped into a bear trap and remained stuck in it for several days.

URBANE (ur BAYN) *adj* poised; sophisticated; refined

The British count was witty and *urbane;* all the hosts and hostesses wanted to have him at their parties.

The new magazine was far too *urbane* to appeal to a wide audience outside the big city.

Urbanity (ur BAN uh tee) is a quality more often acquired in an *urban* setting than in a rural one.

USURP (yoo SURP) *v* to seize wrongfully

The children believed that their mother's new boyfriend had *usurped* their real father's rightful place in their family.

The founder's scheming young nephew *usurped* a position of power in the company.

The noun is *usurpation* (yoo sur PAY shun).

UTILITARIAN (yoo til uh TAR ee un) *adj* stressing usefulness or utility above all other qualities; pragmatic

Jason's interior-decorating philosophy was strictly *utilitarian;* if an object wasn't genuinely useful, he didn't want it in his home.

Utilitarian can also be a noun. Jason, just mentioned, could be called a *utilitarian.*

UTOPIA (yoo TOH pee uh) *n* an ideal society

A country where nobody had to work and *Monday Night Football* was on television every night would be Quentin's idea of *utopia.*

The little town wasn't just a nice place to live, as far as Ed was concerned; it was *utopia.*

A *utopian* is someone with unrealistic or impractical plans or expectations for society. Such plans or expectations are *utopian* plans or expectations.

The opposite of a *utopia* is a *dystopia.*

Q•U•I•C•K • Q•U•I•Z #83

Match each word in the first column with its definition in the second column. Check your answers in the back of the book.

1. ubiquitous	a. oily
2. unconscionable	b. poised and sophisticated
3. unctuous	c. everywhere at once
4. uniform	d. pragmatic
5. unremitting	e. seize wrongfully
6. unwitting	f. unscrupulous
7. urbane	g. an ideal society
8. usurp	h. unintentional
9. utilitarian	i. consistent
10. utopia	j. unceasing

V

VACILLATE (VAS uh layt) v to be indecisive; to waver

We invited James to spend Thanksgiving with us, but he *vacillated* for so long about whether he would be able to come that we finally became annoyed and disinvited him.

Tyler *vacillated* about buying a new car. He couldn't decide whether to get one or not.

The act of *vacillating* is called *vacillation*.

VAPID (VAP id) *adj* without liveliness; dull; spiritless

An apathetic person just doesn't care about anything, and everything he does is *vapid*.

The novelist's prose was so *vapid* that Mary couldn't get beyond the first page.

VEHEMENT (VEE uh munt) *adj* intense; forceful; violent

Shaking his fist and stomping his foot, Gerry was *vehement* in his denial.

The noun is *vehemence*.

VENAL (VEEN ul) *adj* capable of being bribed; willing to do anything for money; corrupt

The *venal* judge reversed his favorable ruling when the defendant refused to make good on his promised bribe.

The young man's interest in helping the sick old woman was strictly *venal*; he figured that if he was kind to her, she would leave him a lot of money in her will.

A *venal* person is a person characterized by *venality* (vee NAL uh tee).

Don't confuse this word with *venial* (VEE nee ul), which means trivial or pardonable. A peccadillo is a *venial*, harmless sin.

VENERATE (VEN uh rayt) v to revere; to treat as something holy, especially because of great age

Lester *venerated* his grandfather; he worshiped the very ground the old man limped on.

The members of the curious religion *venerated* Elvis Presley and hoped that the pope would declare him a saint.

A person who is worthy of being *venerated* is said to be *venerable*.

VERACITY (vuh RAS uh tee) *n* truthfulness

The *veracity* of young George Washington is legendary, but it may be apocryphal.

Veracious is truthful.

VERBOSE (vur BOHS) *adj* using too many words; not succinct; circumlocutory

Someone who is *verbose* uses too many words when fewer words would suffice. Lee handed in a 178-word final assignment; no one ever accused him of *verbosity* (vur BAHS uh tee).

VERISIMILITUDE (ver uh si MIL uh tood) *n* similarity to reality; the appearance of truth; looking like the real thing
   They used pine cones and old truck tires to make statues of Hollywood celebrities that were remarkable for their *verisimilitude.*
   The *verisimilitude* of counterfeit eleven-dollar bills did not fool the eagle-eyed treasury officer, who recognized them immediately for what they were.

VERNACULAR (vur NAK yuh lur) *n* everyday speech; slang; idiom
   Our teacher said that we should save our *vernacular* for the street; in the classroom we should use proper grammar.

VESTIGE (VES tij) *n* a remaining bit of something; a last trace
   The unhappy young man found *vestiges* of his fiancée in the rubble, but the explosion had effectively ended their romance.
   An old uniform and a tattered scrapbook were the only *vestiges* of the old man's career as a professional athlete.
   Your appendix is a *vestige:* it used to have a function, but now this organ does nothing.
   The adjective form of *vestige* is *vestigial* (vuh STIJ ee ul). The appendix is referred to as a *vestigial* organ. It is still in our bodies, although it no longer has a function. It is a mere *vestige* of some function our digestive systems no longer perform.
   Note carefully the pronunciation of both parts of speech.

VEX (veks) *v* to annoy; to pester; to confuse
   Margaret *vexed* me by poking me with a long, sharp stick.
   Stuck at the bottom of a deep well, I found my situation extremely *vexing.*
   The act of *vexing*, or the state of being *vexed*, is *vexation*. Both the person who *vexes* and the person who is *vexed* can be said to exhibit *vexation.*
   A *vexed* issue is one that is troubling or puzzling.

VIABLE (VYE uh bul) *adj* capable of living; workable
   When a doctor says that a patient is no longer *viable*, it's time to begin planning a funeral.
   A fetus is said to be *viable* when it has developed to the point where it is capable of surviving outside the womb.
   Harry's plan for storing marshmallows in the dome of the Capitol just wasn't *viable.*
   Something that is *viable* has *viability* (vye uh BIL uh tee).

VICARIOUS (vye KAR ee us) *adj* experienced, performed, or suffered through someone else; living through the experiences of another as though they were one's own experiences
   To take *vicarious* pleasure in someone else's success is to enjoy that person's success as though it were your own.

We all felt a *vicarious* thrill when the mayor's daughter won fourth prize in the regional kick-boxing competition.

VICISSITUDE (vi SIS uh tood) *n* upheaval; natural change; change in fortune

The *vicissitudes* of the stock market were too much for Penny; she decided to look for a job that would stay the same from one day to the next.

The *vicissitudes* of the local political machine were such that one could never quite be certain whom one was supposed to bribe.

VILIFY (VIL uh fye) *v* to say vile things about; to defame

The teacher was reprimanded for *vilifying* the slow student in front of the rest of the class.

Our taxi driver paused briefly on the way to the airport in order to *vilify* the driver of the car that had nearly forced him off the road.

The political debate was less a debate than a *vilification* contest. At first the candidates took turns saying nasty things about one another; then they stopped taking turns.

Q•U•I•C•K • Q•U•I•Z #84

Match each word in the first column with its definition in the second column. Check your answers in the back of the book.

1. vacillate	a. annoy
2. vapid	b. be indecisive
3. vehement	c. defame
4. venal	d. capable of living
5. venerate	e. experienced through another
6. veracity	f. dull
7. verbose	g. upheaval
8. verisimilitude	h. revere
9. vernacular	i. last trace
10. vestige	j. similarity to reality
11. vex	k. truthfulness
12. viable	l. corrupt
13. vicarious	m. wordy
14. vicissitude	n. slang
15. vilify	o. intense

VINDICATE (VIN duh kayt) *v* to clear from all blame or suspicion; to justify

Tony, having been accused of stealing money from the cash register, was *vindicated* when the store manager counted the money again and found that none was missing after all.

Inez's claim of innocence appeared to be *vindicated* when several dozen inmates at the state mental hospital confessed to the crime of which she had been accused.

A person who has been *vindicated* is a person who has found *vindication*.

VINDICTIVE (vin DIK tiv) *adj* seeking revenge

Jeremy apologized for denting the fender of my car, but I was feeling *vindictive* so I filed a $30 million lawsuit against him.

Samantha's *vindictive* ex-husband drove all the way across the country just to punch her in the nose.

To feel *vindictive* is to be filled with *vindictiveness*.

VIRTUOSO (vur choo WOH soh) *n* a masterful musician; a masterful practitioner in some other field

The concert audience fell silent when the *virtuoso* stepped forward to play the sonata on his electric banjo.

As an artist, he was a *virtuoso;* as a husband, he was a chump.

Virtuoso can also be an adjective. A *virtuoso* performance is a performance worthy of a *virtuoso*.

VIRULENT (VIR uh lunt) *adj* extremely poisonous; malignant; full of hate

The *virulent* disease quickly swept through the community, leaving many people dead and many more people extremely ill.

The snake was a member of a particularly *virulent* breed; its bite could kill an elephant.

Jonathan is a *virulent* antifeminist; he says that all women should sit down and shut up and do what he tells them to.

To be *virulent* is to be characterized by *virulence*. *Virulent* is related to *virus*, not to *virile*, which means manly.

VISIONARY (VIZH uh ner ee) *n* a dreamer; someone with impractical goals or ideas about the future

My uncle was a *visionary,* not a businessman; he spent too much time tinkering with his antigravity generator and not enough time working in his plumbing business.

The candidate was a *visionary;* he had a lot of big ideas but no realistic plan for putting them into practice.

Visionary can also be an adjective. A *visionary* proposal is an idealistic and usually impractical proposal.

VITIATE (VISH ee ayt) *v* to make impure; to pollute

For years a zealous group of individuals has campaigned against the use of fluoride in water, claiming that it has *vitiated* our bodies as well as our morals.

VITRIOLIC (vi tree AHL ik) *adj* caustic; full of bitterness

Vitriol is another name for sulfuric acid. To be *vitriolic* is to say or do something so nasty that your words or actions burn like acid.

The review of the new book was so *vitriolic* that we all wondered whether the reviewer had some personal grudge against the author.

VOCATION (voh KAY shun) *n* an occupation; a job

Your *vocation* is what you do for a living.

If Stan could figure out how to make a *vocation* out of watching television and eating potato chips, he would be one of the most successful people in the world.

Vocational training is job training.

Since your *vocation* is your job, your *avocation* is your hobby. The accountant's *vocation* bored her, but her *avocation* of mountain climbing did not.

VOCIFEROUS (voh SIF ur us) *adj* loud; noisy

Randy often becomes *vociferous* during arguments. He doesn't know what he believes, but he states it loudly nevertheless.

VOLATILE (VAHL uh tul) *adj* quick to evaporate; highly unstable; explosive

A *volatile* liquid is one that evaporates readily. Gasoline is a *volatile* liquid. It evaporates very readily, and then the vapor poses a great danger of explosion.

A *volatile* crowd is one that seems to be in imminent danger of getting out of control, or exploding.

The situation in the Middle East was highly *volatile;* the smallest incident could have set off a war.

To be *volatile* is to be characterized by *volatility.*

VOLITION (voh LISH un) *n* will; conscious choice

Insects, lacking *volition,* simply aren't as interesting as humans are.

The question the jury had to decide was whether the killing had been an accident or an act of *volition.*

Q•U•I•C•K • Q•U•I•Z #85

Match each word in the first column with its definition in the second column. Check your answers in the back of the book.

1. vindicate	a. extremely poisonous
2. vindictive	b. masterful musician
3. virtuoso	c. dreamer
4. virulent	d. caustic
5. visionary	e. clear from suspicion
6. vitiate	f. will
7. vitriolic	g. quick to evaporate
8. vocation	h. seeking revenge
9. vociferous	i. occupation
10. volatile	j. make impure
11. volition	k. noisy

W

WANTON (WAHN tun) *adj* malicious; unjustifiable; unprovoked; egregious

Terrorists commit *wanton* acts on a helpless populace to make their point.

Wanton also means intemperate. A hedonist lives a *wanton* life in the relentless, unremitting pursuit of pleasure; an ascetic does not.

WILLFUL (WIL ful) *adj* deliberate; obstinate; insistent on having one's way

The mother insisted that the killing committed by her son had not been *willful*, but the jury apparently believed that he had known what he was doing.

When her mother told her she couldn't have a cookie, the *willful* little girl simply snatched the cookie jar and ran out of the room with it. She had stolen the cookies *willfully*.

Note carefully the spelling of this word.

WISTFUL (WIST ful) *adj* yearning; sadly longing

I felt *wistful* when I saw Herb's fancy new car. I wished that I had enough money to buy one for myself.

The boys who had been cut from the football team watched *wistfully* as the team put together an undefeated season and won the state championship.

Q•U•I•C•K • Q•U•I•Z #86

Match each word in the first column with its definition in the second column. Check your answers in the back of the book.

1. wanton	a. yearning
2. willful	b. deliberate
3. wistful	c. malicious

Z

ZEALOUS (ZEL us) *adj* enthusiastically devoted to something; fervent

The *zealous* young policeman made so many arrests that the city jail soon became overcrowded.

The dictator's followers were so *zealous* that if he had asked them all to jump off a cliff, most of them would have done so.

To be *zealous* is to be full of zeal, or fervent enthusiasm. An overly *zealous* person is a *zealot*.

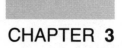

CHAPTER 3

THE
FINAL
EXAM

The following final exam drills contain every word in the *Word Smart* core list. If you get a question wrong, try it again. Perhaps you were careless. If not, look up all the answer choices for that question and review the definitions.

Final Exam Drill #1: COMPLETIONS

For each question below, choose the word that best completes the meaning of the sentence.

1. Because Stan had been preoccupied during his dynamite-juggling demonstration, the jury felt that he was not _____ for the destruction of the audience.
   a. decorous
   b. decimated
   c. indiscreet
   d. culpable
   e. indiscrete

2. Sally was sad because Mr. Reeves, our English teacher, filled the margins of her term paper with _____ remarks about her spelling, grammar, and writing style.
   a. fatuous
   b. heretical
   c. ineffable
   d. prepossessing
   e. derogatory

3. The fans were _____ when the football team lost its fiftieth game in a row.
   a. irascible
   b. despondent
   c. rapacious
   d. stigmatized
   e. precipitous

4. Bill and Harry were given jobs on the stage crew because their _____ voices ruined the sound of the chorus.

a. unremitting
b. paternal
c. wanton
d. laconic
e. dissonant

5. The baby kittens were so _____ that the nursery school children were able to pick them up, carry them around by the scruffs of their necks, and dress them up in doll clothes.

a. abashed
b. peripatetic
c. docile
d. agrarian
e. nefarious

Final Exam Drill #2: BUDDY CHECK

For each question below, match the word on the left with the word most similar in meaning on the right.

1. litigious	a. ingenuous
2. artless	b. querulous
3. taciturn	c. auspicious
4. refute	d. perennial
5. perjure	e. avow
6. allege	f. reticent
7. gauche	g. impugn
8. officious	h. rebut
9. chronic	i. inept
10. propitious	j. solicitous

Final Exam Drill #3: ODD MAN OUT

Each question below consists of four words. Three of them are related in meaning. Find the word that does not fit.

1. address	infer	construe	extrapolate
2. rigorous	punctilious	integral	painstaking
3. consecrate	revere	venerate	delineate
4. abstain	relegate	forbear	forgo
5. insubordinate	willful	didactic	intransigent
6. labyrinthine	profane	secular	atheistic
7. acrid	amoral	sardonic	virulent
8. analogous	perfunctory	cursory	desultory
9. decadent	degenerate	profligate	magnanimous
10. connoisseur	virtuoso	malleable	aesthete

Final Exam Drill #4: RELATIONSHIPS

For each question below, decide whether the pair of words are roughly similar (S) in meaning, roughly opposite (O) in meaning, or unrelated (U) to each other.

1.	sporadic	incessant
2.	beget	spawn
3.	malaise	subversion
4.	coerce	compel
5.	peccadillo	enormity
6.	charismatic	insipid
7.	countenance	condone
8.	usurp	appropriate
9.	espouse	extricate
10.	arbitrate	mediate

Final Exam Drill #5: COMPLETIONS

For each question below, choose the word that best completes the meaning of the sentence.

1. The applicant's credentials were _____, but I didn't like the color of his necktie so I didn't hire him.

   a. irreproachable
   b. aloof
   c. domestic
   d. vitriolic
   e. histrionic

2. Walter's skin took on a(n) _____ cast after his exposure to the pool of radioactive wastes.

   a. artful
   b. squalid
   c. luminous
   d. nebulous
   e. garrulous

3. The police spent seven months working on the crime case but were never able to determine the identity of the _____.

   a. demagogue
   b. dilettante
   c. egotist
   d. malefactor
   e. patriarch

4. The portions at the restaurant were so _____ that immediately after dessert we drove to another restaurant and ordered a second full meal.

a. pertinent
b. minuscule
c. exhaustive
d. futile
e. misanthropic

5. Alan thought that throwing some scraps to the bear would _____ it, but instead the beast tore apart our campsite in search of more to eat.

a. accost
b. mollify
c. preclude
d. efface
e. tout

Final Exam Drill #6: RELATIONSHIPS

For each question below, decide whether the pair of words are roughly similar (S) in meaning, roughly opposite (O) in meaning, or unrelated (U) to each other.

1. debacle	coup
2. amenity	injunction
3. cognizant	unwitting
4. emigrate	expatriate
5. concurrent	anachronistic
6. blithe	morose
7. disinterested	partial
8. anachronism	archaism
9. collusion	complicity
10. insular	hermetic

Final Exam Drill #7: ODD MAN OUT

Each question below consists of four words. Three of them are related in meaning. Find the word that does not fit.

1. sacrilege	renaissance	blasphemy	desecration
2. ambiguous	equivocal	cryptic	requisite
3. apprehensive	martial	contentious	belligerent
4. arcane	esoteric	sacrosanct	recondite
5. incense	replenish	foment	antagonize
6. exacting	onerous	ponderous	arbitrary
7. circumspect	eclectic	scrupulous	fastidious
8. introverted	aloof	reclusive	elliptical
9. allocate	relinquish	capitulate	succumb
10. effusive	histrionic	avuncular	gesticulating

Final Exam Drill #8: RELATIONSHIPS

For each question below, decide whether the pair of words are roughly similar (S) in meaning, roughly opposite (O) in meaning, or unrelated (U) to each other.

1. abyss   chasm
2. substantive   ethereal
3. loquacious   taciturn
4. doctrinaire   dogmatic
5. colloquial   pedantic
6. encroach   transgress
7. amorphous   nebulous
8. domestic   endemic
9. cogent   incisive
10. lethargic   capricious

Final Exam Drill #9: COMPLETIONS

For each question below, choose the word or phrase that best completes the meaning of the sentence.

1. Amanda _____ her daughter for putting the cat in the washing machine.
   a. expropriated
   b. disfranchised
   c. coerced
   d. broached
   e. chastised

2. David's salary was _____ his very limited skills; he was paid nothing.
   a. as vapid as
   b. tenable despite
   c. vehement in view of
   d. commensurate with
   e. acerbic notwithstanding

3. After several decades of peace, the little country grew _____ about defense and let its army slowly drift away.
   a. dissolute
   b. partisan
   c. catholic
   d. adamant
   e. complacent

4. None of us had enough money to undertake the project alone, so we had to depend on the _____ of our parents.
a. postulate
b. vilification
c. largess
d. hedonism
e. veracity

5. The court ruled that Ursula's covert discussions with the Russian ambassador did not _____ treason.
a. comprise
b. abnegate
c. libel
d. broach
e. constitute

Final Exam Drill #10: RELATIONSHIPS

For each question below, decide whether the pair of words are roughly similar (S) in meaning, roughly opposite (O) in meaning, or unrelated (U) to each other.

1.	bureaucracy	hierarchy
2.	extrapolate	infer
3.	mercurial	volatile
4.	impeccable	culpable
5.	corroborate	refute
6.	expedient	utilitarian
7.	censure	approbation
8.	propriety	decorum
9.	emulate	peruse
10.	mandate	touchstone

Final Exam Drill #11: RELATIONSHIPS

For each question below, decide whether the pair of words are roughly similar (S) in meaning, roughly opposite (O) in meaning, or unrelated (U) to each other.

1.	ameliorate	exacerbate
2.	candor	equivocation
3.	caricature	parody
4.	scrupulous	mendacious
5.	apartheid	mentor
6.	bane	panacea
7.	facile	arduous
8.	philistine	erudite
9.	absolute	commensurate
10.	kinetic	stagnant

Final Exam Drill #12: ODD MAN OUT

Each question below consists of four words. Three of them are related in meaning. Find the word that does not fit.

1.	awry	overt	salient	manifest
2.	duplicity	ascendancy	guile	chicanery
3.	contrition	remorse	cadence	penitence
4.	temperance	sobriety	celibacy	oblivion
5.	nominal	amiable	affable	congenial
6.	choleric	querulous	petulant	equitable
7.	dormant	latent	nostalgic	inert
8.	astute	bereft	sagacious	prudent
9.	copious	bourgeois	profuse	myriad
10.	ascetic	austere	frugal	pejorative

Final Exam Drill #13: RELATIONSHIPS

For each question below, decide whether the pair of words are roughly similar (S) in meaning, roughly opposite (O) in meaning, or unrelated (U) to each other.

1.	serendipitous	hapless
2.	lugubrious	facetious
3.	espouse	appease
4.	qualitative	pejorative
5.	exigency	periphery
6.	harbinger	precursor
7.	profound	desecrated
8.	despotic	autocratic
9.	engender	decimate
10.	pristine	unalloyed

Final Exam Drill #14: COMPLETIONS

For each question below, choose the word that best completes the meaning of the sentence.

1. Reginald was as clever as he was unscrupulous, and he knew what he could not obtain by legitimate means he could always obtain through

————.

a. chicanery
b. burlesque
c. nihilism
d. strife
e. theology

2. The visiting professor was so _____ in his field that many of our faculty members became nervous in his presence.
a. antithetical
b. archetypal
c. eminent
d. plebeian
e. pathological

3. The orator _____ a bizarre economic program whose central tenet was the abolition of all forms of money.
a. scintillated
b. espoused
c. vacillated
d. emulated
e. inundated

4. "Kicking the bucket" is a humorous _____ for "dying."
a. dictum
b. stipulation
c. incantation
d. conjecture
e. euphemism

5. The actor, pretending to be inebriated, made a(n) _____ attempt to open his umbrella in a telephone booth.
a. viable
b. enigmatic
c. farcical
d. cognitive
e. aphoristic

Final Exam Drill #15: BUDDY CHECK

For each question below, match the word on the left with the word most similar in meaning on the right.

1. opaque		a. obscure
2. ostensible		b. secular
3. avaricious		c. mellifluous
4. mundane		d. prudent
5. judicious		e. venal
6. mercenary		f. specious
7. ramification		g. rapacious
8. saccharine		h. repercussion
9. archaic		i. dearth
10. paucity		j. anachronism

Final Exam Drill #16: RELATIONSHIPS
For each question below, decide whether the pair of words are roughly similar (S) in meaning, roughly opposite (O) in meaning, or unrelated (U) to each other.

1. belie   aggregate
2. legacy   bequest
3. aptitude   propensity
4. matriculate   purport
5. fatalist   cynic
6. fecund   desiccated
7. exhort   admonish
8. polarize   prevail
9. condescension   adulation
10. discreet   blatant

Final Exam Drill #17: ODD MAN OUT
Each question below consists of four words. Three of them are related in meaning. Find the word that does not fit.

1. uniform   monolithic   existential   homogeneous
2. flaunt   malign   slander   libel
3. felicity   audacity   temerity   impetuosity
4. meager   tenuous   pivotal   paltry
5. indulgent   salutary   prodigal   profligate
6. disparate   incongruous   heterogeneous   ubiquitous
7. apprehensive   diffident   succinct   circumspect
8. cogent   eminent   potent   robust
9. farcical   affected   contrived   ostentatious
10. ennui   satiety   languor   volition

Final Exam Drill #18: RELATIONSHIPS
For each question below, decide whether the pair of words are roughly similar (S) in meaning, roughly opposite (O) in meaning, or unrelated (U) to each other.

1. zealous   catholic
2. aloof   nefarious
3. mitigate   assuage
4. agnostic   atheist
5. clique   consensus
6. coalition   faction
7. husbandry   itinerary
8. coalesce   dissipate
9. slavish   subservient
10. flaunt   reproach

Final Exam Drill #19: COMPLETIONS

For each question below, choose the word that best completes the meaning of the sentence.

1. The Sandersons viewed the flaming image of the devil, which hovered above their house for thirteen days, as a(n) _____ of evil to come.
   a. stratum
   b. portent
   c. periphery
   d. infidelity
   e. aberration

2. There was nothing _____ about Herbert's scientific theories; in fact, they were quite shallow.
   a. sentient
   b. vociferous
   c. peremptory
   d. profound
   e. nepotistic

3. The _____ author turned out a new book every week of his adult life.
   a. prolific
   b. canine
   c. dialectical
   d. implicit
   e. contiguous

4. The _____ boys stubbornly refused to call off their rock fight, despite the pleadings of their mothers.
   a. recalcitrant
   b. pacific
   c. egalitarian
   d. exemplary
   e. fervent

5. Hal's disappointed wife _____ him for being a lazy, foul-smelling, obnoxious slob.
   a. instigated
   b. reproached
   c. flaunted
   d. desecrated
   e. belied

Final Exam Drill #20: RELATIONSHIPS

For each question below, decide whether the pair of words are roughly similar (S) in meaning, roughly opposite (O) in meaning, or unrelated (U) to each other.

1. profess	espouse
2. extrovert	introspective
3. foible	hiatus
4. caricature	touchstone
5. debilitate	enervate
6. placid	frenetic
7. depravity	debauchery
8. infinitesimal	grandiose
9. grandiloquent	rhetorical
10. malefactor	benefactor

Final Exam Drill #21: ODD MAN OUT

Each question below consists of four words. Three of them are related in meaning. Find the word that does not fit.

1. avaricious	covetous	officious	parsimonious
2. reprove	scrutinize	censure	rebuke
3. reprehensible	transient	ephemeral	transitory
4. belittle	depreciate	disparage	founder
5. palpable	resolute	tenacious	steadfast
6. absolve	condone	qualify	exculpate
7. civil	culinary	aristocratic	genteel
8. stricture	reproach	admonishment	corollary
9. fidelity	proximity	steadfastness	resolution
10. circumlocutory	redundant	tautological	vicarious

Final Exam Drill #22: RELATIONSHIPS

For each question below, decide whether the pair of words are roughly similar (S) in meaning, roughly opposite (O) in meaning, or unrelated (U) to each other.

1. elude	circumvent
2. rustic	urbane
3. circuitous	oblique
4. beset	beleaguered
5. imperial	servile
6. pedestrian	prosaic
7. reprisal	reparation
8. daunt	stymie
9. apotheosis	epitome
10. inaugurate	abort

Final Exam Drill #23: COMPLETIONS

For each question below, choose the word that best completes the meaning of the sentence.

1. Sally had already eaten all her cookies, so she _____ mine.
   a. permeated
   b. mortified
   c. protracted
   d. appropriated
   e. defamed

2. The country's _____ ruler required her citizens to receive official permission before changing channels on their television sets.
   a. definitive
   b. dubious
   c. indigenous
   d. autocratic
   e. redolent

3. I don't enjoy oysters myself, but I'm not _____ to letting others eat them.
   a. innate
   b. averse
   c. opaque
   d. adverse
   e. oblique

4. The president was so _____ by international crises that he found it difficult to watch an entire baseball game without being interrupted.
   a. beset
   b. belittled
   c. bereaved
   d. bequeathed
   e. bemused

5. The representative had _____ so many losing causes that he fainted dead away when his proposal was unanimously adopted by the legislature.
   a. championed
   b. caricatured
   c. misappropriated
   d. flouted
   e. mediated

Final Exam Drill #24: RELATIONSHIPS

For each question below, decide whether the pair of words are roughly similar (S) in meaning, roughly opposite (O) in meaning, or unrelated (U) to each other.

1. preempt	usurp
2. turpitude	confluence
3. incipient	culminating
4. burgeon	arbitrate
5. belittle	stymie
6. dictum	paradigm
7. luminous	incandescent
8. mortified	chagrined
9. precipitate	prudent
10. inscrutable	obscure

Final Exam Drill #25: ODD MAN OUT

Each question below consists of four words. Three of them are related in meaning. Find the word that does not fit.

1. intrinsic	innate	omnipotent	inherent
2. fortuitous	gregarious	convivial	amicable
3. cliché	verisimilitude	maxim	epigram
4. belligerent	indignant	pertinent	contentious
5. inane	hackneyed	platitudinous	conducive
6. vitriolic	acrimonious	choleric	prolific
7. gravity	austerity	vicissitude	sobriety
8. noxious	obsequious	pernicious	deleterious
9. finesse	competence	proficiency	euphemism
10. incorrigible	recalcitrant	diffident	obdurate

Final Exam Drill #26: RELATIONSHIPS

For each question below, decide whether the pair of words are roughly similar (S) in meaning, roughly opposite (O) in meaning, or unrelated (U) to each other.

1. catalyst	coherence
2. concord	dissonance
3. discord	consonant
4. ingenuous	urbane
5. infatuated	beguiled
6. categorical	contingent
7. novel	banal
8. parsimony	munificence
9. permeate	pervade
10. tentative	definitive

Final Exam Drill #27: COMPLETIONS

For each question below, choose the word that best completes the meaning of the sentence.

1. The trees, vines, and other plants in the tropical forest were truly remarkable, but it was the exotic _____ that caught the zoologist's attention.
   a. accolade
   b. compendium
   c. acumen
   d. fauna
   e. surfeit

2. Herb hated to pay extra for a fancy name, but he had discovered that he greatly preferred expensive brand-name products to the cheaper _____ ones.
   a. generic
   b. hypothetical
   c. supercilious
   d. amorphous
   e. contentious

3. After several years of disappointing crops, the enormous harvest left the farmers confronting a(n) _____ of soybeans.
   a. alacrity
   b. blight
   c. glut
   d. chasm
   e. debacle

4. The previously undefeated team found it difficult to cope with the _____ of defeat.
   a. attrition
   b. ignominy
   c. prerequisite
   d. penchant
   e. neologism

5. The darkening sky indicated to all of us that a thunderstorm was _____.
   a. ambivalent
   b. imminent
   c. conciliatory
   d. inherent
   e. lugubrious

Final Exam Drill #28: RELATIONSHIPS

For each question below, decide whether the pair of words are roughly similar (S) in meaning, roughly opposite (O) in meaning, or unrelated (U) to each other.

1. hegemony	heyday
2. fortuitous	nominal
3. deride	venerate
4. deduce	infer
5. supercilious	servile
6. placid	nonchalant
7. reverence	insolence
8. extraneous	extrinsic
9. levity	irony
10. onerous	exacting

Final Exam Drill #29: ODD MAN OUT

Each question below consists of four words. Three of them are related in meaning. Find the word that does not fit.

1. comprise	placate	appease	mollify
2. beguile	bemuse	cajole	delude
3. provident	egregious	flagrant	unconscionable
4. adept	adroit	anecdotal	dexterous
5. iconoclast	insurgent	maverick	prodigy
6. cadence	incisiveness	acumen	acuity
7. gratuitous	superfluous	soporific	inordinate
8. incongruous	staunch	anomalous	eccentric
9. vacillate	incense	foment	instigate
10. aberration	vestige	anomaly	singularity

Final Exam Drill #30: RELATIONSHIPS

For each question below, decide whether the pair of words are roughly similar (S) in meaning, roughly opposite (O) in meaning, or unrelated (U) to each other.

1. mandate	martyr
2. laud	defame
3. belabor	complement
4. disdain	supercilious
5. distinguish	distend
6. eulogize	censure
7. apocalypse	covenant
8. segregate	sequester
9. quixotic	utopian
10. microcosm	magnate

Final Exam Drill #31: COMPLETIONS

For each question below, choose the word that best completes the meaning of the sentence.

1. The _____ salesperson bowed deeply and said, "Yes, sir, of course, sir," whenever I requested anything.
   a. verbose
   b. incumbent
   c. evanescent
   d. malingering
   e. obsequious

2. Because he had never lost a tennis match, Luther believed himself to be _____ on the court.
   a. ascetic
   b. deleterious
   c. omnipotent
   d. inane
   e. amorous

3. Our teacher was so _____ in his interpretation of the novel that it was difficult to believe he had taken any pleasure in reading it.
   a. pedantic
   b. laudable
   c. intrepid
   d. inveterate
   e. coherent

4. The prisoners were all _____ as they were led off to the firing squad, but they were shot all the same.
   a. perfunctory
   b. concise
   c. virulent
   d. prosaic
   e. penitent

5. The divisive issue _____ the community; half the residents seemed to be strongly for it, and half strongly against.
   a. circumscribed
   b. polarized
   c. assuaged
   d. castigated
   e. disseminated

Final Exam Drill #32: RELATIONSHIPS

For each question below, decide whether the pair of words are roughly
similar (S) in meaning, roughly opposite (O) in meaning, or unrelated (U) to
each other.

1.	reverence	disdain
2.	conjure	incant
3.	profound	superficial
4.	protract	curtail
5.	fauna	glut
6.	deprecate	lament
7.	abridge	augment
8.	eccentric	orthodox
9.	iconoclast	maverick
10.	idiosyncratic	conventional

Final Exam Drill #33: ODD MAN OUT

Each question below consists of four words. Three of them are related in
meaning. Find the word that does not fit.

1.	infamous	abhorrence	innocuous	nefarious
2.	assimilate	abate	mitigate	alleviate
3.	laconic	unctuous	concise	terse
4.	relinquish	renounce	forsake	exult
5.	axiom	maxim	surrogate	precept
6.	virulent	tantamount	adverse	baneful
7.	catharsis	abhorrence	rancor	animosity
8.	idiosyncrasy	eccentricity	complacency	affectation
9.	antecedent	precursor	precedent	recrimination
10.	exonerate	patronize	exculpate	vindicate

Final Exam Drill #34: RELATIONSHIPS

For each question below, decide whether the pair of words are roughly
similar (S) in meaning, roughly opposite (O) in meaning, or unrelated (U) to
each other.

1.	slothful	assiduous
2.	affluent	opulent
3.	consummate	rudimentary
4.	chastisement	amnesty
5.	sycophant	cajoler
6.	implication	allusion
7.	quantitative	qualitative
8.	agenda	itinerary
9.	pragmatic	quixotic
10.	paradox	anomaly

Final Exam Drill #35: BUDDY CHECK

For each question below, match the word on the left with the word most similar in meaning on the right.

1. torpid	a. subservient
2. sublime	b. astuteness
3. recapitulate	c. ingenuous
4. acuity	d. subtlety
5. replete	e. provincial
6. subordinate	f. inert
7. parochial	g. transcendent
8. credulous	h. reiterate
9. recant	i. satiated
10. nuance	j. repudiate

Final Exam Drill #36: RELATIONSHIPS

For each question below, decide whether the pair of words are roughly similar (S) in meaning, roughly opposite (O) in meaning, or unrelated (U) to each other.

1. colloquial	contiguous
2. auspicious	portentous
3. moribund	viable
4. aristocratic	patrician
5. perquisite	prerogative
6. stagnation	metamorphosis
7. ebullient	roguish
8. turpitude	sordidness
9. cosmopolitan	urbane
10. denizen	lampoon

Final Exam Drill #37: COMPLETIONS

For each question below, choose the word that best completes the meaning of the sentence.

1. The _____ spring weather was a great relief to all of us who had struggled through the long, harsh winter.

a. abortive
b. volatile
c. temperate
d. pragmatic
e. intrinsic

2. I made a(n) _____ effort to repair the leak, but my improvised patch didn't hold and I soon realized that I would have to call a plumber.

a. vindictive
b. tentative
c. pristine
d. acrid
e. caustic

3. The adoring members of the tribe _____ their old king even though he was blind and senile.

a. squandered
b. extrapolated
c. beleaguered
d. exacerbated
e. venerated

4. The hikers were _____ by the billions of mosquitoes that descended upon them as soon as they hit the trail.

a. extolled
b. vitiated
c. palliated
d. vexed
e. promulgated

5. Seeing the pictures of our old home made us feel _____ and nostalgic.

a. adept
b. fastidious
c. wistful
d. infamous
e. impartial

Final Exam Drill #38: RELATIONSHIPS
For each question below, decide whether the pair of words are roughly similar (S) in meaning, roughly opposite (O) in meaning, or unrelated (U) to each other.

1.	ardent	indifferent
2.	adherent	forsaker
3.	poignant	redolent
4.	inundate	reconcile
5.	abject	exalted
6.	proselytize	implement
7.	latent	manifest
8.	burgeon	accost
9.	immutable	static
10.	perfidy	piety

Final Exam Drill #39: ODD MAN OUT
Each question below consists of four words. Three of them are related in meaning. Find the word that does not fit.

1.	quixotic	scintillating	chimerical	visionary
2.	antipathy	malfeasance	digression	malevolence
3.	absolute	unqualified	categorical	wistful
4.	static	cerebral	inert	immutable
5.	destitute	insolvent	affable	indigent
6.	altruist	benevolent	philanthropic	ideological
7.	vexed	unequivocal	unalloyed	unmitigated
8.	comprehensive	stringent	rigorous	exacting
9.	abstract	abstruse	intangible	impervious
10.	discernment	tirade	discrimination	sagacity

Final Exam Drill #40: RELATIONSHIPS
For each question below, decide whether the pair of words are roughly similar (S) in meaning, roughly opposite (O) in meaning, or unrelated (U) to each other.

1.	plethora	dearth
2.	autonomy	subjugation
3.	aggregate	augment
4.	vocation	avocation
5.	extraneous	intrinsic
6.	implicit	inferred
7.	invective	eulogy
8.	acerbic	caustic
9.	insinuation	hyperbole
10.	adulterated	unalloyed

Final Exam Drill #41: COMPLETIONS

For each question below, choose the word that best completes the meaning of the sentence.

1. An _____ current of dissatisfaction among the soldiers indicated to the ambassador that revolution was becoming a possibility.
   a. incipient
   b. inert
   c. impervious
   d. impeccable
   e. inept

2. The _____ surgeon sewed Lana's finger to her forehead.
   a. bucolic
   b. ursine
   c. cosmopolitan
   d. infinitesimal
   e. incompetent

3. Irene's _____ cure for her husband's snoring was a paper bag tied snugly around his head.
   a. agnostic
   b. congenital
   c. extrinsic
   d. ingenious
   e. diffident

4. Myron looked harmless, but there was nothing _____ about his plan to enslave the human race.
   a. terse
   b. innocuous
   c. mendacious
   d. nominal
   e. preeminent

5. Attempting to bask in reflected glory, the candidate _____ the names of eleven past presidents in his speech to the convention of schoolteachers.
   a. absolved
   b. implied
   c. litigated
   d. invoked
   e. allocated

Final Exam Drill #42: RELATIONSHIPS

For each question below, decide whether the pair of words are roughly
similar (S) in meaning, roughly opposite (O) in meaning, or unrelated (U)
to each other.

1.	ambience	milieu
2.	literal	figurative
3.	hypothetical	empirical
4.	subjugate	enfranchise
5.	taciturn	integral
6.	congenital	innate
7.	enfetter	expedite
8.	peripheral	tangential
9.	usurp	abdicate
10.	consummate	abortive

Final Exam Drill #43: ODD MAN OUT

Each question below consists of four words. Three of them are related in
meaning. Find the word that does not fit.

1.	cacophony	antagonism	rancor	antipathy
2.	discord	benefactor	contention	incongruity
3.	apathy	indifference	manifesto	languor
4.	amenable	tractable	docile	reciprocal
5.	clandestine	surreptitious	provisional	furtive
6.	intrepid	blithe	squalid	equanimous
7.	callow	apocryphal	dubious	spurious
8.	putative	overt	explicit	patent
9.	desultory	derisory	cursory	perfunctory
10.	conciliate	proscribe	appease	placate

Final Exam Drill #44: BUDDY CHECK

For each question below, match the word on the left with the word most
nearly its **OPPOSITE** on the right.

1.	deferential	a.	irreverent
2.	remonstrate	b.	assiduous
3.	tacit	c.	amorous
4.	clement	d.	explicit
5.	indolent	e.	acquiesce
6.	ambivalent	f.	intemperate
7.	aloof	g.	aversion
8.	lucid	h.	antagonist
9.	partisan	i.	enigmatic
10.	affinity	j.	resolute

Final Exam Drill #45: RELATIONSHIPS

For each question below, decide whether the pair of words are roughly similar (S) in meaning, roughly opposite (O) in meaning, or unrelated (U) to each other.

1.	artifice	machination
2.	obtuse	myopic
3.	respite	premise
4.	exalt	laud
5.	assimilate	appreciate
6.	edify	obfuscate
7.	pensive	ruminating
8.	narcissist	egocentric
9.	precipitate	stigmatize
10.	polemical	contentious

Final Exam Drill #46: COMPLETIONS

For each question below, choose the word that best completes the meaning of the sentence.

1. The three-year-old was _____ in his refusal to taste the broccoli.
   a. recondite
   b. didactic
   c. fortuitous
   d. resolute
   e. genteel

2. We _____ the fine print in the document but were unable to find the clause the lawyer had mentioned.
   a. scrutinized
   b. reconciled
   c. exculpated
   d. cajoled
   e. accrued

3. A state in which one can see, hear, feel, smell, and taste little or nothing is known as _____ deprivation.
   a. aggregate
   b. subversive
   c. sensory
   d. sensual
   e. sensuous

4. The children tried to be _____ about the fact that their parents couldn't afford to give them Christmas presents, but you could tell that they were really quite depressed inside.

a. tangential
b. abysmal
c. stoic
d. disingenuous
e. eclectic

5. We felt repeatedly _____ by the impersonal and inflexible bureaucracy in our attempt to win an exemption to the rule.

a. vindicated
b. deluged
c. stymied
d. reiterated
e. gesticulated

Final Exam Drill #47: RELATIONSHIPS

For each question below, decide whether the pair of words are roughly similar (S) in meaning, roughly opposite (O) in meaning, or unrelated (U) to each other.

1. cliché   platitude
2. malevolent   macroeconomic
3. juxtaposed   contiguous
4. defame   laud
5. idyllic   bucolic
6. inexorable   irrevocable
7. despondent   sanguine
8. lethargy   zeal
9. dogma   tenet
10. ebullient   stoic

Final Exam Drill #48: COMPLETIONS

For each question below, choose the word that best completes the meaning of the sentence.

1. The gasoline spill had so thoroughly _____ the town's main well that it was possible to run an automobile on tap water.

a. exulted
b. exalted
c. engendered
d. adulterated
e. preempted

2. Mr. Jones _____ the teenagers after they had driven the stolen car into his living room and put a dent in his new color TV.
   a. admonished
   b. usurped
   c. enervated
   d. alleged
   e. professed

3. Henry's legs were so severely injured in the roller-skating accident that he didn't become fully _____ again until more than a year later.
   a. decadent
   b. exemplified
   c. querulous
   d. portentous
   e. ambulatory

4. The kitchen in the new house had an electronic vegetable peeler, an automatic dish scraper, a computerized meat slicer, and dozens of other futuristic _____.
   a. proponents
   b. genres
   c. amenities
   d. mendicants
   e. protagonists

5. When Joe began collecting stamps, he hoped that the value of his collection would _____ rapidly; instead, the collection has slowly become worthless.
   a. qualify
   b. appreciate
   c. polarize
   d. belabor
   e. rebuke

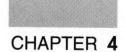

CHAPTER 4

THE
SAT HIT
PARADE

Despite all the talk about "scholastic aptitude" and "reasoning ability," the verbal Scholastic Aptitude Test (SAT) is primarily a vocabulary test. If you don't know the words on the test, you won't earn a good score. It's as simple as that.

If you learn every word on the main word list in this book, you'll have a big advantage on the SAT. The bigger your vocabulary, the better you'll do. But not every word on the main list is the sort of word that is tested on the SAT. If you're getting ready to take the SAT or a similar standardized test, you should focus your attention on the words in the following list, which we call the Hit Parade.

The Hit Parade is a list of the words tested most frequently on the SAT, *in order of their frequency on the SAT.* We created the Hit Parade by using a computer to analyze all released SATs. Princeton Review students use the Hit Parade to get the maximum possible mileage out of their vocabularies and improve their verbal SAT scores. Not all Hit Parade words appear on our main word list, but all of them have appeared on recent SATs.

We've included short definitions to make it easier for you to learn the words. These definitions aren't always exactly like the ones you'll find in the dictionary or the main word list of this book; they're the definitions of the words *as they are tested on the SAT.*

Keep in mind that these are not the *only* words you need to know for the SAT. They're just the words that have been tested most frequently in the past—the words that the Educational Testing Service's question writers tend to come back to over and over again. Also keep in mind that the words near the top of the list are more likely to turn up than the words near the bottom.

Some SATs are absolutely loaded with Hit Parade words; others don't contain as many. One of the most important things the Hit Parade will teach you is the *level* of the vocabulary on the test. Once you get a feel for this level, you'll be able to spot other possible SAT words in your reading.

After you finish the Hit Parade, you might want to memorize the GRE Hit Parade that follows. All the words in *Word Smart,* by the way, are SAT-type words.

indifferent not caring one way or the other; mediocre; lacking a preference; neutral

apathy lack of emotion or interest

obscure unclear; clouded; partially hidden; hard to understand

impartial unbiased; neutral

objective without bias (as opposed to *subjective*)

revere to worship; to honor (think of a reverend)

discriminate to differentiate; to make a clear distinction; to see the difference

denounce to speak out against; to condemn

innovate to be creative; to introduce something new

relevant important; pertinent

candid honest; frank

discernment insight; ability to see things clearly

disdain arrogant scorn; contempt

abstract theoretical; lacking substance (the opposite of *concrete*)

temperate moderate; restrained

enigma mystery

inevitable unavoidable; bound to happen

eccentric not conventional; a little kooky; irregular

provincial limited in outlook to one's own small corner of the world; narrow

futile hopeless; without effect

diverse varied

benevolent kind; good-hearted; generous

pious reverent or devout; outwardly (and sometimes falsely) reverent or devout

conciliatory making peace; attempting to solve a dispute through goodwill

resignation reluctant acceptance of a bad situation (secondary meaning)

resolute determined; firm; unwavering

servile submissive and subservient; like a servant

acute sharp; shrewd

reticent restrained; uncommunicative

anarchy absence of government or control; lawlessness; disorder

virulent extremely poisonous; malignant; full of hate

scrutinize to examine closely

discord disagreement (the opposite of *concord*)

repudiate to reject; to deny

diligent hardworking

superficial on the surface only; shallow; not thorough

contempt reproachful disdain

lucid clear; easy to understand

aesthetic having to do with artistic beauty; artistic (not to be confused with *ascetic*, also on the Hit Parade)

prodigal extravagant; wasteful

augment to add to; to increase; to make bigger

complacent smug; self-satisfied; pleased with oneself; contented to a fault

guile cunning; duplicity

squander to waste

incessant unceasing; never-ending

laudable worthy of praise

deter to prevent; to stop; to keep from doing something

redundant repetitive; unnecessary; excessively wordy

infamous shamefully wicked; having (and deserving) an extremely bad reputation; disgraceful

provocative exciting; attracting attention

depravity moral corruption

gravity seriousness (secondary meaning)

banal unoriginal; ordinary

extol to praise

euphony pleasant sound (the opposite is *cacophony*)

deride to ridicule; to laugh at contemptuously

insipid dull; banal

austere unadorned; stern; forbidding; without much money

expedite to make faster or easier

heresy an opinion violently opposed to established beliefs

novel new; original

philanthropy love of mankind; donating to charity

tentative experimental; temporary; uncertain

deference submission to another's will; respect; courtesy

vacillate to be indecisive; to waver back and forth

fervor passion

dispassionate without passion; objective; neutral

pragmatic practical; down-to-earth; based on experience rather than theory

rigorous strict; harsh; severe

solemn serious; grave

alleviate to lessen; to relieve, usually temporarily or incompletely; to make bearable

negligence carelessness

conspicuous standing out; obvious

advocate to speak in favor of; to support

ascetic hermitlike; practicing self-denial

profound deep; insightful (the opposite of *superficial*)

ironic satiric; unexpected

dogmatic arrogantly assertive of unproven ideas; arrogantly claiming that something (often a system of beliefs) is beyond dispute

condone to overlook; to permit to happen

dissent disagreement

volition will; conscious choice

voluntary willing; unforced

didactic instructive; intended to instruct

disparate different; incompatible

disparage to belittle; to say uncomplimentary things about, usually in a somewhat indirect way

ephemeral short-lived; fleeting; not lasting

compliant yielding; submissive

prosaic dull; unimaginative; like prose

profuse flowing; extravagant

expedient providing an immediate advantage; serving one's immediate self-interest

fastidious meticulous; demanding

belligerent combative; quarrelsome; waging war

astute perceptive; intelligent

languish to become weak, listless, or depressed

censure to condemn severely for doing something bad

stagnation motionlessness; inactivity

mitigate to lessen the severity of something

reprehensible worthy of blame or censure

engender to create; to produce

exemplary outstanding; setting a great example

neutral unbiased; not taking sides; objective

relegate to banish; to send away

anecdote a brief, entertaining story

scanty inadequate; minimal

fallacious false

acclaim praise; applause; admiration

uniform consistent; unchanging; the same for everyone

incoherent jumbled; chaotic; impossible to understand

repress to hold down

articulate speaking clearly and well

solicit to ask for; to seek

reproach to scold

condescend to stoop to someone else's level, usually in an offensive way; to patronize

orthodox conventional; adhering to established principles or doctrines, especially in religion; by the book

indolence laziness

congenial agreeably suitable; pleasant

preclude to prevent; to make impossible; to shut out

apprehensive worried; anxious

elaborate detailed; careful; thorough

arrogant feeling superior to others; snooty

elusive hard to pin down; evasive

efface to erase; to rub away the features of

taciturn untalkative by nature

ameliorate to make better or more tolerable

acquiesce to give in; to agree

atrophy to waste away from lack of use

dubious doubtful; uncertain

flagrant shocking; outstandingly bad

concise brief and to the point; succinct
immutable unchangeable; permanent
static stationary; not changing or moving (not radio fuzz)
credulous believing; gullible
blasphemy irreverence; an insult to something held sacred; profanity
coalesce to come together as one; to fuse; to unite
lax careless; not diligent; relaxed
cryptic mysterious; mystifying
levity lightness; frivolity; unseriousness
ambivalent undecided; blowing hot and cold
innate existing since birth; inborn; inherent
sycophant one who sucks up to others
amiable friendly
esoteric hard to understand; understood by only a select few; peculiar
extraneous irrelevant; extra; unnecessary; unimportant
tedious boring
caustic like acid; corrosive
inadvertent lax; careless; without intention
exhaustive thorough; complete
incongruous not harmonious; not consistent; not appropriate
belittle to make to seem little
unprecedented happening for the first time; novel; never seen before
digress to go off the subject
appease to soothe; to pacify by giving in to
frivolous not serious; not solemn; with levity
instigate to provoke; to stir up
sage wise; possessing wisdom derived from experience or learning
predecessor someone or something that came before another
jeopardy danger
tangible touchable; palpable
indulgent lenient; yielding to desire
remorse sadness; regret
pivotal crucial
scrupulous strict; careful; hesitant for ethical reasons
refute to disprove; to prove to be false
respite a rest; a period of relief
stoic indifferent (at least outwardly) to pleasure or pain, to joy or grief, to fortune or misfortune
volatile quick to evaporate; highly unstable; explosive
peripheral unimportant
hedonistic pleasure-seeking; indulgent
idiom a peculiar expression
benefactor a generous donor
brevity briefness
apocryphal of doubtful origin; false
virtuoso masterful musician; a masterful practitioner in some other field
slander to defame; to speak maliciously of someone

animosity resentment; hostility; ill will
deplete to use up; to reduce; to lessen
amity friendship
stringent strict; restrictive
voluminous very large; spacious (this word has nothing to do with sound)
auspicious favorable; promising; pointing to a good result
fickle capricious; whimsical; unpredictable
lethargy sluggishness; laziness; drowsiness; indifference
hackneyed banal; overused; trite (a *cliché* is a hackneyed expression)
amass to accumulate
willful deliberate; obstinate; insistent on having one's way
bastion stronghold; fortress; fortified place
trepidation fear; apprehension; nervous trembling
desecrate to profane a holy place (the opposite is *consecrate*)
fortuitous accidental; occurring by chance
vehement urgent; passionate
assuage to soothe; to pacify; to ease the pain of; to relieve
prodigious extraordinary; enormous
torpor sluggishness; inactivity; apathy
furtive secretive
supercilious haughty; patronizing
prudent careful; having foresight
verbose wordy; overly talkative
pedestrian common; ordinary; banal (secondary meaning)
innocuous harmless; banal
fanatic one who is extremely devoted to a cause or idea
enhance to make better; to augment
retract to take back; to withdraw; to pull back
ambiguous unclear in meaning; confusing; capable of being interpreted in at least two similarly plausible ways
paucity scarcity
rescind to repeal; to take back formally
subtle not obvious; able to make fine distinctions; ingenious; crafty
zealous fervent; enthusiastically devoted to something
benign gentle; not harmful; kind; mild
compliant yielding; submissive
emulate to strive to equal or excel, usually through imitation
innumerable too many to number or count; many
meander to wander slowly, like a winding river
authoritarian like a dictator
brawn bulk; muscles
contrite deeply apologetic; remorseful
exemplify to serve as an example of
facilitate to make easier
hypothetical uncertain; unproven
recalcitrant stubbornly defiant of authority or control
ambulatory able to walk; walking

diffident timid; lacking in self-confidence
drone to talk on and on in a dull way
gullible overly trusting; willing to believe anything
marred damaged; bruised
nullify to make unimportant
parsimony stinginess
propriety properness; good manners
rejuvenate to make young and strong again
skeptical doubting (opposite of *gullible*)
tenacious tough; hard to defeat
animated alive; moving
authentic real
bias prejudice; tendency; tilt
blithe carefree; cheerful
dearth a lack of; scarcity
divert to change the direction of; to alter the course of; to amuse
enthrall to thrill
heed to listen to
hindrance an obstruction; an annoying interference or delay
irascible irritable
merger a joining or marriage
nostalgia a sentimental longing for the past; homesickness
pretentious pompous; self-important; ETS-like
saccharine sweet; excessively or disgustingly sweet
stanza a section of a poem; verse
venerate to revere; to treat as something holy, especially because of great age
vilify to say vile things about; to defame

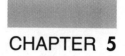

CHAPTER 5

THE
GRE HIT
PARADE

The GRE (Graduate Record Examination) is the SAT for graduate school. Two of the sections on the GRE are verbal. How well you do in these sections is almost exclusively determined by your vocabulary. If you know a lot of words, you'll do fine; if you don't, you'd better start learning some. Today.

The GRE Hit Parade, like the SAT Hit Parade, includes those words most likely to appear on a GRE. We have listed them roughly in order of importance. All of these words appear frequently, but *manifest* is marginally more likely to appear than *conventional,* and so on.

These are not the only words that can appear on the GRE, but they are the most likely. This list is a start. If you know all of these words, get cracking on the other *Word Smart* definitions. (Many GRE Hit Parade words are also on the *Word Smart* core list.)

It should go without saying that you need to know all the words on the SAT Hit Parade, too.

manifest visible; evident
conventional common; customary; unexceptional
partisan one who supports a particular person, cause, or idea
contentious argumentative; quarrelsome
lament to mourn
allusion an indirect reference to something else, especially something in literature; a hint
arbiter one who decides; a judge
inherent part of the essential nature of something; intrinsic
paradox a true statement or phenomenon that nonetheless seems to contradict itself; an untrue statement or phenomenon that nonetheless seems logical
cynic one who deeply distrusts human nature; one who believes people are motivated only by selfishness
exposition expounding or explaining; explanatory treatise
consensus unanimity or near unanimity
comprehensive covering or including everything
sagacious wise; possessing wisdom derived from experience or learning
precipitate to cause to happen abruptly
pervade to spread throughout
discourse to converse; to formally discuss a subject

conjure to summon or bring into being as if by magic
sanction authorize or approve; ratify or confirm
genial cheerful and pleasant; friendly; helpful
indulgent lenient; yielding to desire
inert inactive; sluggish; not reacting chemically
levee an embankment designed to prevent the flooding of a river
erratic unpredictable or wandering
luminous giving off light; glowing; bright
abstinent abstaining; voluntarily not doing something
placid pleasantly calm; peaceful
exuberant extremely joyful or vigorous; profuse in growth
impede to hinder; to obstruct; to slow something down
permeate to spread or seep through; to penetrate
audacity boldness; reckless daring; impertinence
indignant angry, especially as a result of something unjust or unworthy
implicit implied rather than expressly stated
renaissance/renascence a rebirth or revival
superfluous extra; unnecessary
litigate to try in court; to engage in legal proceedings
vex to annoy; to pester; to confuse
anomaly an aberration; an irregularity; a deviation
bereave to deprive or leave desolate, especially through death
connoisseur an expert, particularly in matters of art or taste
corroborate to confirm; to back up with evidence
frenetic frantic; frenzied
polemic a powerful argument made in refutation of something
synthesis the combining of parts to form a whole
feasible able to be done
forbear to refrain from; to abstain
genre an artistic class or category
vindicate to clear from all blame or suspicion
conciliatory making peace; attempting to resolve a dispute through goodwill
squalid filthy; repulsive; wretched; degraded
inept clumsy; incompetent
mandatory authoritatively ordered or commanded; necessary
disseminate to scatter or spread widely
eclectic choosing the best from many sources; drawn from many sources
idyllic charming in a rustic way; naturally peaceful
pristine original; unspoiled; pure
prodigy an extremely talented child; an extraordinary accomplishment or occurrence
frugal economical; penny-pinching
qualify to modify or restrict
decorous in good taste; orderly
infer to conclude; to deduce
ostentatious excessively conspicuous; showing off
pathology the science of diseases; any deviation from a healthy, normal condition

plumb to measure the depth of something
spurious doubtful; bogus; false
subjugate to subdue and dominate; to enslave
visionary a dreamer; someone with impractical goals or ideas about
    the future
reciprocal mutual; shared; interchangeable
antipathy firm dislike; dislike; hatred
dissonant inharmonious; in disagreement
palliate to hide the seriousness of something with excuses or apologies
substantive having substance; real; essential; solid; substantial
surreptitious sneaky; secret
equivocal ambiguous; intentionally confusing; capable of being inter-
    preted in more than one way
flippant frivolously shallow and disrespectful
impervious not allowing anything to pass through; impenetrable
judicious exercising sound judgment
laconic using few words, especially to the point of being rude
piquant pungent
satiric using sarcasm or irony
sullen gloomy or dismal
tacit implied; not spoken
tractable easily managed or controlled; obedient
impromptu without preparation; on the spur of the moment
parallel a comparison made between two things
sterile unimaginative; unfruitful; infertile
debauchery corruption by sensuality; intemperance; wild living
deleterious harmful
disinterested unbiased
fecund fertile; productive
hermetic impervious to external influence; airtight
salubrious promoting health
foster to promote the growth or development of
transitory not staying for a long time; temporary
cacophony a harsh-sounding mixture of words, voices, or sounds
goad to urge forcefully; to taunt someone into doing something
implement to carry out
ingenuous unwarily simple; candid; naive
malleable easy to shape or bend
pungent forceful; sharp or biting to the taste or smell
savor to linger on the taste or smell of something
correlate to find or show the relationship of two things
facetious humorous; not serious; clumsily humorous
kinship natural or family relationship
petulant rude; cranky; ill tempered
rampart a fortification; a bulwark or defense
temerity boldness; recklessness; audacity
truculent savagely brutal; aggressively hostile
incisive cutting right to the heart of the matter

aberration something not typical; a deviation from the standard
abstemious sparing or moderate, especially in eating and drinking
alacrity cheerful readiness; liveliness or eagerness
allocate to distribute; assign; allot
arid extremely dry; unimaginative; dull
beget to cause or produce; to engender
conundrum a puzzle; a riddle
debacle violent breakdown; sudden overthrow
doggerel comic, loose verse
exorbitance an exceedingly large amount
garrulous extremely chatty or talkative; wordy or diffuse
intransigent uncompromising; stubborn
maverick a nonconformist; a rebel
turpitude shameful wickedness or depravity
axiom a self-evident rule or truth; a widely accepted saying
beneficent doing good
capricious unpredictable; likely to change at any moment
circumlocution an indirect expression; use of wordy or evasive language
impugn to attack, especially to attack the truth or integrity of something
incursion a hostile invasion
invective insulting or abusive speech
placate to pacify; to appease; to soothe
temperament one's disposition or character
antiseptic free from germs; exceptionally clean
lax not strict or firm; careless or negligent; loose or slack
accolade an award or honor; high praise
assiduous hardworking; busy; diligent
brook to bear or tolerate; to put up with something
desiccate to dry out
erudite scholarly; deeply learned
flag to weaken; to slow down
impudent bold; impertinent
baleful menacing; harmful
divergent differing in opinion; deviating
effluvium a disagreeable or noxious vapor; an escaping gas
evanescent vanishing or fading; scarcely perceptible
exigent demanding prompt action; urgent
exonerate to free completely from blame
flaunt to show off; to display ostentatiously
improvident lacking prudent foresight; careless
ineluctable inescapable; unavoidable
mellifluous sweetly flowing
oscillate to swing back and forth; to fluctuate
ossify to convert into bone; to become rigid
probity integrity; uprightness; honesty
proselytize to convert someone from one religion or doctrine to another; to recruit converts to a religion or doctrine

pundit a learned person; an expert in a particular field

recondite hard to understand; over one's head

spendthrift extravagant or wasteful, especially with money

vacuous lacking ideas or intelligence

coda a passage concluding a composition (in music)

penchant strong taste or liking

abstruse hard to understand or grasp

cognizant perceptive; observant

gainsay to deny; to speak or act against

garner to gather and store

obdurate stubborn; inflexible

propinquity nearness

ribald vulgar or indecent speech or language, as in a ribald joke

sinuous having many curves

veracity truthfulness

chronology an order of events from earliest to latest

economical frugal; thrifty

conjoin to join or act together

panegyric lofty praise

pedagogue a strict, overly academic teacher

reprobate a wicked, sinful, depraved person

untoward unfavorable or unfortunate; improper

welter a confused mass; a commotion or turmoil

inchoate just beginning; not organized or orderly

problematic doubtful or questionable

timbre the quality of a sound independent of pitch and loudness

disavow to deny

gerrymander to divide a state or county into election districts to gain political advantage

repugnant distasteful or offensive

taut tightly drawn, as a rope; emotionally tense

cajole to deceptively persuade someone to do something he or she doesn't want to do

discomfit to confuse, deject, frustrate, deceive

accrete to increase by growth or addition

contumacious stubbornly rebellious or disobedient

fulsome disgusting or repulsive

homeostasis the tendency of an organic system to maintain internal stability

hone to sharpen

insolvent unable to pay one's bills

ligneous woodlike

motility spontaneous movement

munificent very generous; lavish

neophyte a beginner

rivet to fix one's attention on

saturnine a sluggish, gloomy temperament

viscous thick and sticky

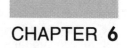

CHAPTER 6

WORD ROOTS YOU SHOULD KNOW

We discussed the use of roots on pages 19–21. Here is a list of the most helpful roots to know. As we said earlier, learning roots helps you memorize words. We've concentrated on roots that will help you learn the *Word Smart* words, but the Root Parade will help you memorize hundreds of other words, too.

When you look up the definition of a word on this list, try to relate that definition to the root. Some students go through this list one root at a time. They look up all the words under one root and learn the definitions together. As always, whatever works for you is best.

You Don't Have to Memorize These Roots— You Already Know Them!

To show you how each root relates to words you already know, each list includes an easy word or two. For example, the letters "spic" come from a Latin word meaning to look or see, as in the easy words *conspicuous* and *suspicious*. Recognizing that will help you memorize the definition of the difficult word *auspicious,* which is on the same list. And you thought you didn't know Latin!

You will notice that the same root can be spelled in different ways. We have included the most common spelling variations in the heading. Remember that roots tell us the common heritage of words thousands of years old, and over the centuries spelling variations occur.

A note to philologists (etymologically: "word lovers"): in keeping with our pragmatic philosophy, we have sometimes taken liberties in compiling this list.

A (without)
amoral
atheist
atypical
anonymous
apathy
amorphous
atrophy
apartheid
anomaly
agnostic

AB/ABS (off, away from, apart, down)
abduct
abhor
abolish
abstract
abnormal
abdicate
abstinent
absolution
abstruse
abrogate

abscond
abjure
abstemious
ablution
abominate
aberrant

AC/ACR (sharp, bitter)
acid
acute
acerbic
exacerbate
acrid
acrimonious
acumen

ACT/AG (to do, to drive, to force, to lead)
act
agent
agile
agitate
exacting
litigate
prodigal
prodigious
pedagogue
demagogue
synagogue
cogent
exigent

AD/AL (to, toward, near)
adapt
adjacent
addict
admire
address
adhere
administer
adore
advice
adjoin
adultery
advocate
allure
alloy

AL/ALI/ALTER (other, another)
alternative
alias
alibi
alien
alter ego
alienation
altruist
altercation
allegory

AM (love)
amateur
amatory
amorous
enamored
amity
paramour
inamorata
amiable
amicable

AMB (to go, to walk)
ambitious
amble
preamble
ambulance
ambulatory
perambulator
circumambulate

AMB/AMPH (around)
amphitheater
ambit
ambience
ambient

AMB/AMPH (both, more than one)
ambiguous
amphibian
ambivalent
ambidextrous

ANIM (life, mind, soul, spirit)
unanimous
animosity
equanimity
magnanimous
pusillanimous

ANTE (before)
ante
anterior
antecedent
antedate
antebellum
antediluvian

ANTHRO/ANDR (man, human)
anthropology
android
misanthrope
philanthropy
anthropomorphic
philander
androgynous
anthropocentric

ANNU/ENNI (year)
annual
anniversary
biannual
biennial
centennial
annuity
perennial
annals
millennium

ANTI (against)
antidote
antiseptic
antipathy
antipodal

APO (away)
apology
apostle
apocalypse
apogee
apocryphal
apotheosis
apostasy
apoplexy

APT/EPT (skill, fitness, ability)
adapt
aptitude
apt
inept
adept

ARCH/ARCHI (chief, principal)
architect
archenemy
archetype
archipelago

ARCHY (ruler)
monarchy
matriarchy
patriarchy
anarchy
hierarchy
oligarchy

ART (skill, craft)
art
artificial
artifice
artisan
artifact
artful
artless

AUC/AUG/AUX (to increase)
auction
auxiliary
augment
august

AUTO (self)
automatic
autopsy
autocrat
autonomy

BE (to be, to have a certain quality)
belittle
belated
bemoan
befriend
bewilder
begrudge
bequeath
bespeak
belie
beguile
beset
bemuse
bereft

BEL/BELL (war)
rebel
belligerent
bellicose
antebellum

BEN/BON (good)
benefit
beneficiary
beneficent
benefactor
benign
benevolent
benediction
bonus
bon vivant
bona fide

BI (twice, doubly)
binoculars
biannual
biennial
bigamy
bilateral
bilingual
bipartisan

BRI/BREV (brief, short)
brief
abbreviate
abridge
brevity

CAD/CID
(to fall, to happen by chance)
accident
coincidence
decadent
cascade
recidivism
cadence

CAND (to burn)
candle
incandescent
candor

CANT/CENT/CHANT (to sing)
chant
enchant

accent
recant
incantation
incentive

CAP/CIP/CEPT (to take, to get)
capture
anticipate
intercept
susceptible
emancipate
recipient
incipient
percipient
precept

CAP/CAPIT/CIPIT
(head, headlong)
capital
cape
captain
disciple
principle
principal
precipice
precipitate
precipitous
capitulate
capitalism
precipitation
caption
recapitulate

CARD/CORD/COUR (heart)
cardiac
courage
encourage
concord
discord
accord
concordance
cordial

CARN (flesh)
carnivorous
carnival
carnal
carnage
reincarnation
incarnation

CAST/CHAST (cut)
caste
castigate
chastise
chaste

CAUST (to burn)
caustic
holocaust

CED/CEED/CESS (to go, to yield, to stop)
exceed
precede
recess
concede
cede
access
predecessor
precedent
antecedent
recede
abscess
cessation
incessant

CENTR (center)
central
concentrate
eccentric
concentric
centrifuge
egocentric

CERN/CERT/CRET/CRIM/CRIT (to separate, to judge, to distinguish, to decide)
concern
critic
secret
crime
discrete
ascertain
certitude
hypocrite
discriminate
criterion
discern
recrimination

CHRON (time)
synchronize
chronicle
chronology
chronic
chronological
anachronism
chronometer

CIRCU (around, on all sides)
circumference
circumstances
circuit
circumspect
circumvent
circumnavigate
circumambulate
circumlocution
circumscribe
circuitous

CIS (to cut)
scissors
precise
exorcise
excise
incision
incisive
concise

CIT (to set in motion)
excite
incite
solicit
solicitous

CLA/CLO/CLU (shut, close)
closet
enclose
conclude
claustrophobia
disclose
exclusive
recluse
preclude
seclude
cloister
foreclose

CLAIM/CLAM
(to shout, to cry out)
exclaim
proclaim
acclaim
clamor
disclaim
reclaim
declaim

CLI (to lean toward)
decline
recline
climax
proclivity
disinclination

CO/COL/COM/CON
(with, together)
connect
confide
concede
coerce
cohesive
cohort
confederate
collaborate
compatible
coherent
comply
conjugal
connubial
congenial
convivial
coalesce
coalition
contrite
conciliate
conclave
commensurate

CRAT/CRACY (to govern)
bureaucracy
democracy
aristocracy
theocracy
plutocracy
autocracy

CRE/CRESC/CRET (to grow)
creation
increase
crescendo
increment
accretion
accrue

CRED (to believe, to trust)
incredible
credibility
credentials
credit
creed
credo
credence
credulity
incredulous

CRYP (hidden)
crypt
cryptic
apocryphal
cryptography

CUB/CUMB (to lie down)
cubicle
succumb
incubate
incumbent
recumbent

CULP (blame)
culprit
culpable
exculpate
inculpate
mea culpa

COUR/CUR (running, a course)
occur
recur
current
curriculum
courier
cursive
excursion
concur
concurrent
incur

incursion
discourse
discursive
precursor
recourse
cursory

DE (away, off, down, completely, reversal)
descend
detract
decipher
deface
defile
defraud
deplete
denounce
decry
defer
defame
delineate
deferential

DEM (people)
democracy
epidemic
endemic
demagogue
demographics
pandemic

DI/DIA (apart, through)
dialogue
diagnose
diameter
dilate
digress
dilatory
diaphanous
dichotomy
dialectic

DIC/DICT/DIT (to say, to tell, to use words)
dictionary
dictate
predict
contradict
verdict
abdicate

edict
dictum
malediction
benediction
indict
indite
diction
interdict
obiter dictum

DIGN (worth)
dignity
dignitary
dignify
deign
indignant
condign
disdain
infra dig

DIS/DIF (away from, apart, reversal, not)
disperse
disseminate
dissipate
dissuade
diffuse

DAC/DOC (to teach)
doctor
doctrine
indoctrinate
doctrinaire
docile
didactic

DOG/DOX (opinion)
orthodox
paradox
dogma
dogmatic

DOL (suffer, pain)
condolence
indolence
doleful
dolorous

DON/DOT/DOW (to give)
donate
donor
pardon
condone
antidote
anecdote
endow
dowry

DUB (doubt)
dubious
dubiety
indubitable

DUC/DUCT (to lead)
conduct
abduct
conducive
seduce
induct
induce
ductile

DUR (hard)
endure
durable
duress
dour
obdurate

DYS (faulty)
dysfunction
dystopia
dyspepsia
dyslexia

EPI (upon)
epidemic
epilogue
epidermis
epistle
epitome
epigram
epithet
epitaph

EQU (equal, even)
equation
adequate

equivalent
equilibrium
equable
equidistant
equity
iniquity
equanimity
equivocate
equivocal

ERR (to wander)
err
error
erratic
erroneous
errant
aberrant

ESCE (becoming)
adolescent
obsolescent
iridescent
luminescent
coalesce
quiescent
acquiescent
effervescent
incandescent
evanescent
convalescent
reminiscent

EU (good, well)
euphoria
euphemism
eulogy
eugenics
euthanasia
euphony

E/EF/EX (out, out of, from, former, completely)
evade
exclude
extricate
exonerate
extort
exhort
expire
exalt

exult
effervesce
extenuate
efface
effusion
egregious

EXTRA (outside of, beyond)
extraordinary
extrasensory
extraneous
extrapolate

FAB/FAM (speak)
fable
fabulous
affable
ineffable
fame
famous
defame
infamous

FAC/FIC/FIG/FAIT/FEIT/FY (to do, to make)
factory
facsimile
benefactor
facile
faction
fiction
factitious
efficient
deficient
proficient
munificent
prolific
soporific
figure
figment
configuration
effigy
magnify
rarefy
ratify
ramification
counterfeit
feign
fait accompli
ex post facto

FER (to bring, to carry, to bear)
offer
transfer
confer
referendum
infer
fertile
proffer
defer
proliferate
vociferous

FERV (to boil, to bubble, to burn)
fervor
fervid
effervescent

FID (faith, trust)
confide
confident
confidant
affidavit
diffident
fidelity
infidelity
perfidy
fiduciary
infidel
semper fidelis
bona fide

FIN (end)
final
finale
confine
define
definitive
infinite
affinity
infinitesimal

FLAG/FLAM (to burn)
flame
flamboyant
flammable
inflammatory
flagrant
conflagration
in flagrante delicto

FLECT/FLEX (to bend)
deflect
flexible
inflect
reflect
genuflect

FLICT (to strike)
afflict
inflict
conflict
profligate

FLU, FLUX (to flow)
fluid
influence
fluent
affluent
fluctuation
influx
effluence
confluence
superfluous
mellifluous

FORE (before)
foresight
foreshadow
forestall
forgo
forbear

FORT (chance)
fortune
fortunate
fortuitous

FRA/FRAC/FRAG/FRING (to break)
fracture
fraction
fragment
fragile
refraction
fractious
infraction
refractory
infringe

FRUIT/FRUG (fruit, produce)
fruitful
fruition
frugal

FUND/FOUND (bottom)
foundation
fundamental
founder
profound

FUS (to pour)
confuse
transfusion
profuse
effusive
diffuse
suffuse
infusion

GEN (birth, creation, race, kind)
generous
generate
genetics
photogenic
degenerate
homogeneous
genealogy
gender
genre
genesis
carcinogenic
genial
congenial
ingenuous
ingenue
indigenous
congenital
progeny
engender
miscegenation
sui generis

GN/GNO (know)
ignore
ignoramus
recognize
incognito
diagnose

prognosis
agnostic
cognitive
cognoscent
cognizant

GRAND (big)
grand
grandeur
grandiose
aggrandize
grandiloquent

GRAT (pleasing)
grateful
ingrate
ingratiate
gratuity
gratuitous

GRAV/GRIEV (heavy, serious)
grave
grief
aggrieve
gravity
grievous

GREG (herd)
congregation
segregation
aggregation
gregarious
egregious

GRAD/GRESS (to step)
progress
graduate
gradual
aggressive
regress
degrade
retrograde
transgress
digress
egress

HER/HES (to stick)
coherent
cohesive
adhesive
adherent

inherent

(H)ETERO (different)
heterosexual
heterogeneous
heterodox

(H)OM (same)
homogeneous
homonym
homosexual
anomaly
homeostasis

HYPER (over, excessive)
hyperactive
hyperbole

HYPO
(under, beneath, less than)
hypodermic
hypochondriac
hypothesis
hypocritical

ID (one's own)
idiot
idiom
idiosyncrasy

IM/IN/EM/EN (in, into)
in
embrace
enclose
ingratiate
intrinsic
influx
incarnate
implicit
indigenous

IM/IN (not, without)
inactive
indifferent
innocuous
insipid
indolence
impartial
inept
indigent

INFRA (beneath)
infrastructure
infrared
infrasonic

INTER (between, among)
interstate
interim
interloper
interlude
intermittent
interplay
intersperse
intervene

INTRA (within)
intramural
intrastate
intravenous

JECT (to throw, to throw down)
inject
eject
project
trajectory
conjecture
dejected
abject

JOIN/JUNCT (to meet, to join)
junction
joint
adjoin
subjugate
juxtapose
injunction
rejoinder
conjugal
junta

JUR (to swear)
jury
perjury
abjure
adjure

LECT/LEG (to select, to choose)
collect
elect
select

electorate
predilection
eclectic
elegant

LEV (lift, light, rise)
elevator
relieve
lever
alleviate
levitate
relevant
levee
levity

LOC/LOG/LOQU (word, speech)
dialogue
eloquent
elocution
locution
interlocutor
prologue
epilogue
soliloquy
eulogy
colloquial
grandiloquent
philology
neologism
tautology
loquacious

LUC/LUM/LUS (light)
illustrate
illuminate
luminous
luminescent
illustrious
lackluster
translucent
lucid
elucidate

LUD/LUS (to play)
illusion
ludicrous
delude
elude
elusive

allude
collusion
prelude
interlude

LUT/LUG/LUV (to wash)
lavatory
dilute
pollute
deluge
antediluvian

MAG/MAJ/MAX (big)
magnify
magnitude
major
maximum
majestic
magnanimous
magnate
maxim
magniloquent

MAL/MALE (bad, ill, evil, wrong)
malfunction
malodorous
malicious
malcontent
malign
malaise
dismal
malapropism
maladroit
malevolent
malinger
malfeasance
malefactor
malediction

MAN (hand)
manual
manufacture
emancipate
manifest
mandate
mandatory

MATER/MATR (woman, mother)
matrimony
maternal

maternity
matriculate
matriarch

MIN (small)
minute
minutiae
diminution
miniature
diminish

MIN (to project, to hang over)
eminent
imminent
prominent
preeminent

MIS/MIT (to send)
transmit
manumit
emissary
missive
intermittent
remit
remission
demise

MISC (mixed)
miscellaneous
miscegenation
promiscuous

MON/MONIT (to warn)
monument
monitor
summons
admonish
remonstrate

MORPH (shape)
amorphous
metamorphosis
polymorphous
anthropomorphic

MORT (death)
immortal
morgue
morbid
moribund
mortify

MUT (change)
commute
mutation
mutant
immutable
transmutation
permutation

NAM/NOM/NOUN/NOWN/ NYM (rule, order)
astronomy
economy
autonomy
antimony
gastronomy
taxonomy

NAT/NAS/NAI (to be born)
natural
native
naive
cognate
nascent
innate
renaissance

NEC/NIC/NOC/NOX (harm, death)
innocent
noxious
obnoxious
pernicious
internecine
innocuous
necromancy

NOM/NYM/NOUN/NOWN (name)
synonym
anonymous
nominate
pseudonym
misnomer
nomenclature
acronym
homonym
nominal
ignominy
denomination
noun

renown
nom de plume
nom de guerre

NOV/NEO/NOU (new)
novice
novel
novelty
renovate
innovate
neologism
neophyte
nouvelle cuisine
nouveau riche

NOUNC/NUNC (to announce)
announce
pronounce
denounce
renounce

OB/OC/OF/OP (toward, to, against, completely, over)
obese
object
obstruct
obstinate
obscure
obtrude
oblique
oblivious
obnoxious
obstreperous
obtuse
opprobrium
obsequious
obfuscate

OMNI (all)
omnipresent
omniscient
omnipotent

PAC/PEAC (peace)
peace
appease
pacify
pacifist
pacifier
pact

PAN (all, everywhere)
panorama
panacea
panegyric
pantheon
panoply
pandemic

PAR (equal)
par
parity
apartheid
disparity
disparate
disparage

PARA (next to, beside)
parallel
paraphrase
parasite
paradox
parody
paragon
parable
paradigm
paramilitary
paranoid
paranormal
parapsychology
paralegal

PAS/PAT/PATH
(feeling, suffering, disease)
apathy
sympathy
empathy
antipathy
passionate
compassion
compatible
dispassionate
impassive
pathos
pathology
sociopath
psychopath

PATER/PATR (father, support)
patron
patronize

paternal
paternalism
expatriate
patrimony
patriarch
patrician

PO/POV/PAU/PU
(few, little, poor)
poor
poverty
paucity
pauper
impoverish
puerile
pusillanimous

PED (child, education)
pedagogue
pediatrician
encyclopedia

PED/POD (foot)
pedal
pedestal
pedestrian
podiatrist
expedite
expedient
impede
impediment
podium
antipodes

PEN/PUN
(to pay, to compensate)
penal
penalty
punitive
repent
penance
penitent
penitentiary
repine
impunity

PEND/PENS
(to hang, to weigh, to pay)
depend
dispense

expend
stipend
spend
expenditure
suspense
compensate
propensity
pensive
indispensable
impending
pendulum
appendix
append
appendage
ponderous
pendant

PER (completely, wrong)
persistent
perforate
perplex
perspire
peruse
pervade
perjury
perturb
perfunctory
perspicacious
permeate
pernicious
perennial
peremptory
pertinacious

PERI (around)
perimeter
periscope
peripheral
peripatetic

PET/PIT (to go, to seek, to strive)
appetite
compete
petition
perpetual
impetuous
petulant
propitious

PHIL (love)
philosophy
philanthropy
philatelist
philology
bibliophile

PHONE (sound)
telephone
symphony
megaphone
euphony
cacophony

PLAC (to please)
placid
placebo
placate
implacable
complacent
complaisant

PLE (to fill)
complete
deplete
complement
supplement
implement
plethora
replete

PLEX/PLIC/PLY (to fold, to twist, to tangle, to bend)
complex
complexion
complicate
duplex
replica
ply
comply
implicit
implicate
explicit
duplicity
complicity
supplicate
accomplice
explicate

PON/POS/POUND
(to put, to place)
component
compound
deposit
dispose
expose
exposition
expound
juxtapose
depose
proponent
repository
transpose
superimpose

PORT (to carry)
import
portable
porter
portfolio
deport
deportment
export
portmanteau
portly
purport
disport
importune

POST (after)
posthumous
posterior
posterity
ex post facto

PRE (before)
precarious
precocious
prelude
premeditate
premonition
presage
presentiment
presume
presuppose
precedent
precept

precipitous
preclude
predilection
preeminent
preempt
prepossess
prerequisite
prerogative

PREHEND/PRISE
(to take, to get, to seize)
surprise
comprehend
enterprise
impregnable
reprehensible
apprehension
comprise
apprise
apprehend
comprehensive
reprisal

PRO (much, for, a lot)
prolific
profuse
propitious
prodigious
profligate
prodigal
protracted
proclivity
proliferate
propensity
prodigy
proselytize
propound
provident
prolix

PROB (to prove, to test)
probe
probation
approbation
probity
opprobrium
reprobate

PUG (to fight)
pugilism
pug
pugnacious
impugn
repugnant

PUNC/PUNG/POIGN/ POINT (to point, to prick)
point
puncture
punctual
punctuate
pungent
poignant
compunction
expunge
punctilious

QUE/QUIS (to seek)
acquire
acquisition
exquisite
acquisitive
request
conquest
inquire
inquisitive
inquest
query
querulous
perquisite

QUI (quiet)
quiet
disquiet
tranquil
acquiesce
quiescent

RID/RIS (to laugh)
ridicule
derision
risible

ROG (to ask)
interrogate
arrogant
prerogative
abrogate

surrogate
derogatory
arrogate

SAL/SIL/SAULT/SULT (to leap, to jump)
insult
assault
somersault
salient
resilient
insolent
desultory
exult

SACR/SANCT/SECR (sacred)
sacred
sacrifice
sanctuary
sanctify
sanction
execrable
sacrament
sacrilege

SCI (to know)
science
conscious
conscience
unconscionable
omniscient
prescient
conscientious
nescient

SCRIBE/SCRIP (to write)
scribble
describe
script
postscript
prescribe
proscribe
ascribe
inscribe
conscription
scripture
transcript
circumscribe
manuscript
scribe

SE (apart)
select
separate
seduce
seclude
segregate
secede
sequester
sedition

SEC/SEQU (to follow)
second
prosecute
sequel
sequence
consequence
inconsequential
obsequious
nonsequitur

SED/SESS/SID (to sit, to be still, to plan, to plot)
preside
resident
sediment
session
dissident
obsession
residual
sedate
subside
subsidy
subsidiary
sedentary
dissident
insidious
assiduous
sedulous

SENS/SENT (to feel, to be aware)
sense
sensual
sensory
sentiment
resent
consent
dissent
assent
consensus

sentinel
insensate
sentient
presentiment

SOL (to loosen, to free)
dissolve
soluble
solve
resolve
resolution
irresolute
solvent
dissolution
dissolute
absolution

SPEC/SPIC/SPIT (to look, to see)
perspective
aspect
spectator
specter
spectacles
speculation
suspicious
auspicious
spectrum
specimen
introspection
retrospective
perspective
perspicacious
circumspect
conspicuous
respite
specious

STA/STI (to stand, to be in a place)
static
stationary
destitute
obstinate
obstacle
stalwart
stagnant
steadfast
constitute
constant

stasis
status
status quo
homeostasis
apostasy

SUA (smooth)
suave
assuage
persuade
dissuade

SUB/SUP (below)
submissive
subsidiary
subjugate
subliminal
subdue
sublime
subtle
subversive
subterfuge
subordinate
suppress
supposition

SUPER/SUR (above)
surpass
supercilious
superstition
superfluous
superlative
supersede
superficial
surmount
surveillance
survey

TAC/TIC (to be silent)
reticent
tacit
taciturn

TAIN/TEN/TENT/TIN (to hold)
contain
detain
pertain
pertinacious
tenacious
abstention

sustain
tenure
pertinent
tenant
tenable
tenet
sustenance

TEND/TENS/TENT/TENU (to stretch, to thin)
tension
extend
tendency
tendon
tent
tentative
contend
contentious
tendentious
contention
contender
tenuous
distend
attenuate
extenuating

THEO (god)
atheist
apotheosis
theocracy
theology

TOM (to cut)
tome
microtome
epitome
dichotomy

TORT (to twist)
tort
extort
torture
tortuous

TRACT (to drag, to pull, to draw)
tractor
attract
contract
detract

tract
tractable
intractable
protract
abstract

TRANS (across)
transfer
transaction
transparent
transport
transition
transitory
transient
transgress
transcendent
intransigent
traduce
translucent

US/UT (to use)
abuse
usage
utensil
usurp
utility
utilitarian

VEN/VENT (to come, to move toward)
adventure
convene
convenient
event
venturesome
avenue
intervene
advent
contravene
circumvent

VER (truth)
verdict
verify
veracious
verisimilitude
aver
verity

VERS/VERT (to turn)
controversy
revert
subvert
invert
divert
diverse
aversion
extrovert
introvert
inadvertent
versatile
traverse
covert
overt
avert
advert

VI (life)
vivid
vicarious
convivial
viable
vivacity
joie de vivre
bon vivant

VID/VIS (to see)
evident
television
video
vision
provision
adviser
provident
survey
vista
visionary
visage

VOC/VOK (to call)
vocabulary
vocal
provocative
advocate
equivocate
equivocal
vocation
avocation

convoke
vociferous
irrevocable
evocative
revoke
convoke
invoke

VOL (to wish)
voluntary
volunteer
volition
malevolent
benevolent

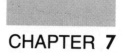

CHAPTER 7

COMMON USAGE ERRORS

Some of the most embarrassing language errors involve words so common and so apparently simple that almost no one would think of looking them up. The following list contains a number of the most frequently misused words and expressions in the language.

ALL RIGHT Not "alright."

AMONG/BETWEEN *Among* is used with three or more; *between* is used with two.
The tin-can telephone line ran between the two houses.
Among the twelve members of the committee were only three women.
Mrs. Downs distributed the candy among the four of us.
"Between you and I" is incorrect; *between you and me* is correct.

ANXIOUS This word properly means "filled with anxiety," not "eager." Don't say you're *anxious* for school to end unless the ending of school makes you feel fearful.

AS FAR AS...IS CONCERNED Not a very stylish expression, but if you use it, don't leave out the *is concerned*. It is not correct to say, "As far as money, I'd like to be rich." Instead, you should say, "As far as money is concerned, I'd like to be rich."

AS/LIKE You can run like a fox, but you can't run like a fox runs.
Like is used only with nouns, pronouns, and grammatical constructions that act like nouns.
Joe runs like a fox.
Joe runs as a fox runs.
Joe runs the way a fox runs.

BIWEEKLY, ETC. *Biweekly* means either twice a week or once every two weeks, depending on who is using it. Likewise with *bimonthly*. If you need to be precise, avoid it (saying "twice a week" or "every other week," instead). *Fortnightly* means once every two weeks.

CAN/MAY *Can* denotes ability; *may* denotes permission. If you can do something, you are able to do it. If you may do something, you are permitted to do it.

CAPITAL/CAPITOL Washington, D.C., is the capital of the United States. The building where Congress meets is the Capitol.

COMMON/MUTUAL *Common* means "shared"; *mutual* means "reciprocal." If Tim and Tom have a common dislike, they both dislike the same thing (anchovies). If Tim and Tom have a mutual dislike, they dislike each other.

COMMONPLACE In careful usage, this word is an adjective meaning "ordinary" or "uninteresting." It can also be used as a noun meaning a "trite or obvious observation" or a "cliché." It should not be used sloppily as a substitute for the word "common."
   To say that French food is the best in the world is a commonplace.
   It is common but neither interesting nor perceptive to say that French food is the best in the world.

COMPARE TO/COMPARE WITH To compare an apple *to* an orange is to say that an apple is like an orange. To compare an apple *with* an orange is to discuss the similarities and differences between the two fruits.
   Jeff compared his girlfriend's voice to the sound of a cat howling in the night; that is, he said his girlfriend sounded like a cat howling in the night.
   I compared my grades with Bud's and discovered that he had done better in every subject except math.

DIFFERENT FROM *Different from* is correct; "different than" is not. My dog is different from your dog.

EACH OTHER/ONE ANOTHER *Each other* is used with two; *one another* is used with three or more.
   A husband and wife should love each other.
   The fifteen members of the group had to learn to get along with one another.

EQUALLY AS Nothing is ever "equally as" anything as anything else. Your car and Dave's car might be equally fast. You should never say that the two cars are equally *as* fast. Nor should you say that your car is equally as fast as Dave's. You should simply say that it is as fast.

FACT THAT/THAT You almost never need to use "the fact that"; *that* alone will suffice.
   Instead of saying, "I was appalled by the fact that he was going to the movies," say, "I was appalled that he was going to the movies."

FARTHER/FURTHER *Farther* refers to actual, literal distance—the kind measured in inches and miles. *Further* refers to figurative distance. Use *farther* if the distance can be measured; use *further* if it cannot.

Paris is farther from New York than London is.

Paris is further from my thoughts than London is.

We hiked seven miles but then were incapable of hiking farther.

I made a nice outline for my thesis but never went any further.

FEWER, LESS *Fewer* is used with things that can be counted, *less* with things that cannot. That is, *fewer* refers to number; *less* refers to quantity.

I have fewer sugar lumps than Henry does.

I have less sugar.

Despite what you hear on television, it is *not* correct to say that one soft drink contains "less calories" than another. It contains *fewer* calories (calories can be counted); it is *less* fattening.

FORMER, LATTER *Former* means the first of two; *latter* means the second of two. If you are referring to three or more things, you shouldn't use former and latter.

It is incorrect to say, "The restaurant had hamburgers, hot dogs, and pizzas; we ordered the former." Instead, say, "We ordered the first," or, "We ordered hamburgers."

IRREGARDLESS This is not a word. Say *regardless* or *irrespective*.

LAY/LIE The only way to "lay down on the beach" is to take small feathers and place them in the sand.

To *lay* is to place or set. Will the widow lay flowers by the grave? She already laid them, or she has already laid them. Who lies in the grave? Her former husband lies there. He lay there yesterday, too. In fact, he has lain there for several days.

PLURALS AND SINGULARS

The following words take plural verbs:

both
criteria
data
media
phenomena

The following words take singular verbs:

criterion
datum
each
either
every, everybody, everyone, etc.
medium

neither
none, no one, nobody, etc.
phenomenon

PRESENTLY *Presently* means "soon," not "now" or "currently."
The mailman should be here presently; in fact, he should be here in about five minutes.
The mailman is here now.

STATIONARY/STATIONERY *Stationary* means not moving; *stationery* is notepaper.

THAT/WHICH Most people confuse these two words. Many people who know the difference have trouble remembering it. Here's a simple rule that will almost always work: *that* can never have a comma in front of it; *which* always will.
There is the car that ran over my foot.
Ed's car, which ran over my foot, is over there.
I like sandwiches that are dripping with mustard.
My sandwich, which was dripping with mustard, was the kind I like.
Which is used in place of *that* if it follows another *that:* "We were fond of that feeling of contentment which follows victory."

WHETHER OR NOT You can almost always just say w*hether.* "I can't decide whether to go to the grocery store" uses fewer words to convey the same meaning as "I can't decide whether or not to go to the grocery store."

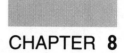

CHAPTER 8

ABBREVIATIONS

Herewith, after an abbreviated introduction, is an abbreviated list of useful abbreviations.

ACT American College Testing Program
ASAP As soon as possible
Assn. Association
Assoc. Associates
asst. Assistant
attn. To the attention of
aux. Auxiliary
AWOL Absent without leave
B.A. Bachelor of Arts
BMOC Big man on campus
B.S. Bachelor of Science
BW Black and white
C Celsius, centigrade
c/o In care of
cc Cubic centimeter; carbon copy
CEEB College Entrance Examination Board
cf. [Latin—*Confer*] See also
CO Commanding officer
Co. Company
COD Cash on delivery
Corp. Corporation
CPA Certified public accountant
CRT Cathode ray tube
DA District Attorney
db Decibels
D.D.S. Doctor of Dental Science
dept. Department
DI Drill instructor
DJ Disk jockey
D.D.M. Doctor of Dental Medicine
DOA Dead on arrival
e.g. [Latin—*Exempli gratia*] For example
EKG Electrocardiogram
EP Extended-play record

ESP Extrasensory perception
et al. [Latin—*Et alii*] And others
et seq. [Latin—*Et sequens*] And following
ETA Estimated time of arrival
etc. [Latin—*Et cetera*] And so on
ETS Educational Testing Service
F Fahrenheit
FF Fred Flintstone
ff. And following pages
FYI For your information
GI Government issue
govt. Government
i.e. [Latin—*Id est*] That is
ibid [Latin—*Ibidem*] In the same place
Inc. Incorporated
IQ Intelligence quotient
IV Intravenous
K [Latin—*kilo*] Thousand
km Kilometer
LP Long-playing record
LPG Liquefied petroleum gas
M.A. Master of Arts
MC Master of Ceremonies
M.D. Doctor of Medicine
Messrs. [French—*Messieurs*] Gentlemen
MIA Missing in action
mm Millimeter
MS Manuscript
M.S. Master of Science
MSS Manuscripts
MVP Most valuable player
op. cit. [Latin—*Opere citato*] In the work previously cited
p. Page
P.S. [Latin—*Postscriptum*] Postscript
PA Public address
PC Personal computer
Ph.D. Doctor of Philosophy
POW Prisoner of war
pp. Pages
QED [Latin—*Quod erat demonstrandum*] Which was to be demonstrated
R & D Research and development
RAM Random access memory
Rep. Representative
RGB Red-green-blue
ROM Read-only memory
ROTC Reserve Officers' Training Corps
RSVP [French—*Répondez s'il vous plâit*] Please reply
SAT Ahem
SDI Strategic Defense Initiative

SRO Standing room only
SWAK Sealed with a kiss
TCB Taking care of business
TKO Technical knockout
TLC Tender loving care
UFO Unidentified flying object
VCR Video-cassette recorder
VIP Very important person
viz. [Latin—*Videlicet*] Namely
w/ With
w/o Without

CHAPTER 9

THE
ARTS

Learn this list, and people will think you paid attention in college.

ABSTRACT EXPRESSIONISM A twentieth-century movement in painting in which the artistic focus is more on the paint itself than on anything it portrays. Jackson Pollock's enormous drip paintings are examples of abstract expressionism.

ALLITERATION A poetic device involving the use of two or more words with the same initial consonant sounds. Big Bird is an alliterative name.

BAUHAUS A German school of art and architecture founded in 1919. Bauhaus style is characterized by harsh geometric form and great austerity of detail.

BLANK VERSE Unrhymed verse, especially *iambic pentameter.*

CHAMBER MUSIC Music written for and performed by small ensembles of players. The string quartet (two violins, viola, and cello) is the most influential form of chamber music ensemble.

CHIAROSCURO An artistic technique in which form is conveyed by light and dark only, not by color.

CONCERTO A musical composition for an orchestra and one or more soloists.

CUBISM An early-twentieth-century artistic movement involving, among other things, the fragmented portrayal of three-dimensional objects, and given its highest expression by Pablo Picasso.

DECONSTRUCTIONISM A recent movement in literary criticism whose popularity on college campuses markedly exceeds its usefulness in the analysis of literary texts.

FREE VERSE Unrhymed and unmetered (or irregularly rhymed and metered) verse.

FRESCO An artistic technique in which paint is applied to wet plaster, causing the painted image to become bound into the decorated surface.

IAMBIC PENTAMETER A poetic metrical form in which each line of verse consists of ten syllables, of which only the even-numbered syllables are stressed.

IMAGISM An early-twentieth-century poetical movement characterized by the rejection of traditional poetic forms. The most prominent imagist was Ezra Pound.

IMPRESSIONISM A late-nineteenth-century French movement in painting that attempted, among other things, to convey the effect of light more vividly than had previously been done. Claude Monet was among the most influential of the Impressionists.

LIBERAL ARTS A general course of study focusing on literature, art, history, philosophy, and related subjects rather than on specifically vocational instruction.

LUMINISM A nineteenth-century American art movement that grew out of Impressionism and that, like Impressionism, was greatly concerned with the portrayal of light.

METAPHOR A figure of speech involving the use of words associated with one thing in connection with another in order to point up some revealing similarity between the two. To refer to someone's nose as his beak is to use metaphor to say something unflattering about the person's nose.

MOSAIC An art form in which designs are produced by inlaying small tiles or pieces of stone, glass, or other materials.

OPERA A drama set to music, in which the dialogue is sung rather than spoken.

OVERTURE An introductory musical piece for an opera or other work of musical drama.

PROSODY The study of meter and other poetic structure.

RENAISSANCE The great blossoming of art, literature, science, and culture in general that transformed Europe between the fourteenth and seventeenth centuries.

ROMAN À CLEF A novel in which the characters and events are disguised versions of real people and events.

ROMANTICISM An anticlassical literary and artistic movement that began in Europe in the late eighteenth century. William Wordsworth and John Keats were perhaps the preeminent Romantic poets.

SIMILE A figure of speech in which one thing is likened to something else. To call someone's nose a beak is to use a *metaphor;* to say that someone's nose is *like* a beak is to use a simile. A simile will always contain the word *like* or *as.*

SONATA An instrumental musical composition consisting of several movements.

SONNET A verse form consisting of fourteen lines of *iambic pentameter* rhymed in a strict scheme or, occasionally, unrhymed.

STILL LIFE An artistic depiction of arranged objects.

STREAM OF CONSCIOUSNESS A literary technique in which an author attempts to reproduce in prose the unstructured rush of real human thought. James Joyce and William Faulkner were among the technique's more successful practitioners.

SURREALISM A primarily French artistic and literary movement of the early twentieth century that attempted to incorporate imagery from dreams and the unconscious into works of art.

SYMPHONY A major work for orchestra, usually consisting of several movements.

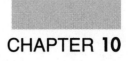

CHAPTER 10

COMPUTERS

The following list of computer terms isn't meant to be exhaustive. If you already know about computers, you won't find much here that isn't familiar. But if you're new to computers, this list should help you hold your own with people who have more experience.

ASCII (pronounced Asky) American National Code of Information Interchange. This is a standard system that assigns a specific number code to each possible keyboard character. Representing data in ASCII code can make it possible to transfer them between otherwise incompatible computer systems.

ASSEMBLY LANGUAGE A *programming language* for professionals only.

BASIC A relatively simple *programming language*.

BINARY The number system on which all computer operation is based. In a binary system there are only two digits, 0 and 1, which are used to represent all possible numbers. (The number system we use in our regular lives is the decimal system, which has ten digits: 0, 1, 2, 3, 4, 5, 6, 7, 8, 9.)

BIT A single *binary* digit.

BOOT To start a computer or a program.

BUG A programming error that causes a program to malfunction.

BYTE Eight bits.

CATHODE RAY TUBE A television screen is a cathode ray tube, or *CRT*. So is a computer *monitor*.

CHIP The small modules of silicon and who-knows-what-else that are the building blocks of any computer.

COBOL A relatively simple *programming language*.

COMPATIBILITY The ability of one computer to run programs written for another.

CORRESPONDENCE QUALITY PRINTER A printer that doesn't quite achieve typewriter quality.

DAISY-WHEEL PRINTER A *letter quality printer* in which the characters are formed much as they are on a typewriter, and whose printing element resembles a many-petaled flower.

DATA BASE A large collection of information that is manipulated by a computer.

DEBUG To eliminate *bugs* from a computer program.

DISK DRIVE A computer information-storage device analogous to a record player but operating at a much higher speed and with a much higher capacity.

DISK OPERATING SYSTEM A disk operating system, or *DOS,* is the set of fundamental *programs* that enables a computer to run other programs compatible with it.

DISKETTE A flexible computer storage medium analogous to a phonograph record. Also called a *floppy disk.* In the past, virtually all diskettes were 5 1/4 inches in diameter. Newer computer systems use 3 1/2-inch diskettes, called *minidiskettes.*

DOT-MATRIX PRINTER A less-than-*letter quality printer* that forms characters out of dozens of closely spaced dots.

DRAFT QUALITY PRINTER A printer whose output doesn't come very close to typewriter quality.

FORTRAN A relatively simple *programming language.*

HARD DISK A rigid computer storage medium that, like a diskette, is analogous to a phonograph record. Unlike a diskette, a hard disk is permanently installed inside a computer and has a vastly larger capacity.

HARDWARE The physical parts of a computer system.

I/O Input/output. Input is what you tell a computer; output is what the computer tells you.

INK-JET PRINTER A usually less-than-*letter quality printer* that forms characters by squirting ink onto the page.

INPUT DEVICE Any device through which a user enters information into a computer. The principal input device among *microcomputers* is the keyboard.

JOYSTICK An *input device* used primarily with computer games.

K One thousand. A computer whose memory has a capacity of 64K can store 64,000 bits of information. (Actually, for reasons too complicated to explain, 64K equals 65,536 bits.)

LAPTOP COMPUTER A portable computer small enough to be held comfortably on a user's lap.

LASER PRINTER A printer, containing an internal laser, that prints text in the same way a photocopier makes copies.

LETTER QUALITY PRINTER A printer that produces copy whose quality is as good as or better than that produced by a typewriter.

MACHINE LANGUAGE What computers think in. A *programming language* for professionals only.

MEMORY A computer's capacity for storing information.

MICROCOMPUTER A personal computer. A step up from a microcomputer is a *minicomputer*. Another step up is a *mainframe,* which is a great big computer capable of doing the thinking for lots of smaller computers. Continuing advances in computer technology have blurred the differences between microcomputers and minicomputers and even between microcomputers and mainframes. Today's personal computers are more powerful than all but the very largest computers of just a few years ago.

MICROPROCESSOR The central brain of the computer.

MODEM A "modulator/demodulator"—a device that enables one computer to communicate with another using ordinary telephone lines.

MONITOR A computer screen or *cathode ray tube.*

MOUSE A hand-held device for moving a computer cursor and entering simple information.

NEAR LETTER-QUALITY PRINTER A printer that comes close to achieving typewriter quality.

PASCAL A relatively simple *programming language.*

PERIPHERAL An accessory, such as a printer or *modem,* that is attached to a computer.

PORTABLE COMPUTER A computer small enough to be carried from one place to another. The earliest portable computers weren't terribly portable by today's standards.

PROGRAM The set of instructions that causes a computer to do something, such as manipulate a *data base.*

PROGRAMMING LANGUAGE An organized system of commands that enables a computer user to create *programs.*

RANDOM ACCESS MEMORY Known as *RAM.* This is the part of the computer's memory that the user can add to and delete from.

READ-ONLY MEMORY Known as *ROM.* A permanent part of a computer's memory, which the user can neither add to nor delete from.

SOFTWARE Computer *programs.*

SPREADSHEET A traditional accounting tool whose electronic counterpart is the basis for some of the most popular *business programs.*

WINCHESTER A *hard disk drive.*

WORD PROCESSING Using a computer to manipulate text. In the olden days, it was known as writing.

CHAPTER 11

FINANCE

Reading the financial pages of the newspaper can be confusing if you don't know the lingo. Here are some of the terms that crop up most often.

ANNUAL PERCENTAGE RATE (APR) A loan's annual percentage rate is the loan's *true* interest rate when all the costs of borrowing are taken into account. Before lending you $10,000 at a nominal interest rate of 12 percent, a bank may charge you a fee of several hundred dollars. The effective interest rate on the loan—its APR—would include the cost of paying this fee and would thus be somewhat higher than 12 percent.

ASSET An *asset* is something you own. A *liability* is something you owe.

BANKRUPTCY A procedure by which a deeply indebted person or company sacrifices most or all remaining *assets* in exchange for being relieved of the obligation to repay any remaining debts.

BEAR MARKET A falling stock market.

BONDS When you buy a bond you are, in effect, lending money to the city, company, or other entity that issued it. In return, the issuer pays you interest.

There are many different kinds of bonds. U.S. government bonds are bonds issued by the federal government. When you buy a government bond, you're helping to finance the federal deficit. *Municipal bonds* are bonds issued by cities, counties, and states. They are often issued to finance specific projects, such as the construction of a highway or an athletic stadium. *Corporate bonds* are bonds issued by companies. *Junk bonds* are high-interest, high-risk bonds issued by relatively uncreditworthy borrowers.

BOOK VALUE A company's book value is what the company would be worth if its *assets* (including office buildings and furniture) were all sold and its *liabilities* were all paid off.

BULL MARKET A rising stock market.

CALL An *option* to buy stock at a certain price within a certain period of time. A *put* is an option to sell stock at a certain price within a certain period of time. *Puts* and *calls* are not for amateurs.

CAPITAL GAIN The profit on the sale of stocks, bonds, real estate, and other so-called capital *assets*. If you buy a stock for $5 a share and sell it a few weeks later for $1,000 a share, you have a capital gain of $995 a share.

A *capital loss* is the same thing in reverse.

COMMODITIES Pork bellies, beef fat, wheat, corn, gold, silver, and other animal, vegetable, and mineral products, contracts for which are traded in highly risky markets that are no place for someone who can't afford to lose a lot of money.

COMMON STOCKS A share of common stock represents a (usually tiny) piece of the company that issues it. If you own a share of stock in a company, you own a fraction of the company itself and are entitled to a corresponding fraction of the company's profits, usually paid in the form of quarterly *dividends*.

COMPOUND INTEREST Compound interest is interest paid on interest that's already been paid. If you put $100 in a savings account and don't withdraw the interest payments, the effective interest rate on your initial investment rises as each new interest payment increases the value of your account. The compounding of interest causes an account earning 10 percent interest to double in value in about seven years instead of the ten you might expect.

CORPORATE BONDS *see Bonds*

DISCOUNT BROKERAGE A stockbrokerage that charges lower commissions than traditional stockbrokerages but provides fewer services.

DIVIDEND When a company earns profits, it typically reinvests some in itself and distributes the rest to its shareholders, who are the company's owners. These profit distributions are typically paid quarterly and are called dividends.

DOW-JONES INDUSTRIAL AVERAGE An index based on the stock prices of thirty big industrial companies. The Dow-Jones isn't a representative sample of either the stock market or the economy in general, but it has traditionally been used as a barometer of both.

EQUITY Equity is the difference between *assets* and *liabilities*. If your house (an *asset*) is worth $100,000 and you owe $45,000 on it (a *liability*), your equity in your house is $55,000.

A *home equity loan* is a loan backed by your *equity* in your home. Home equity loans used to be called *second mortgages*. If you stop paying off your home equity loan, you risk losing your house.

FEDERAL DEPOSIT INSURANCE CORPORATION The *FDIC* is the government agency that insures bank deposits.

HOME EQUITY LOAN *see Equity*

MARGIN Buying stock on margin is buying stock in part with money borrowed from the stockbroker. Buying on margin is risky. If the price of a stock you bought on margin falls below a certain point, the broker will require you to put up more money. If you don't have the money, you may be forced to sell the stock immediately at a loss in order to cover your position.

MORTGAGE When you obtain a mortgage to buy a house, what you are really doing is persuading a bank to buy a house for you and let you live in it in exchange for your promise to pay back the bank, with interest, over a period of years. If you stop paying back the bank, the bank may take back the house. In other words, the bank lends you enough money to buy the house with the understanding that the bank gets the house if you don't pay back the loan. A traditional mortgage runs for thirty years at a fixed interest rate with fixed monthly payments, but there are many variations.

MUTUAL FUND A mutual fund is an investment pool in which a large number of investors put their money together in the hope of making more money than they would have if they had invested on their own. Mutual funds are run by professional managers who may or may not be better than the average person at picking good investments. Some mutual funds invest only in stocks; some invest only in bonds; some invest only in metals; some invest only in Japanese stocks; some invest in a little of everything; some invest in whatever looks good at the moment.

ODD LOT Less than 100 shares of a company's stock. Groups of shares in multiples of 100 are known as *round lots*. Brokerages typically charge slightly higher commissions on transactions involving odd lots.

OPTION The opportunity to do something else (such as buy a certain number of shares at a certain price) at some time in the future.

OVER-THE-COUNTER STOCK An *OTC* stock is one that isn't traded on the New York Stock Exchange or one of several smaller stock exchanges. A stock exchange is a big marketplace where buyers and sellers (or, usually, their representatives) gather to do business within a framework of mutually agreed-upon rules and limitations. But not all stocks are bought and sold through stock exchanges. These stocks (typically those of smaller, less-established companies) are said to be bought and sold "over the counter." To buy or sell such a stock, you have to do business directly with someone who deals in it, or "makes a market" in it. Most stockbrokers of any size have over-the-counter departments that handle such transactions.

PRICE/EARNINGS RATIO A stock's *P/E* is the ratio between its price and the value of the company's earnings in the past year divided by the number of shares outstanding. If a stock sells for $20 a share and had earnings of $2 a share, its P/E is 10 and its share price is said to be "ten times earnings." In theory, if everything else is equal, a stock with a high P/E is a worse buy than a stock with a low P/E, but there are many exceptions.

PRIME RATE The interest rate that banks charge their biggest and best loan customers. Everybody else pays more. Many loan rates are keyed to the prime, which is why a change in the prime rate affects more than just the biggest and best loan customers.

PROXY Ownership of a share of stock entitles the shareholder to vote at the company's annual meeting. Shareholders who can't attend the meeting can still vote by sending in a proxy—essentially, an absentee ballot.

SECURITIES AND EXCHANGE COMMISSION The *SEC* is the government agency that oversees the trading of stocks, bonds, and other securities.

SELLING SHORT To sell a stock short is to sell it before you own it. Sounds impossible? It's not. Selling short is a way to make money on a stock when its price is going down. What you do, technically, is sell stock borrowed from your broker, then buy the same number of shares later, when the price has fallen. What happens if the price doesn't fall? You lose money.

STOCK SPLIT When a stock "splits two for one," shareholders are issued an additional share for every share they own at the time of the split. The effect is to halve the price per share, since each share is now worth half of what it was worth when there were only half as many. Companies generally split their stocks in order to knock the share price down to a level where, the company hopes, it will be more attractive to investors.

Stock splits are sometimes referred to as *stock dividends*. But a stock dividend isn't really a dividend at all, since it doesn't have any value.

TAX SHELTER Any investment that permits the investor to protect income from taxation. Recent tax reform eliminated most of these. Tax shelters that sound too good to be true tend to be not only too good to be true but also illegal. There are still a lot of humbler tax shelters, though. Buying a house is one: interest on mortgage payments is deductible, and the resulting tax savings amounts to a federal housing subsidy for people wealthy enough to buy their own homes.

WARRANT An option to buy a certain amount of stock at a certain price within a certain period of time.

YIELD The annual income generated by an investment expressed as a percentage of its cost. If a *stock* has a yield of 4 percent, it pays dividends equal to 4 percent of purchase price of a share of its *stock*.

CHAPTER **12**

FOREIGN WORDS AND PHRASES

People in France buy their prescriptions at "le drugstore" and look forward to "le weekend"—useful words borrowed from English. We supplement English with many words and phrases borrowed directly from other languages. Here are some of the most useful foreign words and phrases. There is often more than one acceptable pronunciation, usually the foreign pronunciation and an American version.

À PROPOS (ah pruh POH, ap ruh POH) *adj* [French—"to the purpose"] to the point; pertinent
A comment is *à propos* (or *apropos*) if it is exactly appropriate for the situation.

AD HOC (ad HAHK) *adj* [Latin—"for this"] for a particular purpose; only for the matter at hand
An *ad hoc* committee is a committee established for a particular purpose, or to deal with a particular problem.

AFICIONADO (uh fish yuh NAH doh, ah fee syow NAH doh) *n* [Spanish—"affectionate one"] fan
An *aficionado* of football is a football fan. An *aficionado* of theater is a theater fan.

AL FRESCO (al FRES koh) *adj* [Italian—"in the fresh"] outside; in the fresh air
An *al fresco* meal is a picnic.

AU COURANT (oh koo RAWN) *adj* [French—"in the current"] up to date; informed
To be *au courant* is to know all the latest information.

BÊTE NOIRE (bet NWAR) *n* [French—"black beast"] something or someone that one avoids or strongly dislikes
If you absolutely despised your landlord, you might say that he was your *bête noire*.

CARTE BLANCHE (kahrt blanch, kahrt blawnch) *n* [French—"blank card"] the power to do whatever one wants
To give someone *carte blanche* is to give that person the license to do anything.

DE FACTO (dee FAK toh) *adj* [Latin—"from the fact"] actual
Your *de facto* boss is the person who tells you what to do. Your *de jure* (dee JYUR) boss is the person who is technically in charge of you. *De jure* ("from the law") means according to rule of law.

DE RIGUEUR (duh ri GUR, duh ree GUER) *adj* [French—"indispensable"] obligatory; required by fashion or custom
Long hair for men was *de rigueur* in the late 1960s. Evening wear is *de rigueur* at a formal party.

DÉJÀ VU (DAY zhah vu) *n* [French—"already seen"] an illusory feeling of having seen or done something before
To have a *déjà vu* is to believe that one has already done or seen what one is in fact doing or seeing for the first time.

FAIT ACCOMPLI (fet uh kohm PLEE, fayt ah kahm PLEE) *n* [French—"accomplished fact"] something that is already done and that cannot be undone
Our committee spent a long time debating whether to have the building painted, but the project was a *fait accompli;* the chairman had already hired someone to do it.

FAUX PAS (foh PAH) *n* [French—"false step"] an embarrassing social mistake
Henry committed a *faux pas* when he told the hostess that her party had been boring.

IDÉE FIXE (ee day FEEKS) *n* [French—"fixed idea"] a fixed idea; an obsession
An *idée fixe* is an idea that obsesses you or that you can't get out of your mind.

JOIE DE VIVRE (zhwahd uh VEE vruh) *n* [French—"joy of living"] deep and usually contagious enjoyment of life
Henry's *joie de vivre* made his office a pleasant place to work for everyone connected with it.

JUNTA (HOON tuh, JUN tuh) *n* [Spanish—"joined"] a small group that rules a country after its government is overthrown
After the rebels had driven out the president, the Latin American country was ruled by a *junta* of army officers.

LAISSEZ-FAIRE (les ay FER, lay zay FER) *n* [French—"let do"] a doctrine of noninterference by government in the economy; noninterference in general
To believe in *laissez-faire* is to believe the government should exert no control over business. It's also possible to adopt a *laissez-faire* attitude about other matters.

MAÑANA (mah NYAH nah) *n* [Spanish—"tomorrow"] tomorrow

MEA CULPA (may ah KOOL pah, may uh KUL puh) *n* [Latin—"my fault"] my fault
Mea culpa, mea culpa. I was the one who put the dog in the cat's bed.

NOLO CONTENDERE (noh loh kahn TEN duh ree) *n* [Latin—"I do not wish to contend"] no contest
A plea in a court case that is the equivalent of a guilty plea but that doesn't include an actual admission of guilt.

NON SEQUITUR (nahn SEK wi tur) *n* [Latin—"it does not follow"] a statement that does not follow logically from what has gone before
Bill's saying "Forty-three degrees" when Joe asked "May I have the butter?" was a *non sequitur.*

OUTRÉ (oo TRAY) *adj* [French—"carried to excess"] eccentric; bizarre
An *outré* fashion is an unconventional, bizarre fashion.

QUID PRO QUO (kwid proh KWOH) *n* [Latin—"something for something"] something given or done in return for something else
The politician said he would do what we had asked him to do, but there was a *quid pro quo:* he said we had to bribe him first.

RAISON D'ÊTRE (ray zohn DET, ray zohn DET ruh) *n* [French—"reason to be"] reason for being
Money was the greedy rich man's *raison d'être.*

RENDEZVOUS (RAHN day voo, RAHN duh voo) *n* [French—"present yourselves"] a meeting; a meeting place
The young couple met behind the bleachers for a discreet *rendezvous.*

SAVOIR-FAIRE (sav wahr FER) *n* [French—"to know how to do"] tact; ability arising from experience

SEMPER FIDELIS (sem pur fi DAY lis) *n* [Latin—"always loyal"] always loyal
The motto of the United States Marine Corps.

SINE QUA NON (sin ay kwoh NOHN, sye nee kway NAHN) *n* [Latin—"without which not"] something essential
Understanding is the *sine qua non* of a successful marriage.

STATUS QUO (stayt us KWOH, stat us KWOH) *n* [Latin—"state in which"] the current state of affairs
The *status quo* is the way things are now.

SUI GENERIS (soo ee JEN ur is) *adj* [Latin—"of one's own kind"] unique; in a class of one's own
To be *sui generis* is to be unlike anyone else.

TÊTE-À-TÊTE (tayt uh TAYT, tet ah TET) *n* [French—"head to head"] a private conversation between two people
The two attorneys resolved their differences in a brief *tête-à-tête* before the trial began.

VIS-À-VIS (vee zuh VEE) *prep* [French—"face to face"] in relation to; compared with
The students' relationship *vis-à-vis* the administration was one of confrontation.

ZEITGEIST (TSYTE gyste) *n* [German—"time spirit"] the spirit of the times
Bill was always out of step with the *zeitgeist;* he had short hair in 1970 and long hair in 1980.

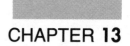

CHAPTER **13**

SCIENCE

Here's a list of scientific terms that crop up in newspapers and magazines with great frequency. You won't learn much science by learning this list, but you'll learn some words that may help you keep your bearings.

ABSOLUTE ZERO The temperature at which atoms become so cold they stop moving around: –459.67°F or –273.15°C. This is theoretically the lowest possible temperature.

ANTIBODY The key part of the immune system. An antibody is a protein produced by the body in response to invasion of the body by a virus, bacterium, or other threatening substance. The antibody attacks the invader and then remains in the bloodstream, providing continuing immunity.

ANTIMATTER In effect, the mirror image of ordinary matter. Each of the *elementary particles* has a corresponding antiparticle, with an opposite electrical charge. When matter and antimatter collide, both are annihilated and energy is released.

ARTIFICIAL INTELLIGENCE The general name for attempts to reproduce human mental processes with computers.

BEHAVIORISM A branch of psychology whose principal tenet is that all behavior consists of reflexive responses to external stimuli.

BIG BANG A massive explosion that theoretically began the universe between 10 billion and 20 billion years ago.

BLACK HOLE The theoretical remnant of a dead star in which the dense collapsed core exerts such a strong gravitational pull that nothing, including light, can escape from it.

CHROMOSOME A structure in the nucleus of a cell that consists of *genes* and carries genetic information.

COSMOLOGY The study of the origins, structure, and future of the universe.

CREATIONISM A fallacious theory holding that the book of Genesis contains a literally accurate account of the beginning of the universe and the origins of human beings.

DNA An abbreviation for deoxyribonucleic acid, the substance that is the principal component of *genes* and, hence, *chromosomes.*

ELECTROMAGNETIC RADIATION Visible light, radio signals, microwaves, ultraviolet light, and X rays are all examples of electromagnetic radiation, which is energy radiated in waves from certain electrically charged *elementary particles.*

ELECTRON MICROSCOPE A device that uses streams of electrons to provide greatly magnified images of objects far too small to be seen by the human eye or even by ordinary optical microscopes.

ELEMENTARY PARTICLES The tiny particles that make up atoms and are thus the building blocks of all matter. Protons, neutrons, and electrons were once believed to be the only elementary particles, but it is now known that these particles are themselves made up of smaller particles and that the list of elementary particles is quite long. Among the newer additions to the list are quarks, muons, pions, gluons, positrons, and neutrinos.

ENDORPHIN Sometimes referred to as the body's own narcotics, endorphins are substances produced by the pituitary gland that can reduce pain, alter moods, and have other effects.

ENZYME Any of a large number of substances in organisms that speed up or make possible various biological processes.

GENE Genes are the building blocks of *chromosomes.* They are made of *DNA* and govern the inheritance of all biological structures and functions.

GENETIC ENGINEERING A relatively new science devoted to altering *genes* in order to produce organisms with more desirable characteristics, such as resistance to disease.

GREENHOUSE EFFECT The phenomenon whereby the earth's atmosphere (especially when altered by the addition of various pollutants) traps some of the heat of the sun and warms the surface of the earth.

HOLOGRAM A three-dimensional image produced by a photographic process called *holography,* which involves *lasers.*

HYDROCARBON Any of a large number of organic compounds composed of hydrogen and carbon. Butane, methane, and propane are three of the lighter hydrocarbons. Gasoline, kerosene, and asphalt are all mixtures of (mostly relatively heavy) hydrocarbons.

IN VITRO FERTILIZATION The fertilization of an egg outside the mother's body.

ISOTOPE An atom with the same number of protons as a second atom but a different number of neutrons is said to be an *isotope* of that second atom.

LASER A device that produces an extraordinarily intense beam of light. The word *laser* is an acronym for Light Amplification by Simulated Emission of Radiation.

LIGHT-YEAR The distance that light travels in a year, or approximately 5,878,000,000,000 miles.

NATURAL SELECTION The theory that species originate and become differentiated one from another as certain characteristics of organisms prove more valuable than others at enabling those organisms to reproduce. These valuable characteristics are in effect "selected" by nature for preservation in succeeding generations, while other characteristics disappear. Natural selection was a key element in Charles Darwin's monumental theory of evolution.

NEBULA An enormous cloud of dust and gas in outer space.

NUCLEAR ENERGY The vast energy locked in the infinitesimal nucleus of an atom. This energy can be released through *fission* (the splitting of certain atomic nuclei) and *fusion* (the combining of certain atomic nuclei). It is also released naturally in a few elements through a process of decomposition called *radioactivity*. Fission, fusion, and radioactivity are all processes involving the conversion of small amounts of matter into enormous amounts of energy. The release of this energy is the basis of nuclear weapons (such as atomic bombs and hydrogen bombs) and nuclear reactors used in the production of electricity.

NUCLEAR WINTER A hypothetical chilling of the earth resulting from the contamination of the atmosphere by radioactive materials, dust, and other substances in the aftermath of a nuclear war.

OSMOSIS The equalization of fluid concentrations on both sides of a permeable membrane.

OZONE LAYER Ozone is a compound of oxygen. The ozone layer is a part of the atmosphere that, among other things, filters out radiation that is harmful to human beings. In recent years the ozone layer has been found to be decomposing at an alarming rate, owing in large part to the release into the atmosphere of certain man-made pollutants.

PASTEURIZATION A sterilization process in which foods are heated in order to kill harmful organisms in them. The process is named for Louis Pasteur, the nineteenth-century French scientist who developed it.

PERIODIC TABLE A chart depicting the known elements arranged according to certain characteristics. If you are a student, there is probably a periodic table in your chemistry classroom.

PHEROMONE Substances secreted by animals that influence the behavior of other animals, primarily through the sense of smell.

PHOTON The smallest unit of *electromagnetic radiation.*

PHOTOSYNTHESIS The process whereby green plants transform energy from the sun into food.

PLATE TECTONICS A revolutionary geological theory holding that the earth's crust consists of enormous moving plates that are constantly shifting position and, among other things, altering the shape and arrangement of the continents.

PULSAR Any of a number of less than thoroughly understood objects in outer space that emit regular pulses of radio waves.

QUASAR Any of a number of starlike objects believed to occupy the very farthest fringes of the universe.

RADIO TELESCOPE A large antenna capable of receiving the radio waves naturally emitted by stars and other objects in outer space. A radio telescope is a telescope capable of "seeing" forms of *electromagnetic radiation* not visible to the human eye or to an ordinary optical telescope.

RELATIVITY Albert Einstein's monumental theory, which holds, among a great many other things, that space and time are not separate entities but elements of a single continuum called *space-time.*

RNA An abbreviation for ribonucleic acid, a substance similar to *DNA* that is a crucial element in the synthesis of proteins.

SEISMOLOGY The study of earthquakes and other tremors (including man-made ones) in the earth's crust.

SOCIOBIOLOGY A relatively new scientific field, which holds that behavior evolves and is inherited in the same way that physical characteristics are.

SPEED OF LIGHT The speed at which light travels through a vacuum, or 186,282 miles per second.

SUPERCONDUCTIVITY The ability of certain substances to conduct electricity unusually readily. Superconductivity has usually been produced by cooling certain substances to temperatures approaching *absolute zero.* More recently, scientists have discovered materials that become superconductive at vastly warmer temperatures.

TEST-TUBE BABY *see In vitro fertilization*

THERMODYNAMICS A branch of science concerned with heat and the conversion of heat into other forms of energy.

VACCINE A substance that, when introduced into an organism, causes the organism to produce *antibodies* against, and hence immunity to, a particular disease.

CHAPTER 14

THE
ANSWERS

Quick Quiz #1
1. j
2. f
3. a
4. i
5. g
6. b
7. k
8. c
9. h
10. e
11. d

Quick Quiz #2
1. b
2. h
3. a
4. c
5. i
6. j
7. d
8. e
9. f
10. d
11. g

Quick Quiz #3
1. a
2. h
3. g
4. e
5. b
6. d
7. f
8. f
9. c

Quick Quiz #4
1. f
2. h
3. a
4. e
5. b
6. d
7. g
8. c
9. i
10. j

Quick Quiz #5
1. g
2. a
3. e
4. b
5. c
6. j
7. i
8. d
9. h
10. f

Quick Quiz #6
1. e
2. b
3. d
4. a
5. c
6. f

Quick Quiz #7
1. f
2. c
3. a
4. j
5. h
6. i
7. d
8. e
9. g
10. k
11. b

Quick Quiz #8
1. i
2. h
3. g
4. f
5. a
6. d
7. e
8. c
9. j
10. b

Quick Quiz #9
1. d
2. i
3. f
4. a
5. h
6. e
7. c
8. g
9. j
10. b

Quick Quiz #10
1. f
2. c
3. a
4. h
5. j
6. i
7. d
8. g
9. e
10. b

Quick Quiz #11
1. i
2. a
3. e
4. b
5. h
6. f
7. c
8. g
9. d

Quick Quiz #12
1. g
2. e
3. a
4. i
5. b
6. d
7. c
8. h
9. f

Quick Quiz #13
1. d
2. a
3. e
4. b
5. f
6. c

Quick Quiz #14
1. b
2. e
3. d
4. h
5. c
6. g
7. f
8. a

Quick Quiz #15
1. g
2. e
3. b
4. i
5. f
6. c
7. d
8. h
9. a
10. j

Quick Quiz #16
1. b
2. e
3. a
4. c
5. f
6. d

Quick Quiz #17
1. n
2. c
3. g
4. e
5. m
6. d
7. h
8. l
9. j
10. b
11. i
12. o
13. f
14. k
15. a
16. p

Quick Quiz #18
1. b
2. l
3. j
4. f
5. a
6. g
7. c
8. i
9. e
10. d
11. k
12. h

Quick Quiz #19
1. a
2. b
3. i
4. g
5. c
6. h
7. d
8. e
9. f

Quick Quiz #20
1. h
2. j
3. d
4. k
5. g
6. i
7. c
8. b
9. a
10. f
11. e

Quick Quiz #21
1. e
2. h
3. b
4. a
5. f
6. d
7. i
8. c
9. j
10. g

Quick Quiz #22
1. b
2. g
3. d
4. h
5. l
6. a
7. f
8. c
9. k
10. e
11. j
12. i

Quick Quiz #23
1. h
2. b
3. g
4. a
5. c
6. d
7. d
8. f
9. e

Quick Quiz #24
1. c
2. i
3. h
4. f
5. g
6. e
7. d
8. a
9. b

WORD SMART

Quick Quiz #25
1. h
2. e
3. g
4. c
5. f
6. d
7. b
8. a

Quick Quiz #26
1. b
2. c
3. h
4. g
5. e
6. a
7. d
8. j
9. i
10. f

Quick Quiz #27
1. g
2. d
3. a
4. b
5. f
6. e
7. h
8. c

Quick Quiz #28
1. e
2. b
3. g
4. f
5. c
6. d
7. i
8. j
9. a
10. h

Quick Quiz #29
1. e
2. a
3. d
4. b
5. c

Quick Quiz #30
1. e
2. b
3. i
4. j
5. h
6. f
7. c
8. g
9. a
10. d

Quick Quiz #31
1. d
2. e
3. a
4. g
5. c
6. i
7. j
8. l
9. h
10. k
11. f
12. b

Quick Quiz #32
1. h
2. g
3. b
4. i
5. e
6. a
7. k
8. l
9. j
10. f
11. d
12. c

Quick Quiz #33
1. a
2. f
3. g
4. c
5. h
6. e
7. d
8. b

Quick Quiz #34
1. j
2. k
3. c
4. l
5. a
6. h
7. i
8. f
9. b
10. g
11. e
12. d

Quick Quiz #35
1. c
2. a
3. b

Quick Quiz #36
1. f
2. d
3. e
4. i
5. g
6. a
7. j
8. h
9. b
10. c

Quick Quiz #37
1. b
2. g
3. c
4. e
5. f
6. a
7. d

Quick Quiz #38
1. g
2. j
3. e
4. d
5. f
6. c
7. a
8. b
9. i
10. h

Quick Quiz #39
1. i
2. e
3. g
4. j
5. a
6. c
7. b
8. d
9. f
10. h

Quick Quiz #40
1. a
2. i
3. h
4. e
5. j
6. b
7. c
8. d
9. g
10. k
11. l
12. f

Quick Quiz #41
1. m
2. d
3. a
4. l
5. i
6. f
7. b
8. c
9. o
10. j
11. g
12. h
13. e
14. k
15. n

Quick Quiz #42
1. i
2. e
3. g
4. h
5. c
6. j
7. d
8. k
9. f
10. a
11. b

Quick Quiz #43
1. j
2. l
3. c
4. a
5. g
6. d
7. i
8. k
9. f
10. h
11. e
12. b

Quick Quiz #44
1. e
2. b
3. d
4. i
5. h
6. f
7. c
8. j
9. a
10. g

Quick Quiz #45
1. g
2. a
3. l
4. h
5. f
6. b
7. j
8. k
9. d
10. e
11. i
12. c

Quick Quiz #46
1. f
2. k
3. d
4. q
5. a
6. r
7. c
8. h
9. n
10. e
11. j
12. m
13. o
14. b
15. i
16. p
17. g
18. l

Quick Quiz #47
1. e
2. h
3. a
4. b
5. j
6. l
7. f
8. k
9. g
10. d
11. c
12. i

Quick Quiz #48
1. d
2. g
3. b
4. c
5. f
6. e
7. a

Quick Quiz #49
1. j
2. d
3. b
4. i
5. c
6. h
7. e
8. f
9. a
10. g

Quick Quiz #50
1. a
2. f
3. h
4. c
5. j
6. k
7. i
8. b
9. g
10. e
11. d

Quick Quiz #51
1. g
2. d
3. j
4. b
5. e
6. c
7. k
8. f
9. i
10. h
11. a

Quick Quiz #52
1. c
2. a
3. h
4. j
5. e
6. f
7. g
8. d
9. b
10. i

Quick Quiz #53
1. e
2. f
3. d
4. b
5. j
6. i
7. g
8. a
9. h
10. c

Quick Quiz #54
1. m
2. e
3. h
4. d
5. c
6. k
7. j
8. i
9. f
10. l
11. g
12. a
13. b

Quick Quiz #55
1. e
2. f
3. b
4. g
5. d
6. c
7. a

Quick Quiz #56
1. e
2. o
3. a
4. n
5. c
6. k
7. g
8. b
9. d
10. h
11. f
12. j
13. m
14. i
15. l

Quick Quiz #57
1. i
2. f
3. b
4. d
5. e
6. c
7. k
8. a
9. j
10. g
11. h

Quick Quiz #58
1. m
2. j
3. h
4. n
5. b
6. f
7. c
8. l
9. i
10. d
11. e
12. k
13. g
14. a

Quick Quiz #59
1. a
2. h
3. e
4. l
5. j
6. k
7. b
8. i
9. g
10. d
11. c
12. f

Quick Quiz #60
1. c
2. l
3. g
4. a
5. b
6. m
7. d
8. o
9. e
10. j
11. f
12. n
13. h
14. i
15. k

Quick Quiz #61
1. i
2. k
3. a
4. h
5. g
6. b
7. e
8. d
9. j
10. f
11. c

Quick Quiz #62
1. i
2. l
3. f
4. a
5. j
6. g
7. k
8. b
9. e
10. c
11. h
12. n
13. m
14. d

Quick Quiz #63
1. k
2. f
3. j
4. b
5. l
6. a
7. d
8. c
9. n
10. e
11. h
12. m
13. g
14. i

Quick Quiz #64
1. b
2. i
3. k
4. d
5. g
6. j
7. c
8. f
9. h
10. l
11. e
12. a

Quick Quiz #65
1. g
2. d
3. a
4. j
5. h
6. k
7. c
8. i
9. b
10. f
11. e

Quick Quiz #66
1. k
2. j
3. f
4. a
5. c
6. i
7. g
8. h
9. b
10. e
11. d

Quick Quiz #67
1. f
2. e
3. b
4. a
5. i
6. j
7. h
8. d
9. k
10. g
11. c

Quick Quiz #68
1. l
2. a
3. j
4. c
5. g
6. b
7. i
8. d
9. k
10. f
11. e
12. h

Quick Quiz #69
1. c
2. f
3. b
4. e
5. d
6. a

Quick Quiz #70
1. d
2. e
3. a
4. c
5. b

Quick Quiz #71
1. c
2. f
3. j
4. b
5. i
6. g
7. h
8. d
9. e
10. a

Quick Quiz #72
1. h
2. e
3. i
4. j
5. g
6. f
7. a
8. d
9. c
10. b

Quick Quiz #73
1. g
2. d
3. j
4. f
5. c
6. a
7. e
8. i
9. k
10. h
11. b

Quick Quiz #74
1. h
2. f
3. d
4. i
5. k
6. e
7. j
8. c
9. l
10. a
11. b
12. g

Quick Quiz #75
1. c
2. a
3. h
4. j
5. b
6. i
7. e
8. d
9. g
10. f

Quick Quiz #76
1. a
2. f
3. h
4. b
5. c
6. d
7. i
8. g
9. j
10. e

Quick Quiz #77
1. a
2. e
3. j
4. i
5. g
6. h
7. c
8. d
9. f
10. b

Quick Quiz #78
1. h
2. g
3. l
4. b
5. m
6. n
7. d
8. k
9. i
10. i
11. a
12. e
13. f
14. j
15. c

Quick Quiz #79
1. k
2. h
3. d
4. e
5. b
6. i
7. g
8. j
9. a
10. f
11. c

Quick Quiz #80
1. b
2. a
3. f
4. e
5. h
6. g
7. d
8. c
9. i

Quick Quiz #81
1. i
2. b
3. e
4. j
5. d
6. f
7. c
8. g
9. h
10. a

Quick Quiz #82
1. h
2. e
3. k
4. a
5. j
6. m
7. g
8. n
9. c
10. b
11. o
12. f
13. f
14. l
15. d
16. i

Quick Quiz #83
1. c
2. f
3. a
4. i
5. j
6. h
7. b
8. e
9. d
10. g

Quick Quiz #84
1. b
2. f
3. o
4. l
5. h
6. k
7. m
8. j
9. n
10. i
11. a
12. d
13. e
14. g
15. c

Quick Quiz #85
1. e
2. h
3. b
4. a
5. c
6. j
7. d
8. i
9. k
10. g
11. f

Quick Quiz #86
1. c
2. b
3. a

Final Exam Drill #1
1. d
2. e
3. b
4. e
5. c

Final Exam Drill #2
1. b
2. a
3. f
4. h
5. g
6. e
7. i
8. j
9. d
10. c

Final Exam Drill #3
1. address
2. integral
3. delineate
4. relegate
5. didactic
6. labyrinthine
7. amoral
8. analogous
9. magnanimous
10. malleable

Final Exam Drill #4
1. O
2. S
3. U
4. S
5. O
6. O
7. S
8. S
9. U
10. S

Final Exam Drill #5
1. a
2. c
3. d
4. b
5. b

Final Exam Drill #6
1. O
2. U
3. O
4. S
5. O
6. O
7. O
8. S
9. S
10. S

Final Exam Drill #7
1. renaissance
2. requisite
3. apprehensive
4. sacrosanct
5. replenish
6. arbitrary
7. eclectic
8. elliptical
9. allocate
10. avuncular

Final Exam Drill #8
1. S
2. O
3. O
4. S
5. O
6. S
7. S
8. U
9. S
10. U

Final Exam Drill #9
1. e
2. d
3. e
4. c
5. e

Final Exam Drill #10
1. U
2. S
3. S
4. O
5. O
6. S
7. O
8. S
9. U
10. U

Final Exam Drill #11
1. O
2. O
3. S
4. O
5. U
6. O
7. O
8. O
9. U
10. O

Final Exam Drill #12
1. awry
2. ascendancy
3. cadence
4. oblivion
5. nominal
6. equitable
7. nostalgic
8. bereft
9. bourgeois
10. pejorative

Final Exam Drill #13
1. O
2. O
3. U
4. U
5. U
6. S
7. U
8. S
9. O
10. S

Final Exam Drill #14
1. a
2. c
3. b
4. e
5. c

Final Exam Drill #15
1. a
2. f
3. g
4. b
5. d
6. e
7. h
8. c
9. j
10. i

Final Exam Drill #16
1. U
2. S
3. S
4. U
5. S
6. O
7. S
8. U
9. O
10. U

Final Exam Drill #17
1. existential
2. flaunt
3. felicity
4. pivotal
5. salutary
6. ubiquitous
7. succinct
8. eminent
9. farcical
10. volition

Final Exam Drill #18
1. U
2. U
3. S
4. S
5. U
6. S
7. U
8. O
9. S
10. U

Final Exam Drill #19
1. b
2. d
3. a
4. a
5. b

Final Exam Drill #20
1. S
2. O
3. U
4. U
5. S
6. O
7. S
8. O
9. S
10. O

Final Exam Drill #21
1. officious
2. scrutinize
3. reprehensible
4. founder
5. palpable
6. qualify
7. culinary
8. corollary
9. proximity
10. vicarious

Final Exam Drill #22
1. S
2. O
3. S
4. S
5. O
6. S
7. O
8. S
9. S
10. O

Final Exam Drill #23
1. d
2. d
3. b
4. a
5. a

Final Exam Drill #24
1. S
2. U
3. O
4. U
5. U
6. U
7. S
8. S
9. O
10. S

Final Exam Drill #25
1. omnipotent
2. fortuitous
3. verisimilitude
4. pertinent
5. conducive
6. prolific
7. vicissitude
8. obsequious
9. euphemism
10. diffident

Final Exam Drill #26
1. U
2. O
3. O
4. O
5. S
6. O
7. O
8. O
9. S
10. O

Final Exam Drill #27
1. d
2. a
3. c
4. b
5. b

Final Exam Drill #28
1. U
2. U
3. O
4. S
5. O
6. S
7. O
8. S
9. S
10. S

Final Exam Drill #29
1. comprise
2. bemuse
3. provident
4. anecdotal
5. prodigy
6. cadence
7. soporific
8. staunch
9. vacillate
10. vestige

Final Exam Drill #30
1. U
2. O
3. U
4. S
5. U
6. O
7. U
8. S
9. S
10. U

Final Exam Drill #31
1. e
2. c
3. a
4. e
5. b

Final Exam Drill #32
1. O
2. S
3. O
4. O
5. U
6. S
7. O
8. O
9. S
10. O

Final Exam Drill #33
1. innocuous
2. assimilate
3. unctuous
4. exult
5. surrogate
6. tantamount
7. catharsis
8. complacency
9. recrimination
10. patronize

Final Exam Drill #34
1. O
2. S
3. O
4. O
5. S
6. S
7. O
8. S
9. O
10. U

Final Exam Drill #35
1. f
2. g
3. h
4. b
5. i
6. a
7. e
8. c
9. j
10. d

Final Exam Drill #36
1. U
2. O
3. O
4. S
5. S
6. O
7. U
8. S
9. S
10. U

Final Exam Drill #37
1. c
2. b
3. e
4. d
5. c

Final Exam Drill #38
1. O
2. O
3. U
4. U
5. O
6. U
7. O
8. U
9. S
10. O

Final Exam Drill #39
1. scintillating
2. digression
3. wistful
4. cerebral
5. affable
6. ideological
7. vexed
8. comprehensive
9. impervious
10. tirade

Final Exam Drill #40
1. O
2. O
3. S
4. O
5. O
6. S
7. O
8. S
9. O
10. O

Final Exam Drill #41
1. a
2. e
3. d
4. b
5. d

Final Exam Drill #42
1. S
2. O
3. O
4. O
5. U
6. S
7. O
8. S
9. O
10. O

Final Exam Drill #43
1. cacophony
2. benefactor
3. manifesto
4. reciprocal
5. provisional
6. squalid
7. callow
8. putative
9. derisory
10. proscribe

Final Exam Drill #44
1. a
2. e
3. d
4. f
5. b
6. i
7. c
8. i
9. h
10. g

Final Exam Drill #45
1. S
2. S
3. U
4. S
5. U
6. O
7. S
8. S
9. U
10. S

Final Exam Drill #46
1. d
2. a
3. c
4. c
5. c

Final Exam Drill #47
1. S
2. U
3. S
4. O
5. S
6. S
7. O
8. O
9. S
10. O

Final Exam Drill #48
1. d
2. a
3. e
4. c
5. b

ABOUT THE AUTHOR

Adam Robinson, with degrees from Wharton and Oxford, worked as a private tutor preparing students from exclusive Manhattan private schools for the SAT. He joined The Princeton Review in 1982. It has since become the fastest-growing test-coaching organization in the United States, with more than thirty test centers from coast to coast. Numerous Princeton Review teachers contributed their suggestions to the content and design of *Word Smart*. Adam Robinson is the coauthor of the national bestsellers *The Princeton Review—Cracking the SAT* and *The Student Access Guide to College Admissions*. He lives in New York City.

More **Bestselling Smart Titles Available**

from ➤ THE PRINCETON REVIEW

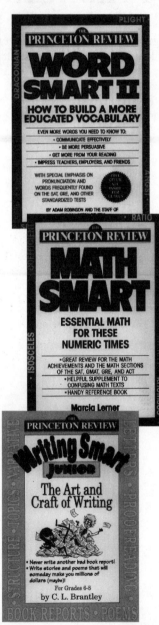